7673

FEMIN

Also by Pam Carter

CHANGING SOCIAL WORK AND WELFARE (*editor with T. Jeffs and M. K. Smith*)

SOCIAL WORKING (*editor with T. Jeffs and M. K. Smith*)

Feminism, Breasts and Breast-Feeding

Pam Carter
Senior Lecturer, Sociology Division
University of Northumbria
Newcastle upon Tyne

Foreword by Mary Evans

Consultant Editor: Jo Campling

First published 1995 by
MACMILLAN PRESS LTD
Houndmills, Basingstoke, Hampshire RG21 6XS
and London
Companies and representatives
throughout the world

ISBN 0-333-62310-X hardcover
ISBN 0-333-62311-8 paperback

A catalogue record for this book is available
from the British Library.

10   9   8   7   6   5   4   3   2
04   03   02   01   00   99   98

Printed and bound in Great Britain by
Antony Rowe Ltd, Chippenham, Wiltshire

 Published in the United States of America 1995 by
ST. MARTIN'S PRESS, INC.,
Scholarly and Reference Division
175 Fifth Avenue, New York, N.Y. 10010

ISBN 0-312-12625-5

Contents

Foreword

Once upon a time all babies in Western societies were breast-fed. They were not, as every reader of eighteenth- and nine-teenth-century literature knows, necessarily fed by their mothers, but the human breast was the sole source of infant feeding. Today, what was universal has become the choice of a minority of mothers. The word 'choice' is central here: what is now taken for granted is that mothers should choose how to feed their babies rather than simply accepting what is naturally given, and possible.

Thus in the context of discussions of breast-feeding the idea of 'a woman's right to choose' becomes a complex, and paradoxical, idea. In one sense, most people would probably defend the possibility of bottle-feeding; after all, breast-feeding is not necessarily positive for the mother, nor is it always necessarily feasible. On the other hand, power-ful lobbies in favour of breast-feeding argue its value for infants and point out the vast commercial interests at stake in the maintenance and continuation of bottle-feeding. Those commercial giants who sell powdered infant food in the non-industrial world implicitly export, this thesis points out, dangers to children through the use of polluted water sup-plies and a further dislocation of traditional feeding and eating patterns.

It is in the context of these debates that Pam Carter's study is such a welcome addition to the literature, since what she does is to demonstrate that even the apparently simple and essential issue of feeding infants is part of political de-bates about the status and role of women, and the general politicisation of the body. We could, therefore, 'read' the rejection of breast-feeding by many Western women as com-plicity with commercial interests, but in doing so we would ignore the powerful argument which suggests that in reject-ing breast-feeding women *may* be refusing the endless re-sponsibility for feeding others which culture assigns to them. Equally, we have to consider that deeply felt emotions are at stake in feeding, and that the sexualization of the breast

vii

by adults fits uneasily, to say the least, with infant needs
and demands.

Of all the many instances of the body as a locus of political struggle, the debates about the breast, and breast-feeding, provide one of the clearest examples of the fragmentation
of the body which is part of Western, twentieth-century,
experience. Thus the female body as a site of adult heterosexual pleasure is divorced from that body as a source of
infant pleasure and gratification. The women interviewed
by Pam Carter, and whose experiences attest to the diverse
pressures about the body experienced by women, demonstrated that they were often distanced from the construction of their bodies as anything other than a resource in
heterosexual relationships. But the crucial issue is then –
and here Pam Carter strikes a radical and important note –
to investigate the cause of this limitation and alienation. It
is not, as she rightly says, that women simply collude with
male sexual fantasies about the breast which exclude real
infants, rather than the infant in men. Rather, that women
are engaged in a complex negotiation about the control
and autonomy of their bodies. All too often, and sadly, the
pressures on women are such that the infant is excluded
from the mother's body. It is not, therefore, that only lit-
eral loss is involved, but equally metaphorical loss of the
experience and understanding of the female body as essentially different, autonomous and empowering. Regaining and
maintaining that sense of female possibility is part of the
project of feminism; within that context Pam Carter's sympathetic and woman-friendly study illuminates the strategies
for constructing and extending real choices about the most
basic of human needs.

University of Kent at Canterbury   MARY EVANS

Acknowledgements

There are a number of people to thank for their help in the production of this book. Mary Mellor and Jeffrey Weeks were encouraging and thoughtful in supervising the research on which it is based. Mary Evans and Michelle Stanworth gave me interesting comments which I have tried to utilise. Thanks also to Jo Campling for enabling the book to become a reality, and to Chris Johnson for being so positive.

Special thanks must go to Angela Everitt who has been unflaggingly enthusiastic even when I've been a bit daunted myself. Jake Carter played an unintentional and unconscious part in my recognition that breast-feeding was not as straightforward as it might seem. Thanks also to Jake and to William Everitt and Sarah Everitt for believing that book writing is just another household chore.

I am also grateful to the women who shared their experiences with me during the research. Interviewing them was probably the most enjoyable bit of the whole process.

PAM CARTER

1 The Great Breast-Feeding Question

Although breast-feeding is a uniquely female activity, and all literature and practices concerned with infant feeding are by definition about women, it has held little interest for feminists. This lack of apparent concern with breast-feeding is in marked contrast with extensive feminist attention to other areas of women's health and reproduction. Indeed one might have expected that Oakley's pathbreaking study of childbirth (Oakley, 1980) would have triggered interest in the closely related area of lactation but this has not been the case. With very few exceptions (e.g. Maher, 1992; Oakley, 1993; Dyball, 1992) feminist energy in relation to the politics of breast-feeding has provided little challenge to the mainstream pre-occupation: how to get more women to breast-feed for longer (Van Esterik, 1989; Palmer, 1988, 1993). The problem of declining breast-feeding rates has been almost universally seen as an assault by baby milk manufacturers on women's natural capacities. Feminists have not been sufficiently alert to what is being said about women in the avalanche of writing and talking about breast-feeding. Nor have we considered breast-feeding in the contexts of gendered relations in widely differing social contexts. This absence of feminist engagement with the politics of infant feeding has left virtually untouched a dominant construction of infant feeding problems as involving an irrational, if natural, woman who needs to be told again and again why breast is best.

INFANT FEEDING: MAINSTREAM POLICY CONCERNS

The central questions of infant feeding, asked by a wide range of policy makers and professionals in the health field, are:

• Why don't more mothers breast-feed their babies?

1

- When they do breast-feed, why don't they do so for longer?
- How can this situation (low incidence and short duration of breast-feeding) be altered?

This has been and still is an international concern, involving organizations like the World Health Organization (WHO, 1981a; WHO, 1981c) and the United Nation's Children's Fund (UNICEF, 1990), as well as national governments, in attempts to devise policies which, they hope, will increase breast-feeding. Concern to promote breast-feeding rests on what has become the dominant understanding of the close relationship between breast-feeding and infant health, as expressed here by UNICEF:

> It has been consistently demonstrated, over many years and in many nations, that bottle-fed babies contract far more illnesses and are as much as 25 times more likely to die in childhood than infants who are exclusively breast-fed for the first six months of life. In those early months even supplementing breast-feeding with powdered milk can bring a ten fold increase in the risk of death. (UNICEF, 1990: 26)

Despite a less dramatic relationship between infant feeding and health in industrialised countries, the British government among many others firmly supports breast-feeding:

> There is no doubt that breastfeeding is the best means of giving infants a healthy start to life. It is natural and provides not only the amount and balance of nutrients for healthy growth and development but also protects against infection and allergy. (Secretary of State for Health, 1991: 81)

Since the mid 1970s, as part of their efforts to encourage breast-feeding, British governments, both Labour and Conservative, have monitored the incidence and patterns of breast-feeding, through four surveys conducted for the Office of Population Censuses and Surveys (OPCS) in 1975, 1980, 1985 and 1990 (Martin, 1978; Martin and Monk, 1982; Martin and White, 1988; White *et al.*, 1992). Initially the focus of this research was on England and Wales but mothers in Scotland and Northern Ireland have now been included. This research, using large representative samples, more than 7000 in the most recent study, has underpinned successive policy documents resulting from working parties set up by the Department of Health Committee on Medical Aspects of Food Policy (COMA) (DHSS, 1974; DHSS, 1980; DHSS, 1988).

In its early stages this research provided some reason for optimism amongst policy makers and professionals. One measure of breast-feeding rates is its incidence, which means those babies who are ever breast-fed, even once. There was a marked increase in incidence between the first two surveys, rising from 51% in 1975 to 67% in 1980 (Martin and Monk, 1982). This change in whether women at least begin to breast-feed initially appeared to be sustained over the babies early infancy. From an apparently all time low in 1974, with 24% of babies wholly or partly breast-fed at six weeks, there was an increase to 42% by 1980. However the two most recent surveys carried out in 1985 (Martin and White, 1988) and 1990 (White *et al.*, 1992) were less optimistic from the policy makers' point of view. There was no increase in the incidence of breast-feeding. In 1985 64% were initially breast-fed. In 1990 the equivalent figure was 63%. This somewhat dashes hopes expressed by some that we have found the true path to almost universal breast-feeding in Britain. What is more, while the figures representing initial breast-feeding remain fairly impressive even if they are not rising, the same cannot be said for the duration of breast-feeding, described in the research as its prevalence at various ages. In the most recent survey 15% of those mothers who began breast-feeding stopped within the first week and there appears to be no increase in the prevalence of breast-feeding at various ages since these surveys began. In the 1985 survey of those women who began breast-feeding (64% of the total) 19% stopped within two weeks and 39% within six weeks. Only two-fifths of those who began breast-feeding continued for four months. This amounted to less than a third of all babies being breast-fed for more than four months, which is the length of time mothers are officially advised to breast-feed for. In the 1990 survey only 25% of mothers met this four month target.

Although the period since 1975 has been subject to particular scrutiny by the British government and has shown at least some, albeit faltering, signs of improvement, there appears overall to have been a decline in breast-feeding rates since the early part of this century. A similar pattern has been observed in the USA. In the 1920s it appears that 90% of babies in the US were being breast-fed at twelve months but there was a decline beginning in the 1920s and 1930s, becoming even more pronounced by the 1950s. Figures noted for the prevalence of breast-feeding on discharge from hospital are 38% in 1946; 21% in 1956; 18% in 1966 (WHO, 1981c). As in the UK, there was an increase in initial breast-feeding rates in the USA in the 1970s, rising from 25% in 1971 to 58% in 1981 (Freeman and Lowe, 1993). As in Britain these positive signs do not appear to have been sustained in the last decade. By 1989 only 52% of US mothers began breast-feeding. Similar patterns of decline during the middle part of this century are evident in Europe, including Eastern Europe, although occurring somewhat later than in the USA (WHO, 1981c). It appears that broadly similar patterns are emerging in developing countries (Jelliffe and Jelliffe, 1978: Chetley, 1986; Jelliffe and Jelliffe, 1988; Palmer, 1988).

It is too early to say whether the somewhat disappointing and stubborn patterns of infant feeding which are beginning to be revealed in Britain and the United States by the early 1990s will be the same elsewhere. However the tendency for breast-feeding patterns to follow similar trends across the industrialised world suggests that the rather optimistic discourse which was emerging in the 1980s may have to be tempered somewhat. In particular duration of breast-feeding appears more resistant to change than initial incidence. For example, although the Netherlands is seen by some UK health practitioners as an exciting example of woman-friendly childbirth arrangements and has a higher initial incidence of breast-feeding, this does not appear to last. By three months Dutch breast-feeding rates are very similar to British ones (Morris, 1993).

CHANGE OR CONTINUITY?

The British 1988 COMA report, *Present Day Practice in Infant Feeding* (DHSS, 1988) picks out the year 1943 for comparison with the contemporary breast-feeding situation. Although breast-feeding rates were certainly higher in 1943 some things have stayed the same. The Ministry of Health report on breast-feeding published in that year expressed disquiet about the decline in breast-feeding after the third month (MoH, 1943). Another problem identified in the 1943 report was that the rates of breast-feeding for babies born in hospital were lower than for babies born at home, signalling some concerns about hospital practices. Hospital routines continue to be identified as problematic in more recent discussions. One particular group of women, unmarried mothers, were specified as failing to reach acceptable rates of breast-feeding and thus potentially damaging their child's development since, the report argued: 'every infant during the first three months of its life is entitled to its mothers milk, to get what has been called the "flying start" which should set it firmly on the road to a healthy childhood' (MoH, 1943: 7). Women without husbands and partners, in the more modern language of the 1988 OPCS report, continue to be considered a problem with regard to infant feeding. But there are other ways in which breast-feeding rates are not evenly distributed amongst different groups of women. There is a strong social class dimension to breast-feeding, alongside other factors which are in themselves also frequently related to social class. This picture is described in this 1988 summary of the research findings:

All three surveys have shown that earlier birth order, education of the mother beyond the age of 18 years, high social class, living in London and the South East, and being a mother of 25 years of age or over, are factors associated with the highest rates of breastfeeding. For example, in 1985, 87 per cent of mothers in social class 1 (professional and managerial) started to breastfeed compared with only 43 per cent of mothers in social class 5 (unskilled). Mothers in the groups which were most likely to start breastfeeding were also those who continued breastfeeding longest. (DHSS, 1988: 10)

Martin and White (1988) also note that there is a considerable difference in the breast-feeding incidence of women in social class III non-manual (76%) and those in social class III manual (61%). Little had changed by 1990. Again there was a significant social class difference in those women who start to breast-feed, 89% in social class I and 50% in social class V. This fourth OPCS survey included Northern Ireland for the first time and revealed that the incidence of breast-feeding there was substantially lower than in the rest of the UK with only 36% of women starting to breast-feed.

Similar variations in breast-feeding rates for different groups of women have also been observed in other countries. In the US, for example: 'Sociodemographic factors associated with breastfeeding for at least 6 months continue to be white ethnicity, some college education, increased maternal age and normal infant birth weight.' (Ryan *et al.*, 1991).

Similar socio-economic patterns are observable in other industrialised nations (Jelliffe and Jelliffe, 1988). It is a pattern which appears to policy makers to be extremely paradoxical: 'Mothers whose babies are in greatest need of the protection afforded by breastfeeding, those from lower social classes, are least likely to initiate lactation' (Jelliffe and Jelliffe, 1988: 19).

What is more, at least at a superficial level, for example without taking into account the nutritional needs of breast-feeding mothers, bottle feeding appears more costly. Hence women in poorer financial circumstances appear to be paying more than they need to feed their babies.

In Britain the information with regard to breast-feeding and ethnicity is less clearcut than that relating to social class. The OPCS studies do not examine the relationship between breast-feeding and ethnicity. However a number of smaller studies have examined the infant feeding practices of different ethnic groups within Britain. The findings of these are somewhat contradictory, but point to an overall decline in breast-feeding rates compared with those in the countries from which the mothers originated. For example, a number of studies have found higher rates of bottle feeding amongst

Asian immigrants to Britain, and to other industrialised countries, than would be the case in their countries of origin (Evans *et al.*, 1976; Jivani, 1978; Costello *et al.*, 1992; Rossiter, 1993). Goel *et al.* (1978) studied Asian, African and Chinese immigrants to Glasgow and found that most were reluctant to breast-feed when they were in Britain. However, Hall and Berry (1985) found that Afro-Caribbean women had higher rates of breast-feeding than white women in the London boroughs which they studied. Jones and Belsey (1977), also studying women in inner London, found that West Indian women (as they described them) retained higher rates of breast-feeding than either white or Asian women. Treuherz *et al.* (1982), in a study of women in east London, found that white women had the lowest rate of breast-feeding, Asians second lowest, and that Jewish women had the highest rates. In most industrialised countries, particularly in urban areas, poorer ethnic groups are least likely to breast-feed. This is certainly the case in the United States as we have seen. In South Africa black women in rural areas tend to breast-feed but black mothers in urban areas are much less likely to do so (Thornton, 1987).

BUT WHY DON'T THEY BREAST-FEED?

Although the decline in breast-feeding rates has been specifically identified as of concern from the 1920s onwards the 'problem' has a much longer history. For example, William Cadogan wrote in his 'Essay on Nursing' in 1749:

> most Mothers of any condition, either cannot or will not undertake the troublesome Task of suckling their own children; which is troublesome only for want of proper Method; were it rightly managed, there would be much Pleasure in it, to every Woman that can prevail upon herself to give up a little of the Beauty of her Breast to feed her Offspring. (Cadogan in Kessen, 1965: 23)

It is apparent here that a concern with infant feeding is also a concern with the behaviour of women. Cadogan's essay was printed in at least ten English editions before 1800. His

8   *Feminism, Breasts and Breast-feeding*

view was, according to Fildes (1986), characteristic of that
period. Fildes suggests that the late eighteenth century was
a turning point in the history of infant feeding. She notes
that the major concern with regard to breast-feeding in the
sixteenth century was the health of the infant, that in the
seventeenth century attention shifted to the mother child
bond, but that: 'The emergence of the *mother* as a major
consideration in the discussions, arguments and persuasions
of the 'mother versus wet nurse' debate is a feature of the
second half of the eighteenth century' (Fildes, 1986: 115)
[emphasis added]. In other words the 'breast versus bottle'
debate has replaced an earlier preoccupation with 'mother
versus wet nurse'. In the eighteenth century this controversy,
according to the evidence gathered by Fildes, began to involve questions about the behaviour of women as mothers.
This preoccupation has remained central as this book will
show.

Asking why women don't breast-feed has become a familar
refrain. There have been many answers. For example in a
large comparative study the WHO gave the following explanations:

> A variety of factors was probably involved, including the
> availability of breast-milk substitutes and their marketing,
> as well as changes in the role of women in society, in
> hospital practices especially with regard to the care and
> delivery of the newborn, and in attitudes of health per-
> sonnel to the preparation of mothers for breast-feeding.
> (WHO, 1981c: 4)

The following is a summary of Jelliffe and Jelliffe's explanations for the decline in breast-feeding (Jelliffe and Jelliffe,
1978: 204):

> i. Rapid urbanization, industrialization, and change in
>   status of women including: increased numbers of
>   women working outside the home; altered family struc-
>   ture with smaller two generational families; alleged con-
>   venience of bottle feeding; apparently scientific nature
>   of bottle feeding; Western urban attitudes to breasts.

ii. Insufficient action by governments to promote breast-feeding including lack of creches and maternity leave; subsidized formula through health services; lack of health education; human milk not appearing in economic balance sheets.

iii. Negative effect of health and nutrition professionals including lack of knowledge about nutrition, increasing hospital deliveries.

iv. Marketing, advertising and promotion of formula.

This a real mixture! Although these ideas may have some general explanatory value they have turned out to be very complex when examined in any particular society or historical period.

In practice the world of infant feeding seems fraught with contradictions and surprises. At face value it may seem obvious that women working outside the home will have more problems with breast-feeding. In fact Martin and White (1988) show that women working outside the home six weeks after their babies were born do not apparently have any lower rates of breast-feeding. Somewhat surprisingly mothers on maternity leave (that is those who intended to return to work) had the highest incidence of breast-feeding, a factor which was probably associated with social class (Martin and White, 1988). Jelliffe and Jelliffe's idea that the break up of extended families is associated with bottle feeding has also turned out to be more complex. Two-generational urban families, separated from their extended families, are not the most 'problematic' as far as breast-feeding is concerned. Hally *et al.* (1981), in their study of Newcastle on Tyne, found that it was those women who were born in Newcastle and who lived very close to their own mothers at the time of their babies birth who were most likely to bottle feed, factors which in that locality are again related to social class. In general in western countries class and income appear to be the most consistent features although they have rarely in themselves been the main focus for intervention.

Hospital practices are also often seen as discouraging breast-feeding but recent findings indicate greater complexity than suggested by Jelliffe and Jelliffe. Martin and White (1988) found that mothers in their 1985 study reported greater levels of breast-feeding advice earlier in pregnancy, and more support after the babies birth in the hospital setting than in their 1980 study. These developments were not however linked to higher rates of breast-feeding. In addition, although the authors were concerned to find that a quarter of mothers had obtained free samples of infant formula, those who received these did not appear more likely to switch to bottle feeding than other mothers. In a recent report on infant feeding in North Tees it was noted that women who had *not* been taught about infant feeding at school were more likely to breast-feed, which is again contrary to common sense expectations, to say the least (Gregson and Bond, 1989)!

The Department of Health is, not surprisingly, less concerned with the causes of the decline than in finding solutions to the 'problem'. It has explored, through postal questionnaires in the OPCS surveys, women's reasons for their choices. Martin and White (1988) report that the most common reason given for choosing breast-feeding was that it was best for the baby and that it was convenient. The most common reasons for choosing bottle feeding were that other people could feed the baby and, for mothers of first babies, that they did not like the 'idea' of breast-feeding. Reasons given for stopping breast-feeding were most often insufficient milk, sore nipples or the baby not sucking properly, as well as breast-feeding taking too long (Martin and Monk, 1982). These reasons, particularly not liking the idea of breast-feeding, indicate great complexity and likely difficulty in finding solutions that can be sustained beyond the very early stages of babies lives. The COMA working groups have made a number of recommendations directed towards improved hospital practices to support breast-feeding. These include: initiating breast-feeding soon after birth: feeding on demand rather than at set times: and the baby remaining with the mother rather than in a nursery. In fact, as suggested above, although at least some of these have been implemented according to Martin and White's study (1988), and may be seen as desirable in themselves, a real shift towards breast-feeding, particularly for those babies seen to be in greatest need has not yet taken place.

What is most important, perhaps, is to think about who is

asking these questions and why. What can we make of the fact that the same questions have apparently been asked over and over again for several centuries? Who decides which questions are to be asked and how do these questions shape the debate?

WOMEN'S LIVED EXPERIENCES OF INFANT FEEDING; THE MISSING DIMENSION?

My initial exploration of infant feeding research suggested that the 'problem' of infant feeding had rarely been looked at from the point of view of women, especially those women who are seen as especially resistant to the breast-feeding messages. This does not mean that women have not been asked for their reasons, views and attitudes. Indeed their attitudes are often seen as containing the answer to the great breast-feeding question. For example one American study examines the differences between high and low income women's breast-feeding rates by comparing the attitudes of the two groups (Leeper *et al.*, 1983). When they fail to find attitudinal differences which indicate why one group breast-feeds and the other doesn't they resort to talking about covert attitudes.

The OPCS studies base their findings largely on information provided by women. However women are asked to respond to an agenda set by policy makers. For example, Martin and White (1988) describe the way in which, although mothers were asked to express reasons for their feeding choice in their own words on the questionnaire, their responses were then coded by the researchers. In the first of the three OPCS studies (Martin, 1978) interviews were conducted and women's attitudes categorized. This involved mothers choosing from a list of 26 statements about breast and bottle feeding, a method unlikely to produce subtle or complex answers. Although this research provides useful comparative data there is little opportunity to explore reasons and experience more fully.

It is not only the specific research technique which is important. The perspective of the researcher can have an impact on the views which women are able to express. Rajan and Oakley in a study of 450 women suggested that pre-set answers to questions about why women do not breast-feed can be useful, since in their study women 'were given permission to express what they may have felt to be an unacceptable attitude' (Rajan and Oakley, 1990: 21). Their particular method resulted in a quarter of women saying that they did not breast-feed because they did not like it, compared with only 14% who expressed this view in Martin and Monk's study (1982).

As well as this large scale mainly quantitative research there have been a number of smaller scale qualitative studies which provide more understanding of the experience of feeding and the complexity of the issues involved (Blaxter and Paterson, 1982; McIntosh, 1985; Hewat and Ellis, 1986). For example Hewat and Ellis discovered that all the women in their study, even those who breast-fed, expressed ambivalence about it, including what they described as 'a loss of self', where they existed only for others in particular the baby, and not for themselves (Hewat and Ellis, 1986: 39).

A feminist perspective however involves more than simply listening to women and drawing on qualitative studies. For example, in relation to Hewat and Ellis's findings noted above, a feminist approach must explore the impact of exhortations to breast-feed alongside the many other demands on women. Feminist approaches necessitate understanding women's experiences in relation to patriarchal social relations. More fundamental than the questions asked by the researcher are the intentions behind the research, the ways in which responses are understood and the theoretical perspectives which frame the discussion. For example, the qualitative studies referred to above, as well as many quantitative studies (Bacon and Wylie, 1976: Martin, 1978; Hally *et al.*, 1981; Martin and Monk, 1982; Martin and White, 1988), indicate the difficulty which women have in breast-feeding in front of others. A feminist approach must examine this within the context of an awareness that such 'feelings' about bodies are likely to be related to patriarchy.

The firm impression from my early explorations of the literature of infant feeding was that the 'problems' stated at the beginning of this chapter were those of the policymakers. Starting with women's experience as they see and live it, and drawing on feminist theory and practice, offers the possibility of asking different questions from those of policy makers and professionals, and therefore of adding to our understanding.

It is not my intention in this book to provide the 'correct' answer to the breast-feeding 'problem', rather to try to illuminate it in a different way. Most research has been conducted in pursuit of increased breast-feeding rates. In order to provide different answers to these breast-feeding questions, and perhaps to reframe them, it seems not only necessary to see it through the eyes of women, it is also important to be more cautious about explicitly adopting a pro-breast-feeding stance. This does not mean that I am simply neutral, that I have no views about breast-feeding. I initiated my own study with positive experiences of, and views about, breast-feeding. But my more fundamental concerns are with how breast and bottle feeding can be understood in relation to gender differences and inequality. It is necessary to hold back on the question of whether, in what ways, and in what circumstances breast-feeding was, or is, in women's interests. This involves not only thinking about how patriarchal social structures affect whether women breast-feed or not, it also necessitates considering the actual experience of infant feeding practices in different social contexts. It is important to examine not simply how many women breast and bottle feed, and what makes them do it, but the meaning of the experience of both forms of feeding within their daily lives.

To understand current breast-feeding policies and practices it is important to place these in a historical context. My own study examined women's memories of feeding in a working class neighbourhood from 1920 onwards. I selected this period for practical reasons (the 1920s and 1930s seemed the earliest period when I would find women still alive and able to discuss this) and because this period saw the start of a major decline in breast-feeding. As well as changes in the incidence of breast-feeding this period has seen significant changes in the practices recommended by health professionals concerned with infant feeding. Amongst many other things these different 'fashions' have included: changes from feeding at set times to feeding 'on demand' (Hardyment,

1983); from separating mothers and babies in hospital to 'rooming in' where mother and baby are together most of the time (Martin and White, 1988); from timing the length of time the baby sucks the breast, giving so many minutes on each 'side', to allowing it to suck for as long as it wants to (Fisher, 1985). In addition to these changes in recommended, if not actual, practices, there have been many other changes which affect the social context of childbirth: increasing numbers of hospital births (from 15% in 1927 to 96% in 1974 and 99% in 1985 [Oakley, 1980: 121; OPCS, 1986]); decreasing infant mortality rates (from 89 per thousand births in 1919 [MoH, 1920] to 14 per thousand in 1975 [Townsend and Davidson, 1982] although with important social class differences throughout that period); maternal mortality rose from the end of the first world war until 1934 and then began to fall (Beddoe, 1989). Concern about why women are not doing their breast-feeding duty seems more constant than anything else during this period.

FEMINISM AND BREAST-FEEDING

Providing a feminist perspective on breast-feeding is not necessarily straightforward however. Although feminists have shown little interest in breast-feeding the reverse is not the case. The breast-feeding literature contains often explicit ideas about feminism. Breast-feeding in fact represents one of the central dilemmas of feminism: should women attempt to minimize gender differences as the path to liberation or should they embrace and enhance gender difference through fighting to remove the constraints placed on them by patriarchy and capitalism, thus becoming more 'truly' women? One might see bottle feeding as freeing women from the demands and restrictions of lactation or, on the other hand, as imposed on women by the manufacturers of baby milk depriving them of a unique womanly experience, based on centuries of skill and knowledge. Feminism has been attributed with both these points of view in the infant feeding literature. The women's movement in the early part of the century has been described as supporting bottle feeding, while the post 1968 women's liberation movement is seen to support the 'naturalness' of breast feeding. For example in a classic and oft-quoted history of infant feeding, Jelliffe and Jelliffe say that feminist movements at the beginning of the century:

> tended to emphasize the need for women to strive for further economic, political and sexual equality with men and to endorse this by encouraging more emancipated roles, especially working outside the home. As with cigarette smoking, bobbing the hair, and the contraceptive diaphragm, the feeding bottle was often visualised by the 'flapper' of the 1920s as a symbol of liberation and freedom. (Jelliffe and Jelliffe, 1978: 189)

This language, gathering together apparently flippant 'fashions' with serious demands, for birth control for example, indicates a tendency in this mainstream literature not to acknowledge the needs of women unless they coincide with the demands of the pro breast-feeding lobby.

Rhodes, writing in the journal *Practical Nursing*, repeats this connection between the earlier women's movement and bottle feeding, a linkage which she sees as negative: 'One of the results of the contemporary women's movement is an increased interest in breast-feeding. Yet ironically, the emancipation of women that began in the 1920s was symbolized by bottle-feeding' (Rhodes, 1982: 19). Present day feminists are credited with support for breast-feeding, as in this comment in a handbook on infant feeding for health workers:

> Women's confidence in their ability to breast-feed is being undermined by many forces in most countries . . . assertive attitudes are still not encouraged in women – particularly about such incontrovertibly female matters as lactation. This may explain why the wave of feminist movements sweeping the world are so positive about breast-feeding. (Helsing and Savage King, 1982: 11)

Given the dearth of feminist analyses of infant feeding which I have already noted, evidence for these statements is slight, and rather more contradictory than suggested here. Some contemporary feminists do explicitly support breast-feeding:

We should stop colluding with the idea that most bottle-feeding mothers have freely chosen to do things the in-dependent modern way and face the fact that this is a fiction the industry would very much like us to believe. (Attar, 1988: 46)

We're deluding ourselves if we think we're supporting women by refusing to say that bottlefeeding is second-best. (Ibid: 46)

Breastfeeding confirms a woman's power to control her own body and challenges medical hegemony. (Van Esterik, 1989: 70)

But Evans writing in the feminist magazine *Spare Rib* believed that breast-feeding is less straightforwardly about the needs and interests of women:

The move towards natural childbirth and support in breastfeeding, with medical and technological help (including formula milk) always available is a move towards reclaiming our bodies and deciding for ourselves what shapes we want to be and how our reproductive powers are to be used . . . But we aren't all clear and united about the question of breastfeeding *as a part of childcare*. Some women have said in discussion that it contradicts all our efforts to make childcare something that can be shared by men and women on equal terms. (Evans, 1980: 52 [emphasis in original])

In an analysis of breast-feeding trends in the United States one writer acknowledges the difficulties for those pursuing women's emancipation: 'On the one hand, there is a distinct concern on the part of liberated women to be free of sex-labelled roles and not to be identified with the exclusive task of being a woman who is breastfeeding. On the other hand, there is a need to feel the importance of being a woman and breastfeeding may well be the essence of this expression' (Brown, 1988). He goes on to say that the 'back to nature' and women's liberation movements have tipped the balance of this quandry in the direction of breast-feeding. Perhaps in support of this we could cite the observation of one writer that 'some communities in California informally report that 90% of new mothers in their area are breastfeeding' (Riordan and Countryman, 1983). However one should not forget that social class and income are much more useful predictors of breast-feeding rates than return to nature sentiments!

Perhaps the lack of a strong feminist movement around breast-feeding also suggests ambivalence and contradiction. Certainly the 1978 version of the feminist health book, *Our Bodies Ourselves* (Phillips and Rakusen, 1978), did not lend its wholehearted support to the pro-breast-feeding lobby: 'The propagandists would have us believe that if we breast feed we are good and if we bottle feed we are bad. They do not take into account the possible disastrous effects of a mother feeding her baby in a way she does not wish or cannot do' (Phillips and Rakusen, 1978: 457–458). The 1989 edition of this text was however rather more positive about breast-feeding (Phillips and Rakusen, 1989). It is possible that the rise of breast-feeding during the 1975–1980 period revealed in the OPCS study (Martin and White, 1988) may indicate some overlap between the concerns of the feminist movements, particularly in relation to women's health, and those of policy makers and others who promote breast-feeding. For example, in their study of the international pro breast-feeding organization, La Leche League, Gorham and Kellner Andrews (1990) noted the similarity between the language of some current feminist writing and those of that organization, with regard to the lack of value which society attaches to mothering.

FEMINISM AND REPRODUCTION

In order to pursue a feminist based analysis of infant feeding it is useful to examine those areas of reproduction – childbirth, contraception and abortion – which have been more extensively explored. Oakley's study of childbirth (1980), in which she researched the experiences of first time mothers in their transition to motherhood, represented a major development in the study of reproduction. The experiences

of women were made central to the research process rather
than being viewed within a taken-for-granted medical framework. Indeed, the medical framework was itself seen as a
major problematic in shaping the reproductive experience
of women. This approach has enabled us to understand that
what had previously been seen as purely biological processes
are actually social in practically every detail. Social as well
as biological factors were seen by Oakley, and the women
whom she researched, as significant in themselves, and as
having a major impact on how they dealt with the complex
feelings aroused by childbirth. For example, women who
were subjected to high levels of technological intervention,
and who had little control over the experience, frequently
experienced depression and feelings of personal inadequacy
after the birth. What is more, Oakley saw the cultural aspects of childbirth as giving important messages about women:
'How a society defines reproduction is closely linked with
its articulation of women's position: the connections between
female citizenship and the procreative role are social not
biological' (Oakley, 1980: 5).

Historical analyses have also added to our understanding
that childbirth is a culturally mediated, rather than biologi-
cally unchanging, experience (Oakley, 1976b; Donnison, 1977;
Ehrenreich and English, 1979). These studies have revealed
that 'The main change in the social and medical management of childbirth and reproductive care in industrialised
cultures over the last century has been the transition from
a structure of control located in a community of untrained
women, to one based on a profession of formally trained
men' (Oakley, 1976: 18). A similar transition has, according to Apple (1987), occurred in relation to infant feeding,
at least in the US which was the subject of her study. This
process has been less systematically charted in relation to
the UK. Attar, writing in the radical feminist journal, *Trouble
and Strife*, wondered what had happened during the period
when breast-feeding declined:

> Did we all spontaneously decide that compared with the
> alleged freedom and joys of bottlefeeding, breastfeeding
> was a drag? In fact we don't know what went on or what
> is happening now. The main responsibility for women's

current loss of confidence in our ability to feed our children, though, lies squarely with the babymilks industry and its aggressive and unethical marketing practices, and with the medical profession with its takeover of childbirth and ignorance of, even hostility towards, breastfeeding as a process not enough under its control. (Attar, 1988: 34)

There can be few mothers of my social class and generation who were not touched in some way by the impact of the criticisms, made since the late 1970s, of the medicalization of childbirth. There is greater complexity with regard to infant feeding however. The path to becoming a mother was fairly well charted by the early 1980s (Beels, 1980; Phillips and Rakusen, 1978; Oakley, 1981a). The women's health movement encouraged women to develop their own knowledge and understanding so that they could challenge medical power and avoid unnecessary interventions. They were advised to try to control things for themselves; 'If you don't prepare for childbirth you won't be able to resist the hospital routine of drugs and interventions' (Phillips and Rakusen, 1978: 382). Choices were to be exercised then in favour of less intervention. Usually the idea of women controlling their own childbirth experience has been conflated with 'natural' childbirth, although Oakley herself makes a distinction between the two, suggesting that natural childbirth has tended to be colonized by medicine (1980: 36).

But no feminist practice has evolved around infant feeding. A number of questions can be raised: is bottle feeding in some way equivalent to medical intervention in childbirth? should it therefore be avoided? does breast-feeding offer greater possibilities of control by women? or is bottle feeding equivalent to contraception in allowing women greater control over their bodies and their lives? should feminists support pro breast-feeding policy in order to strive to recapture the time when infant feeding was within the control of lay women? should they try to recreate the kind of conditions where all women breast-feed? or does a safe and (relatively) healthy alternative offer women more control and autonomy? are middle class women being good girls in breast-feeding their babies realizing that 'doctor knows best' providing a good example to the working class? should feminists campaign for private space for lactating women or should they challenge the dominance of public space by male sexuality and refuse privacy?

An awareness of social class differences between women has been largely absent from research and changing practices in relation to childbirth. In other areas of reproduction however, contraception and abortion are examples, the different experiences of black women, working class and disabled women has resulted in a changed political agenda for feminism. In the 1970s a feminist agenda around abortion had largely formed around the slogan 'a woman's right to choose': free contraception and abortion on demand were two of the original four demands of the women's liberation movement in Britain. However, it has been increasingly recognized that 'choice' is too narrow a concept to encapsulate the broad based social changes needed to enhance women's autonomy and control (Petchesky, 1980: Petchesky, 1986). In relation to contraception and abortion the experiences of black and working class women, as well as disabled women, have been very different from white middle class women. For example, whilst middle class women have fought for access to reproductive controls in order to limit their mothering, black women, working class women, and disabled women have been forced to use contraceptives and to undergo abortions and sterilizations against their will and sometimes without their knowledge (Rakusen, 1981; Arditti *et al.*, 1984; Corea *et al.*, 1985; Morris, 1991; Williams, 1992).

This picture indicates important directions for thinking about infant feeding. One concern is that we have a situation where white middle class women and the medical profession are on one side (pro breast-feeding) and young, working class and some black women are on another (seemingly reluctant breast-feeders). This warrants further investigation. In addition, the pro breast-feeding lobby has, with good reason, focused on the association between infant formula promotion and mortality rates in developing countries (Chetley, 1986; Van Esterik, 1989: Palmer, 1993). But perhaps there is just a hint of romanticism, even a touch of racism, in believing that third world women should be enabled by first world feminists to carry out their breast-feeding duties.

Activism and research with regard to women's health indicate a number of themes which can be examined in relation to infant feeding as an aspect of reproduction. First, it is important to look at the conditions under which different facets of reproduction take place; the hospital setting and use of technology has been shown to be highly problematic in the experience of childbirth. Under what conditions does infant feeding take place? Second, the assumption that 'doctor knows best' has been challenged by women in many different respects, calling into question what Graham and Oakley have described as medical, as opposed to maternal, frames of reference (Graham and Oakley, 1981; Oakley, 1993). In what terms is medical support for breast-feeding being constructed? Third, how can we understand the relationship between the 'natural' and women's demands for control over their reproductive processes? Fourth, it is necessary to recognize and learn from the perspectives of different groups of women. Class, ethnicity, disability, sexual orientation all have profound effects on women's reproductive experiences; infant feeding is unlikely to be an exception to this.

SOCIAL CONTEXTS AND INFANT FEEDING

My own experiences of infant feeding alerted me to the significant differences between infant feeding experiences in disparate settings. For me giving birth and establishing feeding practices in urban Tyneside and, after six weeks, continuing this feeding in rural Zambia provided some startling contrasts. One particular memory is of visting a Tyneside clinic with my two week old baby. I needed to breast-feed him in the clinic waiting room and, as I began the process, was immediately ushered by a somewhat shocked health visitor into a tiny dressing room to conduct the fairly lengthy feed; privacy was apparently essential. Other memories are of sitting breast-feeding next to my Dad and being aware of how profoundly strange the situation seemed. Or of the thirteen year old son of a friend keeping his eyes firmly fixed on the television so he wouldn't have to look at me breast-feeding beside him. In rural Africa, on the other hand, babies sucked their mother's breasts everywhere. They were fed in the market, in bars, on the bus. African friends giggled about the pleasant sensations which came from feeding, open about the sensuality of the experience.

I was not the only meeting point for these two cultures however. I remember on two occasions in Zambia white men walking out of social situations because, they said, the sight of women breast-feeding made them feel sick! Bodies – what they felt like, what they looked like, who got upset about them, who liked them – seemed to me to be central to understanding infant feeding. This is confirmed by the common finding, noted above, that women in the UK find it very difficult to breast feed in public places (Bacon and Wylie, 1976; Martin, 1978; Hally *et al.*, 1981; Martin and Monk, 1982; Martin and White, 1988). During preparations for my own study I interviewed a middle class Asian woman who had her first baby whilst living in Kenya. Her comments offer an interesting illustration of the complexity of different cultural practices as regards feeding in public. She felt that breast-feeding in front of others, even her husband, was deeply embarrassing. But she talked of African women who were far less shy. She strongly disapproved of this: 'They sit in front of everyone, they are not shy. They do it in a public way, it's not right, you can find a secret place, a corner. In Britain women don't breast-feed in public, they're more aware of everything, more aware of right and wrong. This comes with education.' Clearly for this woman cultural influences on infant feeding practices were not one dimensional. Instead beliefs about where breast-feeding should take place were entwined with the complex interconnectedness of class, race and respectability.

The accounts of breast-feeding below are taken from the anthropological work of Mead (1950). They describe breast-feeding in two very different cultures, first in an American hospital in the 1940s and second amongst the Arapesh people of New Guinea. These accounts, like my own experience, indicate again the impact of particular practices on what might simply be seen as a biological activity:

It can suck, but no breast is given it; it can cry for help, but no-one holds it close and feeds it . . . it is taken to its mother at the proper hour for its birth weight, neatly laid out on a moving table, and placed against her fully clothed body, with the carefully sterilized breast exposed just a few inches and persuaded to suck. This persuasion is often a grim business; the nurse knows how to take the baby, who very often is so exhausted with hunger that it no longer wants to eat, and holding it by the scruff of the neck, put it on the mother's breast. Whether it eats or not, it is supposed to be taken away after the appointed number of minutes. (Mead, 1950: 249)

When the mother walks about she carries the child slung beneath her breast in a bark-cloth sling, or in a soft net bag in which the child still curls as he curled in the womb. Whenever it is willing to eat, even if it does not show any signs of hunger, it is fed, gently, interestedly. (Ibid: 79)

Although these accounts are filtered through the gaze of an American anthropologist, it is not difficult to discern the difference in the two experiences from the point of view of the mothers. The two settings also indicate the complexity of specifying one social context for infant feeding. Unlike childbirth infant feeding does not happen in a single place; there are many settings, even if the baby is born in a hospital. For example we might ask of the American mother what she does when she 'escapes' the hospital; surely she doesn't continue these ludicrous hospital rules and practices? Infant feeding isn't an event in the same way that childbirth is; it takes place over months rather than hours. Because of this the range of competing demands on the mother's time and energy is great. We might ask of the Arapesh woman: doesn't she have anything else to do, nowhere she must go without the baby? nowhere she wants to go?

We would probably have little difficulty in describing the Arapesh setting as more 'natural' than the American, but both contexts are part of particular social and economic cultures and we cannot simply recreate Arapesh feeding habits in other environments. Women lead profoundly different ways of life; it is these different ways of life which shape the meaning of infant feeding.

WHICH FEMINISM?

The lack of sustained feminist attention, either in practice or in theory, to infant feeding means that it is difficult to describe clear contributions from particular feminist perspectives. However, despite the lack of explicit work, some points of connection between understandings of infant feeding and both socialist and radical feminist thinking can be sketched out. Moreover mainstream breast-feeding policy, at least in Britain, as well as the activities of organizations like the National Childbirth Trust, overlap with what might be seen as a liberal feminist position, pursuing a pro breast-feeding policy without arguing for any fundamental change in other aspects of gender relations. I will briefly outline examples of what can be seen as socialist and radical feminist influences on thinking about infant feeding. I will then indicate my reasons for making use of poststructuralist feminist perspectives to ask different questions about women and infant feeding.

The influence of socialist feminism can be seen in the main form of activism in relation to infant feeding, which is concerned with reducing the impact of capitalism in the form of baby milk manufacturers. Campbell (1984) provides a Marxist feminist account of infant feeding which she distinguishes from liberal concern about baby milk manufacture which, she says, accepts the fundamental capitalist socio-economic system and sees the rapid rise in third world populations as a major threat. She relates the widespread adoption of infant formula to changing modes of production when women's roles in both production and reproduction were devalued and their role as consumer enhanced. In relation to infant feeding women were persuaded to become consumers of infant formula because 'The alternative to formula is breast milk, a home-made subsistence product which like other such goods, is devalued because it does not permit the extraction of a profit' (Campbell, 1984: 559).

Campbell suggests that 'liberal' pro breast-feeders believe that regulation of baby milk manufacture is necessary to support the long term survival of the system. Breast-feeding is seen as a means of controlling the fertility of the 'dangerous' third world population. Hence she suggests that many pro breast-feeding and other aid programmes are ultimately contained within an ideology which makes the third world useful for capital. Campbell see attempts to regulate the activities of baby milk manufacturers as an accommodation between liberal governments and capital which actually results in more stable and better profits through apparently responsible marketing. Thus: 'Even progressive sounding breast feeding promotions are the result of capital's need to curtail the revolutionary potential of high fertility rates and infant mortality, both of which are affected by breast feeding' (ibid: 565).

A Marxist account, according to Campbell, recognizes that in order to create surplus value capitalism devalues natural products like mother's milk and places women in the position of desiring capitalist commodities, in this case infant formula. Although this provides an important way of understanding the rise of baby milk manufacture the limitation of seeing them as totally the villains of the piece is that women's own experiences are easily left out of the picture. Another comment by Campbell illustrates this: 'The discussion of whether or not breast milk is the ideal infant food is like asking whether or not the kidneys are the ideal means to eliminate wastes from the body and suggests that dialysis machines ought to replace human kidneys' (ibid: 552). One might ask why kidney dialysis has not 'caught on' when bottle feeding has? The answers lie in looking at which facets of women's lives connect with the marketing of baby milk; was a 'false need' created by capitalism, or did needs exist which baby milk manufacturers were able to exploit? Campbell herself suggests that a number of other social changes enabled this market to be created. She identifies the rise of medical 'experts' who undermined women's traditional roles and skills and the sexualization of breasts which are part of women becoming commodities in western societies. These themes are certainly relevant to this book. But the limitation of this Marxist feminist argument is that it provides an account of 'causes' of the decline of breast-feeding at an abstract level rather than rooted in an understanding of women's day to day experience, and in the systems of meaning which surround breasts and breast-feeding.

Campbell also sees these changes as entirely rooted in capitalism, rather than for example, viewing some dimensions, the sexualization of breasts for example, as connected with patriarchal social relations. She tends thus to evoke a rather one dimensional picture of 'natural' pre-capitalist woman who always breast-fed her baby, and always wanted to. The evidence which exists suggests a far more complex picture. For example there was considerable use of 'artificial' feeding devices and extensive wet nursing in many pre-industrial societies (Sussman, 1982; Fildes, 1986; Newall, 1990; Maher, 1992).

The fit between some aspects of radical feminist thinking and strands in the infant feeding literature similarly rests on this picture of the 'natural' woman whose breast-feeding abilities have been undermined. Breast-feeding can be seen as a fundamental part of women's 'true' identity and sexual self. This belief is frequently the kernel of the kind of thinking about infant feeding which sees baby milk manufacturers as having destroyed women's breast-feeding culture. For example, breast-feeding is described as a fundamental human experience both for the baby and for the mother:

> Breastfeeding is really an inadequate word because it is not merely putting food in a stomach, it is also our first experience of love and it works both ways. Brazil has noted a reduction in the numbers of abandoned babies since breastfeeding rates have increased . . . a bit of glass or plastic and rubber does not convey to the baby the primal contact that a soft warm body can. Nor can bottle feeding convey the warm sensual feelings that many women experience through suckling a baby. (Palmer, 1988: 56)

Similarly Van Esterik's book, which I referred to earlier, sees breast-feeding as to do with the notion of Motherpower (part of the title of the book), depicting it as empowering to women (Van Esterik, 1989). These ideas clearly need careful examination, particularly for women in different social contexts.

My caution about accepting this position without looking at the complexity of these claims is partly illustrated by Palmer's observation of Brazil, noted above. She provides no evidence for this assertion but, even if there were data which showed a correlation between breast-feeding rates and a reduction in abandoned babies, it seems to be rather a jump to assume that this is caused by the improved psychological effects of breast-feeding. Rather than seeing breast-feeding as an expression of womanliness or women's culture which has been crushed by the rise of capitalist baby milk manufacture and the sexualization of breasts I have found it more useful, for reasons which I specify below, to make use of poststructuralist feminist approaches.

SEXUAL DIFFERENCE VERSUS GENDER NEUTRALITY

I suggested above that breast-feeding represents what has been a central question throughout modern feminism, that is the extent to which women's best interests are served through either, on the one hand, stressing the insignificance of gender differences or, on the other hand, emphasizing important ways in which men and women, and therefore their needs and interests, differ. I have also indicated the importance of recognizing the different experiences and interests of varied groups of women, particularly with regard to practices concerning reproduction and the body. Poststructuralist feminist thinking has provided valuable ways of re-examining these questions (Weedon, 1987; Diamond and Quinby, 1988; Riley, 1988; Scott, 1988; Fuss, 1989; Hekman, 1990; Nicholson, 1990). Scott (1988) specifies those aspects of poststructuralist thinking which have been appropriated by feminists and which she sees as particularly pertinent to this equality versus difference debate. These include: language; discourse; power and resistance; and difference. These concepts can also usefully illuminate the questions regarding infant feeding which are being pursued here.

First, poststructuralists see language as a system which in itself constitutes meaning rather than a neutral medium of words and grammatical conventions which express previously existing ideas. This focuses attention on examining texts, either in the form of written documents or as spoken words which indicate systems by which meanings and cultural practices are developed and changed in specific contexts. It is helpful, as I show in later chapters, to look at infant feeding texts and practices in terms of systems of meaning concerning women.

Second, the concept of discourse, developed from the work of Foucault (1977; 1979; 1981), is important for feminists using poststructuralist approaches. The idea of discourse refers to specific structures of meanings, categories and beliefs. Poststructuralists see discourses as ways of linking together 'statements' or observations about the world, including biological attributes, giving a notion of unity to what might otherwise be distinct and disparate phenomena. Discourses are frequently expressed in bodies of knowledge, medical knowledge being a prime example, in the social practices that go with them, and in forms of individual subjectivity which are produced through the social relations which these involve. For example, we can ask what kind of linkages are made with the breast-feeding mother? What system of categories is she contained within? What attributes is she reputed to possess? We can identify infant feeding as a discursive field, not contained within one discourse, rather as 'a multiplicity of discourses produced by a whole series of mechanisms operating in different institutions' (Foucault, 1981: 33).

Third, discourses and power are intertwined in mutually reinforcing ways which, according to Foucault, must be analyzed in local, and historically specific, situations. His is a distinctive way of understanding power: 'Power is not an institution, and not a structure; neither is it a certain strength we are endowed with; it is the name that one attributes to a complex strategical situation in a particular society' (Foucault 1981: 93). Power, seen in this way, is within everyday social relations and expressed through them. The multiplicity of discourses within a particular discursive field, and sometimes contradictions between them, offer spaces within which resistance to power and control can form. In this way resistance co-exists with power, it is not outside of it. There are multiple sites of both power and resistance. In relation to infant feeding, we can expect to find both power and resistance within its very relations and practices. Power is not conceived as acting only from outside people but through their subjectivities. People are made 'governable' through this process. Power is seen as a dense web, passing through institutions rather than contained within them. Resistances are also multiple and must be sought as plural, and sometimes unlikely, forms rather than expecting a single act, or form, of rebellion. This approach seems to fit well with infant feeding, where power is complex and contradictory, drawing in discourses concerned with femininity, sexuality, mothering, class, race and gender relations. In his study of sexuality Foucault shaped a set of questions regarding power and discourse which are useful in this analysis:

> In a specific type of discourse on sex, in a specific form of exortion of truth, appearing historically and in specific places (around the child's body, apropos of women's sex, in connection with practices restricting births and so on), what were the most immediate, the most local power relations at work? How did they make possible these kinds of discourses, and conversely how were these discourses used to support power relations? How was the action of these power relations modified by their very exercise, entailing a strengthening of some terms and a weakening of others, with effects of resistance and counterinvestments, so that there has never existed one type of stable subjugation, given once and for all. (Foucault, 1981: 97)

Illuminating the complexity of power relations enables us to recognize that, instead of seeing women as 'driven' by the forces of capitalism to buy infant formula, it is more useful to build an analysis grounded in women's day to day lives, and thus provide what Foucault describes as an 'ascending analysis of power' (Foucault in Gordon, 1980: 99).

Scott (1988) describes the way in which the power of discourses operates through their acquiring the status of objective knowledge, as a set of 'givens' in any debate which means that all arguments accept certain basic assumptions. Conflicts within discursive fields are diminished through this process, whereby even apparently opposing points of view argue from the same first principles, which are not themselves subject to scrutiny. A major difficulty for feminism in relation to infant feeding is that it has been unable to challenge some of the first principles regarding the nature of femininity which are central to infant feeding discourses. Both feminism and mainstream literature suggest that breastfeeding is part of the repressed 'truth' of natural womanhood.

Fourth, the concept of 'difference' in poststructuralist

thinking concerns the way in which meaning is constructed through contrasts, the creation of apparently opposing categories. For feminists the key opposition is that between masculinity and femininity, whereby, within patriarchal discourses 'the meanings of gender become tied to many kinds of cultural representations' (Scott, 1988: 37). But there are other oppositions and categories within the discourses of femininity, women who are proper women, and those who are not. These categories are frequently conflated with differences of race and class. We will see that in relation to infant feeding, for example, discourses of good mothering are frequently linked to notions of naturalness, which is often a vehicle for certain race and class related symbols. Explaining the way in which discourses concerned with femininity construct the meaning and experience of woman, often placing different women in separate and oppositional categories, has become a central feminist project, and is a productive approach to understanding infant feeding. In what ways are breast-feeding and bottle feeding mothers placed in opposition to one another?

Foucault suggests that a particular strategy has been pursued to put women and their sexuality into discourse from the eighteenth century onwards. This has been produced mainly through medical science, and through other forms of 'expertise' which have defined a particular form of femininity. He described this as:

> A hysterization of women's bodies: a threefold process where the feminine body was analyzed – qualified and disqualified – as being thoroughly saturated with sexuality; whereby it was integrated into the sphere of medical practices, by reason of a pathology intrinsic to it; whereby, finally, it was placed in organic communication with the social body (whose regulated fecundity it was supposed to ensure), the family space (of which it had to be a substantial and functional element, and the life of children (which it produced and had to guarantee, by virtue of a biologico-moral responsibility lasting through the entire period of the children's education): the Mother, with her negative image of "nervous woman", constituted the most visible form of this hysterization. (1981: 104)

The discourses of femininity of which this has been a key part are however complex. This view of woman, for example, clearly focuses on the bourgeois woman, 'nervous' often in contrast to her working class sisters, both black and white, who are deemed closer to nature. There are also many sites and practices through which often contrasting discourses of femininity are produced. The contradictions and intricacy of these discourses have been extensively explored by feminists (de Beauvoir 1953; Coward 1984; Weedon, 1987; Butler, 1990b; Hekman, 1990; Young, 1990a).

In Smith's essay, 'Femininity as Discourse', she describes femininity as constructed through an ongoing 'conversation' (Smith, 1988: 39) in various 'texts' such as books, films, magazines and advertisements. As well as these textual discourses of femininity, there are also social and material practices which help to constitute women as feminine subjects, conducted through a multitude of sites and institutions. These include the 'work' that women themselves do to produce their own femininity, encompassing the way in which women talk to each other. Women's construction of their own femininity, individually and with other women, is simultaneously part of the discourses, but can also in some ways subvert, resist and change them. The discourses of infant feeding contain ideas about mothering which often contradict with other codes regarding sexy appearance and availability. Hence infant feeding is a contradictory discursive field, where analyses of power and resistance are complex.

These ways of thinking can help us to find a way through the feminist dilemma stated at the beginning of the preceding section, in which liberation is seen as best pursued either through emphasizing sexual difference or through denying it. In relation to infant feeding the dilemma leads to seeing breast-feeding as a repressed 'truth' of women, a part of our real selves, or as a burden to be avoided through embracing bottle feeding. A third position might be to see choice between these two as important. But this book will show that both breast and bottle feeding are shaped within discursive constructions of femininity. In this sense neither form of infant feeding is necessarily an answer. Rather, feminist strategy as regards infant feeding can be rooted in resistance to dominant discourses. These resistances are not universal but are frequently historically and geographically specific.

THE CATEGORY OF WOMEN

A significant dimension of the recognition of femininity as discourse is that it enables us to question the category of women. We can recognize 'women' as a unity produced through an elaboration of meanings attached to certain bodily differences. Riley's work (1988) concerning the category of women, explores the changing discursive constructions of femininity at different historical periods, leaving us with major questions about how to work with the category of women. This is particularly pertinent in relation to breast-feeding where linkages with nature serve to obscure differences between women and to iron out complexity. As Maher argues: 'The decline in breast-feeding over the last hundred years is interpreted nowadays, particularly in medical circles, as an instance of women's alienation from their biological nature, or from their 'natural' gender roles' (Maher, 1992: 31). It is particularly important, then, to distance ourselves, from any notion that starting from women's experiences will reveal the hidden truth of breast-feeding. They will not simply be able to answer the great breast-feeding question. We need instead to see these experiences as shaped by the discursive field of infant feeding. This discursive field incorporates a number of dimensions: a wide range of literature and policy documents concerned with infant feeding; the conditions under which infant feeding takes place; the kinds of practices and relations it involves; and the ways in which women talk to each other about breast and bottle feeding.

CONCLUSION

Women's accounts, needs and experiences of infant feeding are absent within a paradigm of infant feeding which starts from a concern to increase the incidence of breast-feeding and to prolong it. Neither feminists as activists nor as theorists have provided a critique of this dominant paradigm, in part, as I have argued, because of their reluctance to question the story of the stolen art of breast-feeding. But the absence of feminism from the field of infant feeding has meant that we have not noticed that it is a vibrant arena within which meanings about proper womanliness are constructed. In the next chapter I will examine in more detail what is said about women and how the discursive field of infant feeding is constructed in policies and other literature.

2 A Tidal Wave of Good Advice

In some ways the literature of infant feeding represents the triumph of hope over experience. In 1907 the Medical Officer for the County of Durham, commenting on the use of condensed milk for feeding babies, wrote: 'In my opinion the labels on the tins of such milks should be required to indicate in large letters that the contents are not fit for use as a food for infants' (County Council of Durham 1907: 9). In 1981 the World Health Organization, writing of the marketing of breast milk substitutes, stated: 'Labels should be designed to provide the necessary information about the appropriate use of the product, and so as not to discourage breast-feeding' (WHO, 1981b, Article 9.1). This apparent interest in persuading women to breast-feed, and discouraging the promotion of alternative sources of infant food, might be seen as a substantial failure. The baby milk industry is vast; each year seven billion US dollars worth of baby milk is sold (McConville, 1994). However, as this chapter will show, promotion of breast-feeding can best be seen as symbolic of policy makers' concern with mothering, rather than as a sustained commitment to improve the health of women and their babies. Instead policy and practice have often been deeply ambivalent about breast-feeding and are frequently linked to mechanisms which involve the social control of women.

Rather than examining the case 'for' breast-feeding it is more useful to chart the way in which 'facts' about the virtues of breast feeding have often been connected with certain ideas, images, beliefs and favoured subject positions for women. Although the material in this chapter is organized into specific historical periods they are in some ways false boundaries. Many of the discourses explored can be seen to transcend them. The literature examined includes policy documents and other texts written in the period, as well as more recent material. The final section explores current literature and debate.

34

INFANT FEEDING BEFORE 1900

Many of the building blocks of current discourses have been moulded over several centuries. The changing 'fashions' of infant feeding are frequently expressions of the way in which nature, culture and science are conceptualized within any particular period. These are always in turn linked to particular ways in which femininity is expressed or put into discourse. For example, sometimes nature has been seen as 'a mysterious but nurturing mother' and at other times 'as a wild force that must be subordinated to a dominant mankind' through scientific knowledge and practices (Hekman, 1990: 10).

In chapter one I drew attention to the influential work of Cadogan (Kessen, 1965) as representing the view that children were best breast-fed by their mothers rather than by wet nurses. This aspect of 'naturalness' was linked to others. For example it was also advocated that the child should simultaneously be released from the swaddling clothes which were fashionable at this period, so that it could move its limbs in an unrestricted fashion. Cadogan, writing in 1749, based these views on his observations of the children of poor people who, he said, raised their children 'naturally' and were rewarded with their increased health and vigour. Rousseau's highly popular novel, *Emile*, published in 1762, similarly advocated 'natural' child rearing methods including breast-feeding, preferably by the mother, and unswaddled limbs. Although Rousseau was suspicious of medicine both he and Cadogan (a physician) speak as male experts who, drawing on a particular concept of nature, articulated a set of beliefs about 'good mothering'. This set of beliefs separated 'natural' mothers, often poor women, from 'unnatural' bourgeois women, who failed in their mothering and sent their children to be wet nursed. Thus, although poorer women were praised for their mothering, this was seen as a natural state rather than a chosen direction, and therefore no more a product of their rationality than the irrational behaviour of bourgeois women. Cadogan particularly emphasized the need for the rationality of men to triumph over the irrationality of women: 'In my Opinion, this Business has been too long fatally left to the Management of Women,

who cannot be supposed to have proper Knowledge to fit
them for such a Task, notwithstanding they look upon it to
be their own Province' (Cadogan in Kessen, 1965: 11).

Although the relationship between culture and nature took
on a very specific scientifically framed form within enlightenment thinking from the eighteenth century onwards, this
dichotomy, and the association of women with nature has
much earlier origins, with Aristotle for example (Hekman,
1990). Within enlightenment thinking, such as that represented by Cadogan and Rousseau, science is depicted as
taming and using the irrational forces of nature. From then
on, rather than being linked to the powerful mysteries of
nature, women became the objects of science, to be dis-
sected, understood and managed, crucially different from
men in their embodiment (Laqueur, 1986; Laqueur, 1990).
The social relations of breast-feeding have been shaped within
this understanding since the eighteenth century.

This way of seeing breast-feeding, as natural but as needing management by experts to overcome the irrationality of
women, has influenced the way in which the history of infant feeding has been articulated. One aspect of the notion
of breast-feeding as 'natural' is the common idea of a golden
age, usually seen as pre-industrial or pre-capitalist. For
example, from a textbook for health professionals:

> Our foremothers managed to breast-feed. Our sisters in
> traditional societies still do so, in spite of nutritional stan-
> dards generally far below those of most modern non-breast-
> feeding mothers. How did – and do – they manage? Surely
> they knew – and know – a lot about the art of breast-
> feeding. Today's mothers in urbanized and industrialized
> societies have to rediscover this knowledge (Helsing and
> Savage King, 1982: v).

Whilst this view has an attractive tone in valuing women's
knowledge it is both over simplified and resonates with the
notion of certain kinds of women, in this case pre-industrial
and third world women, being more rooted in nature. Similarly in Palmer's book, *The Politics of Breastfeeding* (1993) she
too suggests that it is only in the present age that breast-
feeding is under threat: 'Why, after more than a million

years of survival, are human beings abandoning one of the principal evolutionary characteristics by which we identify ourselves as mammals?' (Palmer, 1993: 19). Although this statement might be literally correct in that wet nursing, the most common alternative to maternal breast-feeding involved breast milk, Palmer suggests a rather more seamless history than actually exists. In fact the history of infant feeding shows varied, complex practices, influenced by a range of factors: the place of women and children in particular economic and social systems; particular beliefs about child rearing; women's physical condition; and their relationships to each other (Wickes, 1953; Prince, 1976; Sussman, 1982; Silverton, 1985; Fildes, 1986, 1987, 1988). There was diversity even in pre-industrial societies. For example Fildes (1986), describes societies which had a high regard for both babies and lactating mothers citing as examples the 'matriarchal' societies of Babylon and Egypt in the ancient world. In Greek and Roman Egypt, on the other hand, much less value was placed on children and on lactation. In these societies, according to Fildes, social relations were dominated by slavery and wet nurses were often slaves. In addition to wet nursing a great variety of feeding vessels and animal milks have been used throughout history.

Infant feeding practices have also always been shaped by different kinds of beliefs, rather than the straightforward 'lost' body of knowledge inferred by Helsing and Savage King (1982). For example the belief that colostrum was a 'bad' substance which babies should not be allowed to suck was widespread in pre-industrial societies (Wickes, 1953: 151; Fildes, 1986: 81) and remains so in some societies where breast-feeding is still the norm (Maher, 1992: 9). This is in contrast to current advice which stresses that colostrum is if anything more health enhancing than prolonged breast feeding (Kitzinger, 1979; Palmer, 1988; DHSS, 1988). Even in countries which today have high rates of breast-feeding there are considerable variations in actual practices, for example with regard to whether unrestricted or restricted access to the breast is expected and how and when weaning takes place (Riordan, 1983).

Wet nursing involved highly complex sets of social relations and cannot be dismissed as a habit indulged in by the idle rich. Whilst wet nursing certainly had an important relationship to social class, which will be discussed below, there have been many reasons for the use of wet nurses. For example, Sussman (1982) describes the use of wet nurses in France from 1715 to 1914 by urban artisans and shop-keepers, not just by the well-to-do. It was among artisans that women's economic labour was needed to support the family, in ways which were not readily combined with in-fant care. Sussman relates this extensive practice to the com-bination of rapid urbanization but slow industrialization in France. Wet nursing, accompanied by 'boarding out', was thus prolonged in France by this very lengthy transition from a traditional pre-industrial society to an industrial one. One interesting comment in Sussman's account is that 'wet nursing' survived the technological changes in sterilisation techniques which made bottle feeding somewhat safer. What Sussman means is that by 1899 nearly 20% of infants were being dry nursed rather than wet nursed (1982: 165). It thus becomes clear that the term 'wet nursing' has implications beyond the actual feeding method. In this account 'wet nursing' might equally be described as 'fostering' or 'childminding', a method of feeding being used as a shorthand to describe a particular arrangement for the care of children, and one with negative connotations. Infant feeding frequently oper-ates as a symbol for a more fundamental and long term pre-occupation with whether and in what ways women carry out their mothering responsibilities.

Fildes (1988) has now greatly expanded our knowledge about wet nursing, uncovering a hidden history, much more extensive, even in Britain, than had previously been believed, and surviving in many countries into the present century. One interesting dimension of her study is the recognition of wet nursing as an important early occupation for women, as she describes it, following prostitution as 'the second oldest profession' (1988: 158). The employment of wet nurses however, as opposed to informal wet nursing, has frequently been shot through with discourses about women which are class and race related. As indicated at the beginning of this section these frequently drew on sets of beliefs which de-pict women as closer to nature, particularly those seen as less 'civilized'. For example, the habit of white women em-

ploying black women as wet nurses for their children continued in the southern states of America until the 1930s, a
remnant of slavery. Fildes notes that the milk of black women
was said to be produced in greater quantities than that of
white women. Similarly women in the British colonies, India for example, were encouraged to employ 'native' wet
nurses (Fildes, 1988). It might be possible to read these
practices as simply to do with social class, yet another expression of the culture/nature dichotomy which places lower
status women closer to nature. This would be something of
an over simplification. Our attention is readily drawn to the
image of the 'unnatural' bourgeois woman using other women
to carry out her responsibilities, or following the fashions
of the day. This may well be in part an accurate picture,
but there was often greater complexity arising from the relatively powerless position of even affluent women in relation
to men. For example, Fildes explores the reasons behind
the custom, amongst the well-to-do in seventeenth century
London, of sending children to be wet nursed. This was
often the result of husbands' wishes, particularly their desire to produce heirs, a possibility which would have been
limited by the contraceptive effect of lactation. Mary Woll-
stonecraft noted that desire for sexual relations on the part
of husbands was a key reason for wet nursing (Fildes, 1986).

The early history of infant feeding is therefore more complex than sometimes presented. There was no tidy epoch of
'natural' feeding existing prior to the development of large
scale baby milk manufacture. Throughout history there have
been many reasons why some children have not been breast-
fed by their mothers including: the death or illness of the
mother; being of royal birth; as a status symbol; 'parish'
children such as foundlings (Fildes, 1988). This history has
important implications for subsequent infant feeding discourses and relations. The supposed links between particular groups of women, black women and those of lower social
status, and 'nature' have been inscribed into the infant feeding
debates. Whilst wet nurses sometimes enjoyed high social
standing, their personal behaviour has always been subject
to the scrutiny of others, either parents or, in the case of
eighteenth century Prussia or nineteenth century France,
of the state (Sussman 1982; Schiebinger 1989). In Britain

in 1235 a law was passed which forbade Christian wet nurses suckling Jews. What began to change in the eighteenth century, and which Cadogan and Rousseau represent, was the sustained intervention of male (usually medical) experts. This development at this period was not accidental. It was accompanied by, and part of the same discursive field as, women being excluded from the public world and confined to the household. For example, Laqueur writes: 'no one was very interested in looking at the anatomical differences between the sexes until such differences became politically important' (Laqueur, 1986: 3–4). Sexual difference was emphasized and embedded in discourses of femininity, as part of a reinforcement of male authority over women, at a time when emerging liberal political discourses were rooted in a sexless neutral body.

Cadogan and Rousseau cannot be seen as straightforwardly conservative. They were actually writing critically about the dominant social order of the day, which involved the development of an extensive discourse, often in written form, concerning bourgeois femininity and behaviour (Poovey, 1984). The discourse of the 'natural' as applied to women represented an opposition to a culture which was seen by Cadogan and Rousseau as 'artificial'. Nevertheless, for Rousseau, women's sexuality (and in his view women were essentially sexual) was dangerous and therefore in need of control (Walters, 1976; Poovey, 1984; Schiebinger, 1989).

Cadogan's work was not an isolated incident as a piece of medical intervention. This period saw the intensification of the centuries long struggle between midwives and medical men for the control of childbirth with an increase in male supervision of childbirth and the first use of forceps by such male attendants in 1720 (Oakley, 1976b; Donnison, 1977; Schiebinger, 1989). This changing professional control was to have implications for infant feeding, as it did for childbirth.

By the early part of this century key elements of infant feeding discourses were already in place. These concerned the links made between good mothering, breast-feeding and nature. This was however a deeply ambivalent discourse since the women deemed closest to this position were those least valued socially, that is poor women and often black women.

Their worth as mothers derived from characteristics which were not of their making and hence their value was readily dissipated if their behaviour did not fit with their designated position and supposed nature. All women could be found wanting in this discourse, women of different classes and races were held up as both negative and positive examples to each other. Remedies for these pitfalls lay in the work of experts. Infant feeding and women who were deemed responsible for it increasingly became the subject of expert intervention (Hardyment, 1983).

IGNORANCE AND CARELESSNESS: 1900–1918

From about 1900 onwards infant feeding in many industrialised and industrialising countries became an issue for the state as well as experts as part of broader population policies. In fact women's failure to breast-feed had been a concern of the British state, as well as others, from the mid nineteenth century. Medical Officers of Health at that time maintained that women were prevented from breast-feeding by their work outside the home and that this was, in their view, a major cause of infant mortality (Hewitt, 1958; Lewis, 1980). The evidence for this link between women's work, early weaning and high levels of infant deaths was certainly not conclusive, but failure to breast-feed came to symbolize one aspect of poor mothering, expressed here in 1906 by Newman, who became the first Minister of Health in 1919: 'Expressed bluntly, it is the ignorance and carelessness of mothers which causes a large proportion of the infant mortality' (Newman, 1906, in Dyhouse, 1981: 96).

As well as poor hygiene and lack of household skills, Newman picked out the reluctance of young women to breast-feed as an example of 'ignorance and carelessness'. Similarly a report concerning Infant Welfare in the Newcastle area echoes the phrase maternal 'ignorance and carelessness' as a cause of infant mortality in 1924, once again commenting on the 'disinclination to breast feed' linked to the 'prevailing desire for amusement' (Bureau of Social Research for Tyneside, 1927: 6). The mother's ignorance and her work outside the home (as well as her desire for pleasure!), were commonly seen as the causes of infant mortality. If these were removed, it was suggested, women would go about their 'natural' business: child care, symbolized by breast-feeding, in the home. It is interesting that it was women in Lancashire who were particularly subject to these panics about mothering. In that region factory work for women was in abundance during the nineteenth century. A very different image of women's work at that period is quoted by Elizabeth Wilson. Women of Lancashire were described as 'higher in the social scale than in any other part of the world' (Hickson, 1840, in Wilson, 1977). This is a noticeable contrast with the picture of women, degraded by their work, and neglecting their children, expressed in the debates which had surrounded the Factory Acts of the 1840s (Davidoff, 1983). A failure to breast-feed, it seems, was associated with women who were not proper mothers, and who might also be too independent.

Some of the earliest interventions by the state into infant feeding were developed alongside, and symbolized, moves to keep women out of the workplace. Breast-feeding became more firmly linked to a discourse of good, and natural, mothering. The surveillance of working class families by the state, which was set firmly in place during the late nineteenth and early twentieth century (Donzelot, 1980; Lasch, 1977; Walkerdine and Lucey, 1989; Williams, 1989), has frequently focused specifically on the mother. The special place of mothers in this relationship between working class families and the state has been seen differently by various commentators. Donzelot has gone as far as to suggest that it is through mothers that the state carries out its surveillance and control of working class families. He suggested that social provision was, in France anyway, given to the woman so that she in her turn would exercise control over her husband and children. Some feminists have viewed this notion of surveillance of, and by, working class mothers rather differently from Donzelot. Barrett and McIntosh are uneasy about his portrayal of working class women as colluding with the bourgeoisie against the interests of their own class: 'The authoritarian patriarchal family is mourned, and women are blamed for the passing of this organic basis of social order. The text is incipiently anti-feminist, and even at times conjures up the readers sympathy for the "poor family" and the henpecked husband' (Barrett and McIntosh, 1982: 104).

Donzelot is again drawing on a nature/culture dichotomy in his approach, implying an original set of natural social relations unfettered by state interference or bourgeois culture. He refers specifically to breast-feeding in this context, arguing that medicine: 'attached a great importance in the explanation of illnesses to all frauds in the performance of the reproductive functions. The withholding of the mother's milk, the refusal to breast-feed – a tendency commonly found in women who were drawn into the artificial concerns of society life – was designated as the cause of a litany of ills' (Donzelot 1980: 171–2). Donzelot recognizes here that breast-feeding often becomes the vehicle for much wider concerns. But he fails to address the different implications of social provision for men and women. Donzelot's concern about the part which medicine has played in the disciplining of working class people is shared with many feminists, but his characterization of women as 'drawn into the artificial concerns of society life' conveys a notion of working class women as simultaneously duped, 'drawn into', but also as traitors to their class, participating in the 'artificial concerns of society'. In other words, he fails to account for the implications of biology within patriarchal social relations. Women's dependence on others is at least partly the result of their reproductive capacity, and the way this is used in any particular social situation. Women therefore have potentially different relationships to all social and collective forms. Because of this, feminist activism in relation to social policies has been driven to oscillate between emphasizing biological difference or ignoring it. The state in all its facets offers both policing of women through their construction as mothers, but at the same time some protection and resources in relation to needs which are linked to 'biology' particularly as this is constructed in a patriarchal society (Lewis, 1992).

i. Infant Welfare Movements

As we explore the implications of social policy and provision for infant feeding we confront this central dilemma for feminists: what can women get from the state and at what cost? Since the early part of this century organized women's groups have played a part in the development of infant feeding policies. In relation to infant feeding, as in other areas of welfare, war has been a catalyst which has brought together discourses of nation, race, and mother-hood with the demands of women themselves for relief from poverty and poor health. These have for the most part been shaped into a mixture of philanthropy and surveillance, rather than material assistance.

All countries, whatever their dominant political ideologies, attempt to influence and shape population growth, either through welfare or market mechanisms (Heitlinger, 1987) and infant feeding policies are best understood within these policies and practices. Perhaps the earliest infant feeding policy in Britain was the development of municipal milk depots. These 'milk dispensaries' (Poor Law Commission Minority Report, 1912) supplied at reduced costs pure milk and hygienic teats to mothers whose babies 'needed' arti-ficial feeding. The first such centre in Britain was established in St Helens in 1899 and by 1905 there were twelve such depots. These depots were developing in other European countries as well as in the US, and had their origins in France. In 1892 Pierre Baton, an obstetrician had founded a 'con-sultation des nourrissons' in Paris where babies were brought to the hospital for weekly weighings and for supplies of ster-ilized milk (this clinic was also said to encourage breast-feeding). In 1894 a similar centre called a 'Goutte de Lait' was founded by Dr Leon Dufour at Fecamp (Sussman, 1982). This approach began to expand in France in the context of the growing infant welfare movement, an international movement which took off at this relatively early stage in France because of concern about the falling birth rate and slowing population growth. In the USA compulsory sterilization of milk had been pioneered by Nathan Straus, whose first milk depot was set up in New York in 1903. The New York City Health Department operated 77 of these by 1913 (Oakley, 1984). Similar developments followed in other US cities (Apple, 1987).

In the United States these developments in making milk safer paved the way for doctors and later baby milk manufacturers to make themselves apparently indispensible to women trying to do their best for their babies. Oakley argues that in Britain these depots represented from the beginning both the supposed collectivism of the public health movement, and the individualism of weighing, advice and home visiting. She identifies these milk dispensaries as part of the development of 'lady visitors' and the health visiting profession and hence, as she sees it, of surveillance:

> The safe milk movement was, then, never merely a collection of milk shops, but from the start a systematic investment in the monitoring of maternal behaviour. Once networks of lady health visitors and sanitary inspectors had been established for the purpose of ensuring hygienic infant feeding, it was easy for their duties to extend beyond nutritional advice into every crevice of the whole realm of housewifery and motherhood. (Oakley, 1984: 42)

The Poor Law Commission Minority report was indeed enthusiastic about milk depots for this very reason:

> But the special interest of the 'milk dispensary' to the sanitarian is the personal supervision which it enables the Medical Officer of Health to exercise over those ailing babies. At Finsbury the supply of milk is made conditional on the babies being brought regularly for inspection, accurate weighing, and hygienic advice. Those who cannot be brought are visited in their homes. At Glasgow a qualified medical practitioner (lady) visits every home as a matter of course. (1912: 125)

Policy makers frequently saw working class people as *both* poor *and* ignorant. Milk depots, with assistance conditional on accepting middle class intervention, represented this dual concern. Women were expected to breast-feed but might be provided with alternatives if adequate excuses were given, and supervision accepted. 'Collective' policies were often simultaneously authoritarian and underpinned by beliefs about women, seeing them as being 'enabled' to carry out their 'natural', that is correct, functions through collective effort.

ii. Support for Motherhood

The developing infant welfare movement in the early years
of this century was informed by these discourses of scientific solutions to ignorant mothering practices. There was a
recognition of the need for some material help but also for
the intervention and educational efforts of the professions.
In Britain the Boer war, followed by the Inter-Departmen-
tal Committee on Physical Deterioration in 1904–5, focussed
attention on the welfare of infants and school children and
hence on mothers. Concern about these groups was expressed
very much in the language of race and imperialism, key
themes in British social policy particularly in war time
(Williams, 1989). Support for motherhood was essentially a
eugenicist and pro-natalist one, a concern with the quality
of the race. This period was one in which the state's responsibility for social welfare expanded; midwives became
more regulated and better trained (Midwives Act 1902); meals
could be provided at school for those who needed them
(The Education [Provision of Meals] Act 1906); and medical inspection began to take place in schools (Education
[Administrative Provisions] Act 1907). The first World War
reinforced these approaches and provided the basis for the
Maternity and Child Welfare Act of 1918 and for including
a Maternal and Child Welfare Department as one of the six
departments when the Ministry of Health was established in
1919.

Lewis has demonstrated that these policies were partly the
result of feminist campaigns for better services by groups
such as the Women's Co-operative Guild (Lewis, 1980). She
suggests that these groups did not separate broader improve-
ments in social conditions from more medical intervention.
However it was the latter, along with education for mothers,
which became the dominant form of assistance. Hence the
demands of these groups for material assistance in the form
of cash, meals, and for better birth control, were not met.
The expansion of state welfare was underpinned by beliefs
that family responsibilities should not be undermined; and,
of course, within the notion of family responsibility, mothers had a special place. Ambivalence characterized state
policies in relation to infant care and motherhood. There

was concern about the health of mothers and children, but the eugenicist language of race and nation also invoked notions of 'good mothers', who could improve their children's health through their own efforts. Milk depots became infant welfare centres in 1915 and these, along with 'schools for mothers', which had mainly been run by voluntary agencies, engaged in individual consultations as well as educational activities with mothers about health, cookery and housework. Lewis notes that, where breast-feeding advice was given, women were encouraged to follow strict feeding routines, which were thought at the time to build character (Lewis, 1984). However, the mixing of dried milk was also often taught. This perhaps indicates a lack of confidence in working class mothers, preferring, at this time when infant life was to be safeguarded, to apply 'scientific' solutions. It also enabled as Oakley (1984) indicates, greater control and surveillance.

American milk depots were also increasingly used for educational purposes. As Apple (1987) shows bourgeois women played a role in trying to shape the mothering of their poorer sisters. A group of women philanthropists in Madison, Wisconsin called the Attic Angels established a centre for well babies involving weighing and advice in 1915. An educational agency, Little Mothers' Clubs, attempted to educate young girls about baby care so that they could pass on what they learned to their mothers (Apple, 1987). There were numerous outlets for advice about mothering within which feeding played a major part.

In Britain World War One brought a more direct relationship to mothers and babies, reinforcing the role of the state in the feeding of babies. Local Authorities received assistance from central government in distributing milk to mothers and babies through a 'free milk order' whereby The Local Government Board paid 50% of the cost of milk distributed. These various policies resulted in increased bottle feeding even though this was not usually their expressed intention. It is important to consider why women may have gone along with this apparent undermining of their breast-feeding abilities. During this period exhaustion, poverty and poor health were linked with frequent pregnancy and breast-feeding. The poor health of working class women described in the 386 letters sent to the Women's Co-operative Guild in 1914 graphically depict the reality of their lives (Llewelyn Davies, 1978). It is not difficult to see that breast-feeding was a burden for many women. Lewis (1990) has shown how women actively sought anaesthesia in childbirth and hospitalization, in the social context in the early part of the century, as offering some respite from the hard labour of their ordinary lives. Bottle feeding can similarly be seen as a bargain offered by the state in return for keeping up the birth rate.

iii. Infant Feeding and Medicalization

Despite the fact that bottle feeding and sometimes the supply of cheap milk may have eased a small amount of the burden of child care carried by women this state provision also involved the undermining of women's knowledge and opened the door for greater medicalization of their lives. Apple describes this process in the United States: 'within barely three generations – between the late nineteenth and the mid-twentieth century – mothers lost their central position; babies were regularly bottle-fed under medical supervision' (Apple, 1987: 3). This transition was achieved, in Apple's view, through an alliance of infant formula manufacturers and physicians undermining women's knowledge and skills through ideologies of scientific motherhood which: 'defined women in terms of their maternal role centered in the domestic sphere. At the same time, however, it increasingly emphasized the importance of scientific and medical expertise to the development of proper childrearing techniques' (ibid: 97). According to Apple, these processes meant that 'official' insistence on breast-feeding became less adamant and it came to be believed that bottle fed babies were just as healthy as breast-fed ones. Opportunities for this belief to be reinforced came through increasing hospitalization for childbirth.

Apple's account also reveals a familiar class based discourse of breast-feeding. 'Civilized' women were assumed to be less and less able to breast-feed successfully because they were nervous and highly strung. In the US context, this alliance between physicians and baby milk manufacturers was strengthened by, for example, powdered milk not being accompanied

by instructions, so that mothers had to seek medical advice.
This ensured that physicians increased their status and expanded the scope of their practice. The supervision of bottle feeding then had direct material benefits for physicians
given the organization of health care in the US. It is possible to identify similar ideologies and social processes in
Britain, but there are also differences resulting from the
different organization of health care. The state intervenes
in motherhood in different ways in Britain, for example,
through the semi-professions, health visiting and midwifery.
Nevertheless a similar process of medical 'knowledge' and
influence overriding that of mothers and midwives occurred
in both countries (Donnison, 1977; Robinson, 1990). In
America this led to the virtual obliteration of the profession
of midwifery (Gaskin, 1988).

Fisher relates the undermining of women's breast-feeding skills to the concerns about infant mortality in the early
years of this century:

> Out of these concerns arose a new category of medical
> expert – one who has concerned himself with the nutri-
> tion of infants, but who, in practice, concentrated exclusively
> on artificial feeding. It was these experts who were then
> expected to produce the material to form the basis for
> the education programmes to be taken to the 'ignorant'
> women. (Fisher, 1986: 194)

According to both Fisher and Apple, this medicalization did
not just apply to bottle feeding, it also applied to breast-
feeding. For example, four hourly feeds for bottle fed babies
began to be applied to breast-fed babies as well.

BETWEEN THE WARS: THE POLITICS OF FEMININITY

In Britain the milk order which subsidized milk for mothers
and babies during world war one was revoked in 1921 and
gave way to a means tested system as a way of cutting costs.
However, nutrition became a key political issue in the inter
war years, with attention focused particularly on the health
of mothers and babies. The effects of poverty on diet and

health were extensively debated and became central to the campaigns of women's groups. Women had limited access to medical care, given that the 1911 National Insurance Act covered only working people. There were high maternal mortality rates, increasing in the 1920s. The kinds of lives led by working class women in this period, and the effect on their health were eventually documented in the 1939 Women's Health Enquiry which investigated the lives of 1,250 women (Spring Rice, 1981). This showed that the conditions in which women lived had hardly improved since the time when similar accounts were elicited by the Women's Co-operative Guild in 1914. Again breast-feeding is depicted as a burden additional to many others. In my study women said that their mothers 'had done enough' after breast-feeding several children. One woman, described in the Women's Health Enquiry, had five children under the age of four and a half, and was unable to breast-feed (Spring Rice, 1981: 53). Breast-feeding also added to an already long day, often starting at six am: 'If there is a suckling baby as well (and it must be remembered that the woman who has had seven or eight children before the age of 35 has never been without a tiny baby or very young child) she will have had to nurse him at least as late as ten the night before.' (Spring Rice, 1981: 97)

'Realistic' goals for improving nutrition rather than ideals had to be shaped by women's campaign groups. Free good quality milk became a primary aim, along with increased unemployment benefit, of the Children's Minimum Council (CMC) a broad based campaigning organisation established in 1934. These goals received broader support than 'Family Allowances' which many in the labour movement were suspicious of because of the perceived threat to the family wage. Throughout this period the struggles about whether poor child and maternal health was best remedied through material assistance or educating mothers continued. The preoccupation with children and the future of the race was always more popular than any concerns with the health of mothers themselves, despite these extensive campaigns and research concerning women's health. For example, many Labour women had campaigned for mothers to receive dinners for themselves so that they would not have to pool these with other family members. However such obvious benefit to women was the subject of continual dispute and the dinners were phased out in the 1920s. Another example of the narrow view of women's needs and of the dominance of pro-natalism is that a major aspect of 'ignorance' about which women themselves were concerned was birth control. There was a struggle over many years for this to be openly debated and tackled (Hall, 1981; Dale and Foster, 1986; Lewis, 1992).

Perhaps in order to maximize the benefit to women of this dominant discourse of concern for children, feminists, in the 1920s and 1930s, began to emphasize the dignity of motherhood as a service to the state. For example, Rathbone (who had founded the CMC), through the National Union of Societies for Equal Citizenship, began to emphasize the different 'natures' of women and the special job of motherhood which must therefore be supported. This discourse, which can be read in part as a pragmatic attempt to improve the lot of women, had other outcomes however, most notably in the treatment of women as housewives and mothers in the Beveridge report, which has been subject to extensive criticism (Wilson, 1977; Dale and Foster, 1986; Pascall, 1986). This discourse of natural mothering was also connected with other linked discourses about heterosexuality as we shall see below.

As Lewis (1980) observes, milk was increasingly seen as 'medicinal' during 1930s debates about health and poverty, in the sense that it was seen as a 'cure' for many ills. This view, combined with a large milk surplus, meant that cheap milk became increasingly acceptable as a social policy. This was not explicitly intended of course to reduce breast-feeding, at least as far as 'official' policy was concerned. Once again we can see bottle feeding, subsidized by the state, as a payment in kind over which women had control in the family setting, and which left them less exhausted than did breast-feeding. This, combined with its supposed 'medicinal qualities', must have brought at least apparent benefits, even though breast-feeding might be seen superficially as cheaper.

The reinforcement of a discourse of natural mothering was paralleled by a changing discourse of sexuality. This can also be seen as having an impact on breast-feeding attitudes and practices. It is of course the case that the female breast has long been associated with sexuality in various European cultures, probably since classical Greece (Henriques, 1959). What changes, however, are the particular discourses of female sexuality in which the breast becomes embedded at any particular time. Discourses regarding female sexuality had, earlier in the century, begun to be influenced by sexologists such as Havelock Ellis (1903), who depicted the female body as composed of a hierarchy of erogenous zones, with minor ones such as the nipples, culminating in the vagina and in sexual intercourse with men. Female sexuality began to be labelled, understood and endorsed through a particular form of science which saw women as having sexual bodies and appetites which complemented those of the male.

Feminists remain deeply divided about the lengthy period of so called 'sexual liberation' in which sexologists such as Ellis, and later, Kinsey, Masters and Johnson and Comfort have played a prominent part. On the one hand, these experts are seen as legitimating the existence of female sexuality, but on the other hand as framing it within patriarchy and compulsory heterosexuality (Coveney *et al.*, 1984; Campbell, 1987). According to Mort, it was particularly from the 1920s that sexual hygiene represented by 'the white coated male scientist and the plump, happy mother' (1987: 208) replaced social purity as the dominant discourse of sexuality in social policy. He suggests that: 'The purity movement – an amalgam of evangelical, patriarchal morality and biting feminist politics – was forced aside by a highly professionalised discourse on sex' (1987: 209).

Sexual hygiene was pursued by professionals and voluntary bodies through marriage manuals and sex education extolling the virtues of sexual intercourse in marriage, combined with pregnancy, as the source of fulfillment for women. For some contemporary feminists the social purity movement of the nineteenth century represents a radical critique of male sexuality, which was later discredited because of its real threat to male sexual power and privilege (Coveney *et al.*, 1984; Jeffreys, 1985). Other feminists have seen these movements as allowing increased state intervention into the lives of the poor and coercive practices directed at working class women, which imposed bourgeois norms of femininity

(Hunt, 1990). Whilst acknowledging the 'tension in feminism between disciplining and self-determination' (Mort, 1987: 211), Mort observes that feminism was, in the early part of this century, incorporated into a far less radical sexual politics, involving the professional reinforcement of heterosexuality which was, in the 1940s and 50s, 'written into the rubric of the welfare state' (ibid: 209). Weeks also recognizes the way in which sexology, science and the professions gradually created a discourse of 'sexuality in married love' (1989a: 200) involving a two fold process; on the one hand greater emphasis on sexuality within marriage and on the other greater control of sexuality outside the norm.

As noted above, Rathbone, in arguing for women as mothers depicted their needs as products of their biology and 'special' nature, and wanted them to fulfil their potential through womanliness in much the same way as advocated by Havelock Ellis. In other words, what might be seen as the pragmatic adoption of the discourse of natural motherhood in order to pursue the welfare of women, brought with it the demands of a linked discourse of active heterosexuality within marriage. In the 1930s, 1940s and 1950s there was increasing emphasis on love, sex and marriage. Women, even those who were 'respectable', were expected to be sexual.

Thus a range of new discourses around breasts and later about breast-feeding began to be added to the discursive field. Breast-feeding was no longer merely a duty when breasts began to have potential for fulfillment and pleasure. We will see in chapter five that breast-feeding itself became subject to sexualization, in the sense that particular sorts of sexual meaning developed around what for some women is a pleasurable physical activity.

If sensuality was emphasized in relation to the breasts as sexual objects, the opposite was the case in relation to breast-feeding at least as far as child care experts and baby care manuals were concerned. The period between the wars was characterized by the idea that babies should be trained in regular habits and this, rather than responsive intimacy and sensuality, was the sign of a good mother. Truby King and Watson advocated baby care, including, in the case of Truby King, breast-feeding, by the clock (Hardyment, 1983). Many women did not of course follow this advice but nevertheless were required to respond in some way to these expectations even if only in hospital or in reply to the questions of health professionals. In order to resist this some women emphasised breast-feeding as an important and special female activity. For example, Hardyment notes that in the 1930s, Marie Stopes (who can be seen as a part of the sexual hygiene movement), utilising evocative natural symbolism, rebelled against medical interference into 'the rhythmic response between your flow of breast milk and his happy and lusty development' (Stopes, 1939, in Hardyment, 1983: 182). In order to resist medical control and scientific intrusion, claims that women are especially natural and embodied creatures are frequently made by feminists, as they were by Rousseau and Cadogan. In accepting this oppositional relationship of science, or the artificiality of culture, to nature, feminists have been forced to work within the limitations of this fundamentally gendered discourse.

WORLD WAR TWO: PUTTING MILK INTO BABIES

Once again war brought cheap milk for British babies. One week after Dunkirk in 1940 a national milk scheme was announced. With treasury help, milk marketing boards were, under the Milk Industry Act (1940), to supply milk at cheap rates to school children and to expectant and nursing mothers and children under five years (Bruce, 1968; Darke, 1988). By September that year 70% of eligible mothers and children were taking part, nearly 30% of mothers receiving their milk free. A milk powder for babies, National Dried Milk, was similarly subsidised. In fact, infant feeding specialists such as Truby King had produced their own milk powders for some years and Cow and Gate were marketing their products fairly vigorously since at least 1920 (Lewis, 1980: 73–74), although of course these would have been available initially only to more affluent women. Perhaps most significant as an alternative to breast milk for poorer women until world war one was tinned condensed milk. Although it is difficult to be sure about its impact, National Dried Milk was undoubtedly of major significance in offering alternative acceptable feeding.

Government investment in baby milk was clearly a symbolic political strategy, as Churchill's words quoted below indicate: 'there is no finer investment for any community than putting milk into babies' (Winston Churchill broadcast 1943, quoted in Bruce, 1968: 300). More overtly eugenicist arguments were also used by government to support this investment, 'the raw material of the race is too valuable to put at risk' (House of Commons 1943 in Bruce, 1968: 300). In parallel with this high level political support, the Minister of Health had a year earlier set up a committee to 'consider what could be done to intensify the effort to secure more breast feeding' (MoH, 1943: 1). This report, mentioned in the previous chapter, can be read on two levels. First, it is a carefully argued document and considers a range of perspectives and possible influences on feeding. The approach to breast-feeding is a rather cautious one, stating that it 'is not a panacea for all the evils of infancy' and that 'our ultimate desire must be that infant health should be on the highest possible level, no matter what form of infant feeding is employed' (MoH 1943: 14). The evidence on breast-feeding is carefully weighed and, although the report finds in its favour, it suggests that 'appeals to nature can be overworked' (ibid: 9). It is critical of hospital procedures particularly of medical students with no real knowledge of breast-feeding. The report is also dismissive of the practices engaged in to prepare women for breast-feeding (scrubbing the nipples for example), describing these as a discouraging 'elaborate daily ritual' (ibid: 4).

Secondly, the report can be read as a discourse on women and in this respect it adopts a much more moralistic tone. As noted in chapter one, illegitimacy was a major concern and, although the report recognised the special difficulties of this, it considered some unmarried mothers of 'such an irresponsible type that even if they wish to keep their babies with them they wish to keep as few ties for themselves as possible' and that health professionals should consider it a 'moral duty to persuade her to begin breast feeding' (ibid: 4). Other 'categories' of mothers were mentioned. Some had 'an over-sophisticated outlook on life which leads them to reject this natural and instinctive function as unworthy of a civilized woman' (ibid: 3). Others had a nervous temperament and 'failed out of over anxiety' (ibid: 6). A third category represented the 'natural' mother, perhaps the same one who caught the eye of Cadogan! She was the woman with 'fifteen children who had quite easily and "automatically" borne and fed each of them' (ibid: 6). Thus women were stereotyped and set up each as a judgment on the other.

We therefore reach the end of world war two with a set of complex and sometimes contradictory discourses about breast-feeding. It was symbolically supported as the 'natural' behaviour of the good mother. It was then quietly traded off through the provision of an alternative method, via which women were encouraged to ensure the 'quality of the race' in war time. The trade off also brought further opportunities for surveillance and control of mothering habits. Although breast-feeding is supposedly 'instinctive' it required expert advice and intervention. Breast and bottle feeding were both subject to medicalisation. Breasts themselves were to be used for the 'natural' function of breast-feeding, but the 'real' woman also recognized their heterosexual potential as a good wife or 'partner'. Breast-feeding also drew on discourses concerned with the categorization of women as indicated above, specifying which women might be 'excused' breast-feeding, and which were irresponsible if they did so.

1945–1970: HOUSEWIVES AND MOTHERS – A JOB TO BE DONE

Women's position as workers during the second world war had not undermined their more fundamental role as mothers. Although women had been given help with feeding in war time this had not negated the belief that this responsibility nevertheless belonged to them since they were 'naturally' fitted for the task. The period at the end of the second world war involved a reinforcement of this mothering role. This was part of a shift of interest towards what went on inside families, as Wilson notes: 'The period since the second world war is marked off from what went before by an intensification of state interest in family life and in the child' (Wilson, 1977: 35). For women this meant that their behaviour as mothers and housewives became more carefully ob-

served and monitored, albeit to a large extent self-moni-
tored through women's own awareness of motherhood as a
job to be worked at. Riley (1983) describes the values of
'mother' and 'family' as promoted during this period as part
of an underlying pro-natalism which had been a prominent
part of pre-war and war time discourse. This did not mean
any greater actual support for breast-feeding than previously,
although symbolic endorsement remained. Rather, infant
feeding became more and more a part of the natural 'job'
of the housewife and mother. Anxiety about it prevailed, it
was complex and difficult, it involved thought, planning and
checking. Most particularly it could involve outside intervention. It was part of a mother's 'work' even though it was
simultaneously 'natural'.

An important aspect of this approach to child rearing was
increased emphasis on the psychological care of children,
of which breast-feeding was seen to represent one dimension. Riley (1983) draws attention to the influence of Klein,
Bowlby and Winnicot on discourses about mother–child
relationships. They frequently invoked metaphors of breast-
feeding to represent good mothering. These discourses added
weight to the importance of mothering but simultaneously
imbued it with potentially dangerous complexity and therefore anxiety. Feeding was often the channel for these anxieties.
This was a new kind of scientific endorsement of the 'natural',
now more fundamentally child centred, mother.

It is difficult to assess the impact of such thinking on
mothering and feeding experiences. Women, especially working class women, are likely to have experienced such changes
in expert-recommended feeding regimes in rather muddled
ways. For them there would be no clear movement from one
set of expert advice to another and it is much more likely
to have been experienced as a set of confusing and often
contradictory expectations, best not taken too seriously. Although many women in my study thought that breast-feeding
was probably best for the mother's relationship with the baby
few were seriously disturbed by the implications of not having done so. The Newson's study of infant care in the early
1960s suggests that it was middle class women, with their
higher rates of breast-feeding who were 'psychology conscious'
whereas working class ones 'feel free to suit themselves'

(Newson and Newson, 1963: 175), although such sharply drawn class divisions are likely to exaggerate the reality.

Growing hospitalisation for, and medicalisation of, childbirth (in Britain rising from 15% in 1927 to 66% in 1958) clearly had an impact on feeding experiences during this period. Although breast-feeding remained official policy little real attention was paid to it. The deskilling of midwives which greater hospitalisation for childbirth involved undoubtedly also contributed to this (Donnison, 1977). What is more, nutrition disappeared from the political agenda partly because poverty was perceived to have been tackled through welfare state provision (Lang, 1986/87; Blackburn, 1991).

There was however some resistance to the medical control of feeding and childbirth at this time. Most importantly the La Leche League, now an international pro breast-feeding organization, began in Illinois in 1956 (Apple, 1987; Gorham and Kellner Andrews, 1990). In the same year the National Childbirth Trust (NCT) supporting 'natural' or 'prepared' childbirth was formed in England (Kitzinger, 1990). This organization also became increasingly interested in breast-feeding, offering education and support systems. Neither of these organizations challenged dominant views of femininity however. In fact the La Leche League specifically supported the 'natural' mothers of large families who did not work outside the home and made mothering a full time job. For them the discursive connection between breast-feeding and the 'real' mother-at-home was a comfortable one, perhaps as a reaction against the dominance of scientific discourse regarding mothering. These organisations did however make some inroads into the medical control of childbirth albeit, at least in the 1960s, using, 'a very conventional image of femininity' (Kitzinger, 1990: 106). Moreover the NCT was, and has remained, an organization with a very middle class style and membership. These 'grass roots' pro breast-feeding movements are not for the most part shaped by the interests and needs of working class women. Neither are they feminist. Gorman and Kellner Andrews (1990) show, in fact, that the La Leche League often opposes what it sees as feminism and distances itself from feminists. Nevertheless both these organizations have been important in support for large numbers of women, and in at least prodding the medical establishment. They do so however within a basically similar discourse about women and mothering to that of the medical profession itself.

1970 TO THE PRESENT: BREAST-FEEDING CENTRE STAGE

As noted above the post war years had increasingly engendered a discourse of child-centredness for women. This was the case despite increasing numbers of women working at least part time outside the home. The concept of women's dual role, particularly dominant in post war Britain, according to Wilson (1977), inferred that women were satisfactory in neither role. Riley (1983) suggests that the dominance of motherhood as a 'value' meant that women as workers remain in a separate category from women as mothers, and hence their needs in both categories were not taken seriously.

It is interesting in this context that the period 1964–74 saw bottle feeding at its peak. Scowen, in a recent analysis of the changing fortunes of breast-feeding, related increased bottle feeding in that period to women's wish for greater freedom: 'Perhaps it had something to do with the growth of the permissive society and the individual doing his or her "own thing", but the mother was certainly given a choice of how she wished to feed her baby and her choice was usually accepted' (Scowen, 1989: 296). The use of the term 'permissive' also suggests some linkage with changing sexual practices. Although the form of heterosexuality envisaged and written into welfare policy in the 1940s was concerned with married love and sex, this did not stand still. Instead, within this post 1970s period, it began to move on to incorporate more 'liberated' (albeit firmly heterosexual) sex outside marriage. But for some women at least it may have added to their disinclination to breast-feed, a disinclination which had earlier been, perhaps unintentionally, reinforced by government action in providing subsidised baby milk and by rigid hospital practices. It is also interesting in the context of this low ebb in breast-feeding rates that in 1965 Britain had one of the lowest infant mortality rates in Europe, a situation which, as we shall see below was not maintained into the 1970s. Nevertheless the influence of the dominant discourse of child-centredness gradually took the form, in relation to infant feeding, of clear recommendations from government and child care experts of breast-feeding on demand. This even went so far with Dr Hugh Jolly, author of a popular baby care manual, as to recommend a family bed, where babies had constant access to the breast to facilitate this (Jolly, 1980). African women were called on as models of good natural mothering to be emulated by women in the developed world. This revival of ideas of natural mothering was seen by some as influencing rising breast-feeding rates amongst middle class women (Knauer, 1985; Manderson, 1985; Cunningham, 1988). This is an interesting reworking of Cadogan and Rousseau. And once again it is said to be backed up by sound scientific evidence. The 1970s and 1980s were dominated by research into infant feeding, both investigating the finer points of its health giving qualities (DHSS, 1974; DHSS, 1980; Hally *et al.*, 1981; Narayanan *et al.*, 1984; DHSS, 1988) and trying to pin down the recalcitrant mothers who still have not heard the message (Bacon and Wylie, 1976; Jones *et al.*, 1986; Leslie, 1986).

In most industrialised countries official policy and government backed research has increasingly endorsed breast-feeding. Fewer doubts about the importance of breast-feeding are now expressed than in the British government's 1943 report. As described in chapter one, there have been four large scale studies of infant feeding in Britain (Martin, 1978; Martin and Monk, 1982; Martin and White, 1988; White *et al.*, 1992). Government working parties have endorsed breast-feeding (DHSS, 1974; DHSS, 1980; DHSS, 1988). Breast-feeding seems to have been revived as an important part of government health policy. The most recent example of this was that increasing the incidence of breast-feeding was one of the proposed targets in the government green paper, *The Health of the Nation* published in June 1991 (Secretary of State for Health, 1991) although it was not in the end agreed as a target for change, perhaps because it may well prove too difficult to achieve. In a similar target setting exercise for public health the US government proposed increasing breast-feeding incidence from 54% to 75% by the year 2000 (US DHHS, 1990). There are a number of strands in this renewed interest in breast-feeding. One is a widespread recognition across the world that health policies need to have a preventive strand (DHSS, 1976; WHO, 1988: HMSO, 1992: US DHHS, 1990). Politically this has a number of dimensions including a perception that cost cutting might be served by endorsing prevention. Ideologically the language of prevention has almost universal popularity, cloaking support for individualism on the one hand, and greater collectivism and deprofessionalisation on the other (Crawford, 1977; Ashton and Seymour, 1988; Klein, 1989; Leathard, 1990). Breast-feeding also hung onto the coat tails of challenges to the medicalisation of childbirth, though it has never become anything like so prominent an issue.

Two aspects of this new commitment to breast-feeding are of particular interest here. The first is that explanations need to be sought for why breast-feeding has become significant enough in Britain to warrant four large scale surveys. At face value this seems a positive move, given the weight of evidence which supports breast-feeding as a means of improving health. However this needs to be placed in the context of other research and debate about health during this period. In the same decade as concerns about breast-feeding were being reactivated other worries about health were being expressed; in fact they were sometimes similar concerns. For example, there were growing worries about Britain's poor performance in improving its infant mortality rate compared with other developed countries. Britain ranked eighth in the world for infant mortality in 1960 but had slipped to fifteenth by 1978 (Townsend and Davidson, 1982). Also disturbing was the perception that there were still major inequalities in health related to social class and region within Britain. This led to the setting up of a working group by the Secretary of State for Health in 1977 to investigate these. What happened to this report has now become well known. By the time the findings were published in 1979 there had been a change of government. The Tory government, under Thatcher, was committed to cuts in public expenditure and to a very different form of welfare system than the report recommended. The report, known as the Black report, documented the differences in mortality and morbidity levels on the basis of occupational class and region (Townsend and

Davidson, 1982). These it attributed to material, rather than attitudinal, 'lifestyle' differences between the social classes and proposed anti-poverty strategies to tackle them. The report was played down by government. Nevertheless it has had a very considerable impact on research and sometimes on policy and practice at local levels. It has been followed up by other research and reports which have also found considerable evidence of widespread class inequalities in mortality and morbidity (Townsend *et al.*, 1988; Whitehead, 1988; Wilkinson, 1989; Phillimore *et al.*, 1994).

The British government, during the 1980s, continued to do its best to hide these views and reinterpret findings about poor health as products of individual choices. The political agenda around nutrition has become increasingly polarised between those who see structural and material causes of poor diet, and those who see these things as a result of the 'carelessness and ignorance' beloved of policy makers earlier in the century. Breast-feeding research and policy must be seen in this context. Although non breast-feeders are not explicitly labelled as ignorant breast-feeding must nevertheless be seen as representing a relatively safe political issue. This particular pro breast-feeding approach is narrowly based as far as babies' and mothers' health is concerned. For example, in the OPCS research mothers who experienced problems with childbirth are recognized as being unlikely to continue breast-feeding; but once this has been noted there is little further mention of these mothers (Martin and White, 1988). There is no discussion of the social class and regional pattern of these problems. Low birth weight babies for example, one of the types of 'problems' with birth mentioned, are known to be associated with deprivation (Townsend *et al.*, 1984; Townsend *et al.*, 1988). Instead of focusing on these broader health issues the policy agenda is limited to feeding habits and attitudes.

CURRENT LITERATURE AND DEBATE

Rather than a broader concern with women's health, 'scientific' attention goes towards providing increasing evidence to mothers that to breast-feed is to do your best for your baby. And there is certainly a wealth of evidence. For example, immunology has identified the chemical and cellular elements of human milk, particularly colostrum produced in the first few days after birth, which helps protect babies from disease. These qualities of breast milk, coupled with the reduced danger of infection which can accompany bottle feeding through dirty feeding equipment and water, suggest that breast-feeding can protect babies from mortality and various forms of morbidity. As well as the extensively documented protection against diarrhoeal diseases breast-feeding has been said to offer resistance to bronchitis and pneumonia (Hally *et al.*, 1981). It has also been thought to safeguard against 'cot deaths' and other more minor though still significant ailments such as eczema and asthma. In other words the supposed positive qualities of breast-feeding seem endless. From one short article (Rhodes, 1982):

> the mother-child interaction that develops during breast-feeding provides immense psychological satisfaction for both mother and child. (Ibid: 19)

> Compared to cow's milk, breast milk is higher in lactose. . . for rapid brain growth. The ratio of amino acids . . . also appears to favour rapid brain growth. . . better source of essential fatty acids. . . . important for skin integrity and proper nerve cell functioning . . . provides cell building material from non protein sources . . . more easily digested . . . enhances calcium absorption, becomes critical in preventing rickets. . . . ideal electrolyte and mineral composition for human growth . . . cow's milk associated with dehydration and the development of hypertension. . . tetany can result in the newborn from decreased calcium levels. (Ibid: 20)

> Both the placenta and colostrum are important sources of antibodies. . . Breast milk also contains antibodies against chicken pox, mumps, measles and polio . . . a lower incidence of respiratory infections . . . constipation is rare . . . feeding difficulties such as colic, spitting up, and allergic reactions are much less common . . . strong bacteriostatic effect on staphylococci and E. coli. . . protection against

infectious invaders . . . number of pathogens is further kept down. (Ibid: 21)

Besides the psychological bonding that takes place during breast-feeding, physiological bonding takes place as well. (Ibid: 21)

In the face of this bombardment of goodness some remain sceptical. One midwife wrote: 'My main concern is with the over-interpretation of the merits of breast feeding and the stress applied to some mothers to breast feed' (Kwakwa, 1984: 126). Under the huge weight of pro breast-feeding literature there is some concern about the narrow base of infant feeding policy. For example, Billingham (1986), a practising health visitor, notes the relationships between social class and inequality and that working class women are least likely to 'offer' maximum health opportunity to their infants through breast-feeding. She considers in this context what material resources might be needed for breast-feeding, identifying 'adequate diet, privacy, warmth, access to knowledgeable support and advice and time' (ibid: 159). She goes on to look at the material contexts of life for many working class women and suggests that their diet may not be adequate, that their housing may militate against privacy and they may lack support from the health services, for example through lack of transport. In such situations, she suggests, the supposed benefits of breast-feeding (going so far as, she says 'a reduction in child abuse, stronger mother/child relationships and increased intelligence' – ibid: 186) have been overstated.

This concern that the benefits of breast-feeding have been overplayed has also been noted with regard to developing countries. One of the most important criticisms is that the difficulty in separating breast-feeding from other factors in a baby's environment is frequently not acknowledged:

The positive association between breast feeding and survival is not in question. A problem of interpretation arises because the association could be generated by any of several causal mechanisms. Only a few studies have confronted these complexities and attempted to separate the actual

effects of breastfeeding from other mechanisms contributing
to its association with mortality. (Millman, 1985: 67)

Millman cites a number of problems with the apparent link
between breast-feeding and survival. For example, some babies
die before breast-feeding begins and on this basis those who
are breast-fed are already a smaller group than the total
number of babies born. Another difficulty is that babies'
health may affect the feeding method; some may be too
weak or ill to establish breast-feeding. Hence breast-fed babies
may represent stronger babies from the beginning. She examines alternative research strategies and looks at those pieces
of work which have taken these multiple factors into account. From this she concludes: 'although there is good
reason to expect breast feeding to affect the infant's survival chances, the quantitative, empirical evidence is less
impressive than it first appears . . . it seems likely that the
extent to which breast feeding protects health may have been
somewhat overstated in much of this research' (ibid: 76).

Maher (1992) also expresses disquiet that pro breast-feeding
messages may be offering an over simplified picture. In poorer
countries babies whose parents have a somewhat higher than
average income are relatively protected from health problems whether or not they are breast-fed. In any case breast-
feeding can only protect for the first four to six months. In
fact in many situations babies who are exclusively breast-fed
after six months are likely to have problems (Maher, 1992).
Campaigns against the sale of baby milk in third world countries might obscure the real causes of infant mortality which
are a wide range of material factors resulting from poverty.
This is not of course an argument in favour of infant formula promotion but rather against singling out breast-feeding from other factors affecting health. In addition it is in
those areas of third world countries where breast-feeding is
still the norm that infant mortality is also high. Again this
is not to deny the dangers of bottle feeding in some circumstances, rather to suggest that overstating its significance
can lead to a denial of the range of material influences on
health, many of which are not the 'choice' of mothers in
the way that breast and bottle feeding appear to be. Even
some pro breast-feeding campaigners have had 'second

thoughts' and acknowledged the importance of broader aims (Raphael, 1978). In addition, there is evidence in relation to health inequality generally that broader social circumstances are more important than particular instances of health behaviour (Blaxter, 1990).

The second linked aspect of this new commitment to breast-feeding is the reworking of the science mediated culture/nature dichotomy which it involves. This appears at the present time to leave very little room for critical analysis. Breast-feeding, human milk, mothering and breasts are talked of as part of nature, are pure, essential to the origins, and the future, of the species: 'Nature gives a mother the very best for her baby' (Stanway and Stanway, 1978: 44); 'opportunity can be taken (in schools) to portray breast feeding as a *natural function* which is enjoyable and convenient' (DHSS, 1988: 48 [emphasis added]). Coward describes breast milk as central to the nature/health discourse which, she argues, has become deeply embedded in our culture and beliefs: 'Produced by the mother's body and sought by the new-born child, it can be construed as the ultimate symbol of an original health and purity' (Coward, 1989: 30).

This natural substance and feeding method is however analyzed and labelled scientifically, recreating 'natural' on-demand feeding through expert intervention. This is 'modern' as opposed to old fashioned science. Doctors may have made some mistakes whilst, in the best interests of women and children, they tried to find alternative feeding methods. But in the future scientific rationality will find ways of recreating nature, 'if feeding practices (and with them the health and welfare of children) are to be improved, it will be through the application of scientific findings' (WHO, 1981c: 8). This view that science has finally got the 'right' answer with 'natural' demand feeding as practised by 'primitive' women leaving only irrational women to be convinced has been around for some time: 'When this regime becomes universally adopted so the last chapter on the history of infant feeding will be concluded' (Wickes, 1953: 501).

The research methodology arising from this paradigm is for the main part a positivist one, an attempt to get beyond the irrationality of women, to devise a rational and effective pro-breast-feeding strategy, based on the 'facts' of the health of breast milk, combined with increasingly well defined predictive categories of breast and bottle feeders and casting the net of influence wider, for example into schools (Hally *et al.*, 1981; Hellings, 1985; Brockway, 1986; Leslie, 1986; Sweeney and Gulino, 1987; Hawkins *et al.*, 1987; Alder and Bancroft, 1988; Coreil and Murphy, 1988; Kurinji *et al.*, 1988; Wright *et al.*, 1988). Although the 'natural' has come to have a very powerful appeal in modern Western society, particularly in its connection to health, it is very much a natural world mediated through science. Women remain linked with nature; the culture/nature dichotomy intact. In relation to infant feeding though, women's irrationality is doubly remarkable since they have to be reminded about, and retaught, the 'natural' through scientific and professional intervention. There is a constant assumption that women have to be told again and again the benefits of breast-feeding. Ironically women in poorer countries are now being advised about proper breast-feeding practice when current scientific recommendations 'are probably derived from women's actual practice in many developing countries, rather than from some Western discovery' (Maher, 1992: 5).

The idea that breast milk is self evidently pure and natural has also been questioned:

> Breast feeding is undoubtedly 'natural'– it is one of the few unequivocally natural female capacities. But the fact that it is natural does not necessarily make it good. After all hookworm is a perfectly natural phenomena but we do not recommend it as a good thing, nor do we suggest that infestation with lice would be a good thing for human beings because in monkeys mutual grooming facilitates physical contact and group bonding between individuals. (Gomm, 1976: 318)

While this is somewhat facetious it nicely raises the point that 'natural' substances and phenomena do not have some essential purity. We are dealing with a very particular interpretation of nature. A peculiar, somewhat contradictory view of this is evident in the breast-feeding literature. Breast milk is vaunted as always of the right quality despite the nutritional status of the mother: 'Experience has shown, however, that mothers with nutritional deficiencies can, and often do, produce amounts of milk that are only slightly less than average. More importantly, their milk does not vary significantly in composition from that of other mothers and can thus make a vital contribution to infant health and well being' (WHO, 1981c: 1).

This 'fact' is repeated in much of the literature. It is suggested then that even where women are starving their breast milk is still of good quality, and they should therefore still breast-feed. This is in contrast with the view that women need to carefully manage their diet if benefits are really to be gained from breast-feeding. For example, the article referred to earlier which extolled the virtues of breast milk (Rhodes, 1982) went on to give complex instructions for the management of breast-feeding including the mother's diet:

> An adequate fluid intake must be maintained to produce an adequate milk supply. Besides drinking 4 to 6 eight-ounce glasses of milk daily, at least four glasses of other fluids should be consumed . . . one or two additional servings of meat or other high protein food such as peanut butter; one additional serving of a dark green or yellow vegetable; one additional serving of either a vegetable or fruit; and one or two additional slices of enriched or whole grain bread. (Ibid: 55)

In addition a range of foods is forbidden because they might not be tolerated by the baby – garlic, onions, cabbage, turnips, broccoli, and beans. Kitzinger is more liberal, 'You do not need a special diet in order to breastfeed' (1979: 149) but then devotes a whole chapter to discussion of diet. Of course this contradiction might be to do with minimal versus ideal standards but it also suggests perhaps that women need to be carefully managed or to manage themselves if they are to fulfil their 'natural' functions. Breast milk then is only as pure as the mother who produces it. HIV and AIDS have made the 'natural' even more problematic in this respect, since there is a possibility that the virus can be passed through breast milk (DHSS, 1988). Other enviromental influences may also make breast-feeding hazardous. For example in Eastern European countries caution has been expressed about wholehearted support for breast-feeding: 'it has recently become clear that under current environmental conditions in Czechoslovakia, prolonged breastfeeding is not the panacea it is sometimes thought to be for the physical and mental health of babies and mothers' (Heitlinger, 1987: 239). This is because pesticides and other agricultural chemicals contaminate water supplies which then affect breast milk. Similarly drugs can be passed through breast milk, also indicating that breast milk does not exist in some separate 'pure' natural world. The US government states that it is not appropriate for mothers who are drug users of various kinds to breast-feed.

The idea that breast-feeding is what 'real' women do naturally has been with us for many centuries, even if it is accompanied by the belief that those who do it best are of little value within 'culture'. As in the eighteenth century the 'natural' is currently constructed as a positive alternative to an 'artificial' civilisation, but one endorsed and managed by science.

That breast-feeding is as 'good' for women as it is for babies is also part of the scientifically endorsed health/nature discourse. There is an assumption that the mother and baby pair can be seen as a unit, and that mothers will 'naturally' put the babies needs before their own wishes. Indeed mothers are not expected to have separate needs or wishes of their own. It is a daring mother who suggests that the baby's needs may not be all: 'From the moment you know you are pregnant you are bombarded with advice to breast-feed – from the doctor, at the ante-natal clinic, at birth classes, in hospital when you have the baby, from the health visitor, from books and from many friends too. The argument is put entirely in terms of the baby's physiological and psychological needs' (Bisset, 1986: 28).

It appears to have been very rare in the social policies of many industrialised countries for mothers to be seen as having needs of their own. A report for the Food and Agriculture Organization of the United Nations (FAO) tried to express the complex relationship between women's needs and those of their children: 'it must be considered a human right of women to be able to fulfil their reproductive functions in ways that imply no detrimental effects to themselves or their offspring, nor interfere with their other roles and their own personal development' (FAO, 1979: 60). This is not a value which has informed infant feeding policy in many countries. There has even been mention that receiving its mothers milk may be part of a child's civil rights (Lawrence, 1988). Breast-feeding has been embedded in discourses of femininity, which specify what women ought to be and infer that if women are not like this it is because of some moral failing. Women are not expected to need any resources or particular conditions to perform this function since they are only after all doing what ought to come naturally. They are in the phrase of Parsons and Bales, part of the 'lactating class', the fundamental gender division from which follows all manner of 'natural' requirements (Parsons and Bales, 1956). However since Western women have seemingly lost the ability to readily perform this natural function special attention in the form of professional intervention has been provided. This is not however to argue that breast-feeding is unnatural, rather to try to explore the discourses of which it is a part, and to disrupt the particular scientifically endorsed culture versus nature dichotomy which has become fundamental to gender divisions. This necessitates looking for ways to reinforce women's own control of infant feeding and of how their breasts are 'used'.

3 Infant Feeding in Women's Lives

I asked women who had babies between 1920 and 1980 in a particular part of one city in the North of England to tell me about their experience. I did not treat their accounts as 'true' in some objective sense. Rather, I saw them as 'stories' in the sense of accounts arising from complex combinations of experience, understanding, reflection and discussion. There were various layers in the production of these stories. My interviews were interventions into a set of memories, beliefs, thoughts and feelings. The stories which were told were affected by: the accuracy of each woman's memories; whether and how she has processed and understood her own experience; how much opportunity she has had, or currently has in her life for thinking about her own experience and feelings; what kind of use she wishes to make of the interview – social chat, reassurance, learning, influencing change; how she perceives my intentions and wishes; whether the interview provokes a tidy response to an area of life now finished or locks into complex 'unfinished business' in the sense of uneasy or uncomfortable feelings. My hearing and recording of the stories is also important; my biography and my perspective as a feminist affects what I hear.

But to describe the stories as 'theirs' in any simple sense is also problematic. For women to be the 'I' of their own story is not straightforward. In many areas of women's lives the scripts, in the sense of discourses of femininity, are already written at least in outline (Urwin, 1985; MacCannell and MacCannell, 1987; Weedon, 1987; Smith, 1988; Butler, 1990b; Flax, 1990; Cosslett, 1994). It is within, and in spite of, these already written scripts that women understand and talk about their own experiences. For example, in relation to infant feeding, there is an assumption, shared at least at a superficial level by policy makers, health professionals and women themselves that women ought to breast-feed in order to do mothering properly. This affects the way in which women themselves talk about their experiences.

My intention was not simply, however, to produce a set of individual stories but to explore ways of understanding these stories at a more general level. This is intended to be an inside story (told by an outsider) of the type of community which has for long been seen as inadequate with regard to how it feeds its babies. Whilst the study supposed considerable unity with regard to class and locality, a point I will return to in the concluding section of this chapter, potential variation was included through looking at different groups of women; differences of generation and ethnicity for example. This is not a search for the 'causes' of either bottle or breast-feeding. My purpose is to identify and examine the structures and discourses which shape choice, decision making, experience and practice. In this chapter the women's stories, and particularly changes, continuities and differences in these, are the starting point for specifying these structures and discourses. It is these which give the study significance beyond its geographical location.

As indicated in chapter one, there have been many social changes affecting women's lives which might be expected to have an effect on infant feeding during this period. Some of these changes – medical intervention in childbirth, promotion of infant formula followed, in more recent years, by restrictions on this promotion – relate fairly directly to infant feeding. Other – numbers of women working outside the home, changing expectations regarding sexuality – while less immediate, might also be expected to influence the experience. As well as these broad changes, each woman also has her own context, including a generational one – how she relates her experience to that of her mother and possibly her daughter. In this way I am able to look at a part of the process through which generational change occurs. I include women whose origins lie in India and Pakistan in order to reflect the changing nature of the population of this city and of others. I neither assume that their experience of infant feeding will be different from white women in the study, nor do I assume that it will be the same. Rather I look at the ways in which their experiences have been shaped by their ethnicity and their social position as 'Asian' women living in Britain, as well as through the same structures and discourses which shape the experience of white women.

The focus of the chapter then is on continuity and change with regard to infant feeding. Within this and other chapters, where I have quoted from a woman's account I have given in brackets her name (a false one) and the year in which she had her first child.

BREAST AND BOTTLE FEEDING 'CATEGORIES'

The most basic requirement of infant feeding studies is to say how many women bottle fed, how many breast-fed and for how long. The OPCS studies discussed in chapter one (Martin, 1978; Martin and Monk, 1982; Martin and White, 1988; White *et al.*, 1992), along with most other infant feeding research, make this a central part of their work. The world is thus divided into bottle feeders and breast-feeders, according to some specified criteria. This division is both based on, and reinforces, 'common sense' language. For example, women ask each other, 'did you breast-feed yours?'. Similarly, 'do you know if you were breast-fed?' is a readily understood question. Despite difficulties in devising these categories most studies continue to try to do so because they have either an implicit, or more often, an explicit commitment to 'success', as measured by numbers of breast-feeders. Prevalence of breast-feeding at particular ages of the baby helps measure and compare one group, one region, one generation, one nation with another. And the comparison is made in order to try to identify which group, region or generation is 'better'. Whilst such comparisons are not without meaning, their value in understanding women's experiences is limited. Women's stories are more complex, as we will see, even though they may be able to slot themselves into the breast-feeders or bottle feeders categories.

Simple divisions by bottle feeding and breast-feeding categories would not do justice to the experiences of women in this study. There were only a few women for whom bottle feeding played no part. Hence the overlaps, the complexities, and the meaning of infant feeding is disguised by the construction of categories based on breast-feeders and bottle feeders. Most of the women experienced both breast and bottle feeding. The assumption that studies will reveal tidy categories of breast and bottle feeders is not simply an inevitable error of positivist research. It is also based on the assumption that 'natural' feeding practice, unadulterated by Western 'civilization' or 'ignorant' women, is for women to breast-feed totally, giving the baby no other food for about six months. In an important, though remarkably unnoticed, anthropological study of infant feeding in several cultures, Raphael disputed this assumption: 'early on in our study, as the fieldworkers' notes began to come in, we were struck by the evidence that breastfeeding women in traditional cultures gave their babies all kinds of food in very small amounts at an early age, in some cases when the infant was just two weeks old' (Raphael, 1985: 141)

Raphael's study casts doubt then on the simple notion of 'traditional' exclusive breast-feeding patterns. Women in the five different cultures she studied adopted different feeding habits depending on specific resources available to them balanced against demands on their time and energy. That women gave their babies all sorts of other foods even when they were supposedly breast-feeding was only revealed through observations by fieldworkers, since women *said* that they gave their babies nothing other than breast milk. It may well be that the few exclusive breast-feeders in my study also used other foods without deeming themselves to have moved from the breast-feeding category. Maher (1992) also questions the notion of a universal, unchanging definition of successful breast-feeding. This kind of thinking, she suggests, stems from seeing breast-feeding as purely a physical and psychological relationship between two individuals rather than as existing in complex social and economic contexts.

My intention was to listen to stories including the nuances, complexities and feelings involved in feeding babies, rather than gathering 'facts' about the numbers of women who breast or bottle fed. Through what social process did the women arrive at their own practice of infant feeding? My first question in the 'feeding story' was: 'Had you already made your mind up before the baby was born how you were going to feed it?'. Thus I introduced the discussion using a form of language which is about 'decision making' expressed colloquially. Starting before the birth in this way at first seemed an obvious way to begin. Since decision making forms the basic focus of many infant feeding studies and policies I had, presumably, accepted that women make some kind of 'decision', even though it might not be in line with the policy makers wishes. In retrospect it is odd that I had been so much influenced by this approach since, from the beginning, I had understood that women do not necessarily 'make decisions' in the positivist way implied by the language. I had seen their 'decision making' as understandable only within the context of their own lives, as they understood their lives to be. I had seen much of their practices around infant feeding as an extremely complex process of making decisions and accounting for them by reference to very specific facets of their context, perhaps using the language of dominant discourses. In the pilot stage of the study I had already begun to identify the way in which women conceptualized decision making. One example, an answer to my question about whether this woman's daughter breastfed, demonstrates this:

> Well she was very poorly carrying both her children. She was in hospital for a few weeks before the delivery and they had to give her an epidural, but she wanted the second one. She had to plead with her husband. He said 'Jean, I'm not having you going through that again'. She was in a lot before the first was born but with the second she was only in twice. She brought the second one herself, but they had to bring the first because her blood pressure was so high. I was staying with her when she had the second. She's fine after she's had the baby. (Mary Anderson, 1939)

I did not experience this in the interview as a lengthy digression. It was clearly relevant to my question which she later returned to with a more straightforward answer, 'She bottle fed straight away'. What she was expressing was the context of feeding, both in terms of her daughter's health, and the emotional and social events surrounding the birth. It could also of course have been a defensive response to a 'snoopy' question, and she clearly dealt with the moral tone of my later question about whether she thought her daughter was doing 'the right thing' in a more defensive way:

'Yes, in her condition. She would have liked to have fed them but the hospital put the baby straight on the bottle.'

The way in which decisions arise from complex situations, rather than being actively 'made', was reflected in later interviews. Two examples illustrate this:

> When I got out of bed and was busy and that I got a milk infection, the midwife advised the milk be taken away. She gave me pills and put her on the bottle. I had very sore breasts, very painful. I drifted onto the bottle. (Jean Richards, 1949)

> I was going to breast-feed and in fact I did when I was in hospital and for a week when I got home. But the circumstances in the flat were such that I didn't feel relaxed. And of course I had to go somewhere else to feed him. (Beatrice Callender, 1968)

Beatrice's last sentence was uttered in a heavily ironic tone. When explored further, it concerned the fact that she and her husband were living with her mother-in-law, and Beatrice was embarrassed about feeding in front of her. Even this, though, is too simple. Beatrice, as she put it, 'had to get married' and her mother-in-law disapproved of her, 'she thought I was a snob'. Embarrassment then did not simply result from the breast-feeding activity but was an expression of tensions and discomforts in the relationship.

Such accounts indicate that the processes by which infant feeding practices develop for any individual woman are a complex mixture of: her health; the assessment by others of her health; the perceived impact of her health on feeding; and a range of social factors including household membership and other demands for work and energy. Maher (1992) notes that, in making decisions about how long to breast-feed women take into account not only the welfare of the child and of other children but also, 'their own physical and psychological health, the availability of food and the pressures of work' (ibid: 29). The relationships between practices adopted and initial plans and decisions are complex. A woman may account for a practice which she drifted into, or which arose from her situation, by producing 'a reason' in retrospect. There are also several stages in decision making which may or may not connect very directly with each other. So an intention to breast-feed may still be accompanied by almost immediate bottle feeding. There were several examples of this: 'I'd said I would breast-feed. I just wanted to I don't know why. I talked about it to my husband but I just made my own mind up in the end' (Mandy Scott, 1970).

Nevertheless Mandy bottle fed more or less immediately saying 'she just wouldn't take it, believe it or not'. This was not expressed as failure; she had already kept her options open by buying a sterilizer in advance of the birth. This might be seen as someone starting off with the 'right' answer and quickly reverting to her preferred one. But it appeared more complex than that. Her confidence in herself and her commitment to pursue her intentions were clearly shaped by what happened immediately after the birth: 'They took her away straight after the birth. I had a go the next day. Whether I was nervous and projected this I don't know. I never had a big bust but I did then. There was plenty of milk. She just wouldn't open her mouth.'

Another example of the difference between stated intentions and outcome illustrates the subtle effects of the context on eventual practice: I had decided to breast-feed. I hadn't discussed it. It just seemed the right thing to do, better for the baby, cheaper, the natural way to do it' (Gina Godfrey, 1969). However this woman's positively stated intentions turned into complete bottle feeding within six weeks. A range of contextual factors influenced this: 'In hospital it wasn't easy as there was no-one to show us. Only one nurse took an interest – a middle aged woman who offered some encouragement. When I came home I gave him top up bottles to stop him crying. I thought, this is ridiculous, I wasn't getting anything else done in the house. I wasn't doing anything but feeding.' The baby's colic, which she found very difficult to handle, clearly contributed to this. But her husband's attitude, albeit not openly expressed, didn't help: 'I don't think he was very happy. He never said anything apart from once. He woke up in the middle of the night and said, "are you feeding him *again?*" Funny how these things stick in your mind.'

COPING WITH THE 'WORKING CONDITIONS'

In the last section I noted that any simple categorization of breast-feeders and bottle feeders is, for the most part, false. Most women experience both. What is more, the path to eventual feeding practice is a complex one, involving a range of factors, both emotional and material. In this section I take this discussion further by exploring the way in which much of the research on infant feeding sidesteps this complexity and pays scant attention to the conditions under which infant feeding take place. It is useful to conceptualize the situations in which feeding occurs as 'working conditions' in order to avoid the tendency to see tasks undertaken by women as simply arising from their natural biological capacities. Many activities routinely undertaken by women, particularly those which are unpaid, are seen as expressions of their femininity. Feminists, through research and activism, have redefined these as work. A number of areas including housework (Oakley, 1974) and the care of children, elderly people and those with disabilities (Finch and Groves, 1983; Graham, 1984) have been subject to this kind of redefinition and scrutiny. Conceptualizing such activities as work, rather than as extensions of biology, is both an important political strategy and opens up these areas for sociological enquiry. The notion that the conditions under which women's unpaid labour takes place are as important as working conditions in the 'public' world has been an important part of feminist scholarship, particularly regarding the effect of these on women's health (Brown and Harris, 1978; Doyal, 1983; Graham, 1984; Doyal, 1990). There are some problems, however, with describing these varied experiences as 'work'. For example, Gieve (1987) questions feminist representations of mothering as labour. For her this omits many of the most significant dimensions of being a mother, most importantly that it is about a relationship which cannot be limited, contained and controlled, a relationship which is so fundamental to both people that it cannot be reduced to a set of tasks. Morris (1993) is similarly critical of the way in which feminists have labelled 'caring' for older and disabled people as work rather than as a relationship involving much more than just labour. Hence I am using this formulation of infant feeding as work tentatively in order to provide a disruptive reading of the dominant narrative of femininity. I will return to these debates about work and non-work in the next chapter to show how particular public/private divisions have shaped infant feeding.

The methodology of infant feeding studies such as those carried out under the auspices of the OPCS (Martin, 1978; Martin and Monk, 1982; Martin and White, 1988; White *et al.*, 1992) tends to direct our attention away from the social contexts or 'working conditions' of infant feeding and towards individual attitudes. Where they do address contextual factors these relate mainly to hospital practices in ways which reflect the concerns of those who devise the policies. In these studies a number of categories are used as 'reasons for stopping breast feeding' (Martin and White, 1988: 29) by those who had started. The most common reason was 'insufficient milk' followed in descending order of frequency by: painful nipples; baby would not suck; breast-feeding took too long; the mother's illness. Other slightly less common reasons were: did not like breast-feeding; inverted nipples; babies illness; embarrassment. These categories are recognizable amongst the women in my own study. Fifteen (half) of the women in my study had started breast-feeding but had ceased before one month and would thus have had to provide an explanation and be slotted into a category by the OPCS research team. It is useful to compare the category to which they would have been assigned with the story from their point of view. Two very different examples are given here. Lucy Cooper in 1930 would have been in the most common category of 'insufficient milk'. She said that after six weeks 'the milk left us'. She saw this as a result of her poor health and the loss of an earlier baby. The baby she had given birth to a year earlier had died at two weeks of age because Lucy herself had a poisoned knee when she was seven months pregnant 'which went right through to the baby'. Lucy became pregnant very soon afterwards. She had very poor circumstances, her husband was unemployed and they were living on means tested 'dole'. She and her husband lived in an upstairs flat with the only running water outside in the back yard. Lucy took in washing to supplement the 'dole'. Her husband, although 'he loved his children, didn't bother with them really' and Lucy undertook all housework and child care in difficult conditions.

Naheed Ahktar (1970) would also have been placed in the 'insufficient milk' category after three months of breast-feeding. Naheed was basically unhappy about breast-feed-ing but felt she should do what the hospital said. She was embarrassed about breast-feeding and uneasy about discuss-ing anything to do with the body. What is more she said that she felt unhealthy all the time in this country. She told me that the only time she had felt well in recent years was when she spent one year in Pakistan and helped her rela-tives to build a house! This was despite the worry of having left her children here. Her second child had died and she felt worried about the health of all her children. She was very young, sixteen or seventeen, when she had her first child soon after coming to this country. Germaine Greer wrote evocatively of the experiences, as she saw them, of Asian women as mothers in Britain. One feels she might be talking of Naheed:

> Transplanted from their villages to the decaying inner suburbs of dull industrial towns, these women suffer greatly, despite the fact that they have a better chance of bearing healthy children than they had at home. Their misery is not simply explained by their ignorance of the language or the thinly disguised racial hostility they encounter. Their entire support system has vanished: from being never alone they have moved into a situation of utter solitude. (Greer, 1984: 22)

These two examples, as well as those of Jean Richards, Beatrice Callender and Mandy Scott discussed in the pre-ceding section, indicate a number of 'working conditions' which are pertinent to infant feeding practices. The woman's own health is an important consideration. The particularly poor health of working class women at certain historical periods (Llewelyn Davies, 1978; Spring Rice, 1981; Kenner, 1985) is both a product of the 'working conditions' of women's domestic labour and in itself provides the context for infant feeding. Having a heavy burden of other work to do, especially when this is combined with poverty and a lack of support, is similarly important. Lack of confidence and unhappiness are also significant, for example in the case of Naheed. Having to please other people – mothers-in-law, husbands, health professionals – is similarly relevant. Embarrassment must also be recognized as a 'working condition' in that it arises not simply from women's individual attitudes but from the expectations of modesty common in this culture and across much of the Western world with regard to breast-feeding (Jelliffe and Jelliffe, 1978; Raphael, 1985; Van Esterik, 1989).

It is possible then to see that the catch all category 'insufficient milk' covers a wide range of social circumstances and working conditions. Although these conditions affect individual women differently they nevertheless arise from their social location as working class women in a particular geographical area and historical period. As a group these women did not live in situations which were able to offer very much support and care for new mothers. Some individuals undoubtedly had better circumstances than others. The notion of 'working conditions' however directs our attention towards more general underpinning circumstances rather than to individual attitudes and situations. Doyal (1983) uses the notion of 'domestic hazards', drawing on the language of health and safety, as a way of directing attention to the unhealthy conditions under which many aspects of women's work are carried out. The cases noted here suggest situations which are hazardous to breast-feeding in the sense that it is embarrassing, time consuming, tiring, and difficult to do, rather than supportive of it except in a somewhat symbolic, often medically oriented way, for example being expected to do it whilst in hospital.

Raphael's cross cultural anthropological study, referred to above, offers interesting examples of societies which are organized to support breast-feeding (1985). This is mainly because they have to be; there is no realistic alternative for feeding babies. Raphael uses the term 'doula' to describe the arrangement in many societies whereby the new mother will have someone to help her with the new baby and relieve her from other responsibilities and from stress over a period long enough to establish breast-feeding. She argues that some kind of doula system is essential to successful breast-feeding.

Raphael's account of the childbirth experiences of a woman in a very poor area of the Philippines provides an example of a doula system. Odani told the researcher that, during each pregnancy, she works in the fields until the time of the birth, but afterwards her life undergoes a dramatic change. For a week both she and her husband do no work. This is done by grandparents and other relatives. After childbirth in this community the grandmother usually visits daily to help the husband with housework and to give the new mother herbal baths. After the cord drops off in about a week, a naming ceremony is carried out and special food is eaten. For two months Odani's fields are tended by others and she is encouraged to feel serene and have a sense of well being. A young mother will feel highly valued during this period. Women in her community, as in the West, often experience painful nipples and the other problems of breast-feeding but have lots of support and encouragement from relatives. Their families and others in the community are very knowledgeable about breast-feeding. In Odani's language there is only one word for breast, nipple, breast milk and breast-feeding. The female breast is not seen as decorative or sexual; its meaning is entirely connected with breast feeding. Despite all of this, two out of Odani's five children have died. Although they have clean water the environment is contaminated by rats and insects, as well as by the pigs which are kept as a source of food. Poverty means that nutrition is more of a problem once children are weaned. Hence systems which successfully support breast-feeding cannot always overcome these negative features.

What are the equivalents to a doula system for women in the industrialised world? In my study the major source of support was from the women's own mothers. Studies of women in working class communities have frequently observed the close contact between mothers and daughters particularly at the time of childbirth and in relation to advice and support about childrearing (Young and Willmott, 1957; Kerr, 1958; Blaxter and Paterson, 1982). In my study, although this general support was observable, help from grandmothers was not directed towards breast-feeding itself. For example, Polly Williams (1932) stayed in hospital for a few weeks after the birth since she had a septic breast. Her mother, who lived three streets away from Polly was an informal midwife, 'she used to go out bringing babies into the world', and came in every day to help her with the baby. Nevertheless Polly did not breast-feed and her mother did not try to encourage her to do so, because of the breast problem. In other cases, having support with other responsibilities was connected with breast-feeding in a rather indirect way since it provided a context where women did not have too many competing demands. For example, Mary Moreland (1936) had her baby at home and appeared to receive substantial support afterwards with the midwife's daughter calling in daily for several weeks. In addition both her own mother and her mother-in-law lived very nearby and she saw them often. In these circumstances, and with no health problems, Mary breast-fed for seven months. Jane Harrison (1936) had her baby at home and lived with her parents. Her mother did the cooking and was very supportive. Initially breast-feeding went well. However her mother went for a visit to Ireland when the baby was three weeks old and it was after that that she 'failed' at breast-feeding: she felt the baby wasn't getting enough milk.

Some women had little support from their own mother and here breast-feeding was not even attempted. Florence Hope (1941) lived with her mother and sister. But her mother did not help with the baby, 'you had to get on with it. I did my mother's washing and cleaning as well as my own'. Florence didn't breast-feed, ostensibly because of inverted nipples. She did not recall this period of her life as a positive one because of the hard work involved and lack of help. Breast-feeding would clearly have been an added difficulty in such circumstances. Similarly Monica Andrews (1951) breast-fed for four weeks but found she didn't have enough milk. She got little help, 'I had a stepmother, she was a lady who didn't put herself out'. Patricia Poole (1965) also had very little support. Although the midwife visited her, she resented what she saw as interference. Her own mother wasn't well enough to offer any help although she did get advice and support from a friend and the friend's mother. She didn't breast-feed at all because she found it distasteful. Patricia found the transition to motherhood very difficult. It is hard to imagine her thinking it worthwhile to overcome her uneasy feelings about breast-feeding in such circumstances.

These brief examples do not indicate a set of customs geared towards the support of breast-feeding as in Odani's community. Support and help were nevertheless sometimes available to women, mainly from their own mothers. But, as other studies of mother/daughter relationships have indicated, such help is not always forthcoming (Lewis and Meredith, 1988; Finch, 1989). There is a firm belief, including from women themselves, that this is an expected source of advice and support. Where women did not have mothers able to offer support, for whatever reason, they always commented on this and saw it as a problem. In a community such as this, as in most others in the industrialised world, where breast-feeding is not seen as essential to life, resources, help and support tend to be directed towards relieving the mother of too much work, caring for her health or offering advice about the baby, rather than towards breast-feeding as such.

For women in this study it was their extended family rather than official services who were called on for support. Many of the women actually lived with their extended family at the time of the birth of their first baby. Less than half of the women were living in 'nuclear family' households, composed of themselves and their husband, at the time of the birth. An accurate count even of this is difficult, given the close involvement with extended family. For example a number went to stay with their parents for considerable periods before the birth or just after. Others had husbands who were away in the armed forces; some of these were living in their own home and some with parents. This picture of close contact with extended family is unsurprising in some respects given that the birth of a first child marks for many people a transition from family of origin to a new family. But housing availability and policy have also contributed to this picture. A history of poor housing and overcrowding in this area (Benwell Community Project, 1978a; Benwell Community Project, 1978b) clearly contributes to the number of shared households. It is also likely that direct and indirect racial discrimination on the part of housing departments has led to all the Asian women in the study

being housed in owner occupied extended family households.
This is frequently attributed only to cultural preference but
it has been demonstrated that discrimination in housing policy
has played an important part nationally in such housing situations for black people (Luthera, 1988).

In order to better understand the experience of family
life and household arrangements as part of the 'working
conditions' of infant feeding I explored the sharing of domestic work and money both in general terms and more specifically in the period immediately following the birth. The
arrangements in the extended family households were usually ones in which women shared domestic work such as
cooking and other household tasks with others. Expenses
were also shared. Five of the women specifically described
themselves as being part of a household where their mothers
did the cooking and was in charge of the household. Some
described the household as one run by their parents or in-
laws in which they helped their mother or mother-in-law.
For example, 'Mother did the cooking. We were one big
family and a happy family an' all' (Jane Harrison, 1936);
'Mother did all the cooking' (Florence Hope, 1943); 'We
were all in together. I was young you see' (Elizabeth White,
1939). Some of the Asian women emphasized the shared
nature of the household and particularly of all the women
cooking together. 'My mother-in-law and the other women
cook together' (Naheed Akhtar, 1970); 'I share cooking with
mother-in-law. We have no separate money' (Rukhsana
Rehman, 1980). For many of the women extended family
relationships were clearly close and supportive, although as
noted above this sharing of resources was not geared towards
helping women to breast-feed, since this was no longer a
necessity as it was in Odani's village. However, whilst often
supportive, living in extended family households made breast-
feeding more difficult in other respects. For example, discussions about where, and in whose presence, women felt
comfortable about breast-feeding indicated that such households may have created problems in this respect. This is
explored further in the next chapter.

Supportive grandmothers and/or other family members
were significant, but material circumstances were also important. For some women housing conditions had a negative

effect on mothering experiences. For example, Eleanor Kershaw's housing conditions (1940) were extremely poor, a damp tenement block with shared toilets. She talked a lot about these conditions, and still felt strongly about how dreadful they were. Her circumstances had clearly been very poor and they were made worse because her husband, who worked for the brewery, was a heavy drinker. She had supplemented their income by 'homeworking'; taking in washing. She couldn't go out to work because: 'My mother would never mind the children'. There were compensations, though, from these tenements, 'I used to stand a lot at the door with the other women just watching the children playing . . . it was better, you're on your own when you're on your own now'. She took a pride in keeping her children clean, despite these conditions, and described at length her elaborate arrangements for their frequent baths. She felt she'd survived these conditions partly because she'd only had two children. Her husband, despite his other failings, had been careful about this. Although it is difficult to be precise about the relationship between these housing conditions and her feeding habits, she certainly worked to a notion of modesty which would have made this tenement social life less pleasant if she'd breast-fed and had to conduct all feeding in private. She was also very health conscious and was advised by the Doctor that the baby would be better if bottle fed. And she got low cost milk from the clinic. Trying to be a good mother in such difficult circumstances pushed Eleanor towards bottle feeding.

Annie Sinclair (1947) also felt that her life in the first few months was severely affected by housing. When asked about her experiences at that time, she said, 'life was terrible'. Annie had suffered from post natal depression. She was unmarried and her mother had gone to the doctor about Annie's depression. Annie was then sent to see a psychiatrist. He apparently agreed that the housing conditions were to blame: 'Really it was the house. We had to go right downstairs for the water to wash the nappies. It had only one bedroom and mam was sleeping on the settee. Also it had them bugs and was really smelly.' The psychiatrist later got them a new house on a nearby more modern housing estate. Annie felt that this terrible housing had affected her feeding experience. Her answers are interesting when thinking about the complexity of the reasons for women making infant feeding decisions. Her 'official' reason was 'sore nipples' but the housing and social context add other dimensions. The pregnancy and birth were very difficult. She had been unmarried and felt, 'really I didn't want him'. However despite the difficult birth her feelings changed after the baby was born. In my interview with her forty years later, it was the only time she became animated when she said, 'I loved him in hospital, picking him up and feeding him, I fed him that much'. The context then provides a picture of a woman whose confidence and self esteem were affected by a much more complex set of dimensions than sore nipples. Her temporary animation in recounting this story ended with, 'I picked him up that much I got sore nipples and they had to take the milk away. They removed the milk with a tube for two days. I was disappointed. I'd like to have fed him'. Sore nipples might have been coped with by a woman in different social and material circumstances.

For other women though, not having their own home and living with others, which might be seen as a difficult housing situation, added to positive feelings in the post birth period. Ada Brown's housing conditions (1959) were in some ways 'objectively' quite poor, certainly overcrowded, with herself, her parents and six unmarried siblings in a two bedroomed flat. However she described her life after the baby's birth as 'exceptional, I used to wake up at six o'clock in the morning and feed her and mam came in and topped and tailed her and put her out in the pram'. Ada's husband was away in the navy, but she was surrounded by her large and helpful family who were positive about breast-feeding without putting pressure on her. Her sister hadn't breast-fed as she wanted to go out to work and this decision was as much accepted in the family as was Ada's decision to breast-feed. What was important for Ada in identifying this part of her life as particularly happy was the support, encouragement and practical help she received, rather than the fact that she managed to breast-feed. Ada was one of the few women in this study who breast-fed for a substantial period. In the next section we explore the situations of those women who 'successfully' breast-fed.

ARE 'BREAST-FEEDERS' DIFFERENT?

In examining the contexts and experiences of infant feeding it is useful to look at those described by Hally *et al.* as '"deviant" working-class women who breast fed' (1981: 95). My intention is not to artificially separate out these women – the successful ones – from the rest. Rather I wish to suggest that we should not see culture as monolithic. Working class culture does not *cause* bottle feeding. Instead life in these communities makes a whole range of demands on women. But there are also 'ways out' of particular demands, there are resources which can be used, there is the necessity to balance one requirement against another and, sometimes, even opportunities for pleasure to be grasped. I make a distinction here between those who breast-fed for more than four months and those who breast-fed for between one and four months. Women in both these categories have a stated intention to breast-feed.

Although this four month boundary might at first sight seem relatively arbitrary it did appear to make sense in these women's stories. Those who breast-fed for less than four months clearly recognized the need to explain why they switched to bottle feeding. Martin and White's study also notes that it was only women who breast-fed for more than four months who said that their reason for stopping was that they had done so for as long as they had intended (1988: xviii). Three points can be made about these two groups of women. First, some of those who breast-fed for more than four months saw breast feeding as 'what everyone did', although from other accounts in this study this is no by means straightforward – others in the same periods clearly found their way to bottle feeding. However the fact that most of the women who breast-fed for more than four months were in the older age group suggests that a ready alternative for younger women played a part even if it did not determine the outcome. Second, only one woman breast-fed for more than four months against the odds; the odds in this case being unhelpful hospital practices. Third, the 'more than four month' breast-feeders appear to have had somewhat more fortunate circumstances than the other women. These circumstances included fewer health problems, rather better material circumstances and more support from key people.

There also appears to be some element of contingency. The circumstances which result in particular women breast-feeding or not cannot be honed into causal relationships. This does not mean that women are merely victims of chance circumstances. Such a view would be inadequate in two ways. First, the circumstances are not chance. They are individual experiences of the broader practices and material circumstances which surround infant feeding, which I have described as the 'working conditions'. What happens in any one case is shaped and patterned, although not determined, by these. Second, women are not victims in the sense of having no part to play. They appear to try to retain control and to make decisions.

It is interesting to return to the question of whether the women who succeeded had some kind of 'doula'. It appears that more support and better conditions may well lead to breast-feeding, although so might lack of choice. In this community in the period covered, the importance of a 'doula' (in the sense of supportive people and reasonable material conditions) for these women was in making a slightly easier transition to motherhood. This may in turn facilitate breast-feeding. However, breast-feeding was not seen as a priority in the face of other demands and constraints.

CONTINUITY AND CHANGE: WHAT IS A GENERATION?

One element of continuity across the generations is that breast-feeding is perceived by many women in this community as difficult to achieve and is often added to other problems most of which are outside their control. Poor health played a part in feeding practices over the whole period of the study, although this appeared less central from the 1960s onwards. A considerable number of the women explained their lack of breast-feeding in terms of health problems, either their own general poor health or other health problems connected with childbirth and breast-feeding – breast abscesses, caesareans, septic breasts. When there was some choice about feeding method, these health problems led women towards bottle feeding. Often these health problems were also connected with poverty and poor housing. Elizabeth White in 1939 thought she hadn't enough milk because she didn't have enough food for herself. Jean Richards in 1949 thought she got a milk infection because she was working too hard looking after her younger brothers and sisters. Even when poor health wasn't specified as a reason, 'getting out of bed' and the work which women then took on, was enough to make 'the milk go away'. This was particularly the case when women did not have supportive relatives. Although the poor health of working class women has been of particular concern at certain specific periods, class inequality in morbidity rates has remained a feature throughout the period (Graham, 1984; Whitehead, 1988; Blackburn, 1991; Payne, 1991).

One of the clearest generational changes is that the category 'totally bottle fed' was almost completely a post 1965 one. It was in these later years that women forcefully rejected the very idea of breast-feeding during their pregnancy or at the time of the birth. The restrictions which breast-feeding imposed due to embarrassment were major factors in this.

For many women across the whole period breast-feeding was associated with exhaustion, poverty, discomfort, embarrassment and restriction, as well as authoritarian hospital practices. Being 'made to feed' in hospital was common at least for those women who had babies in the earlier years covered by the study. Throughout the whole period few saw hospital staff as helpful. Hospital contexts, even when they are apparently pro breast-feeding, are anything but a substitute for a 'doula' system. The main change, as I have noted above, was that from 1965 onwards women became more confident about rejecting breast-feeding when they did not want to do it. Some women did of course wish to breast-feed but they too were often discouraged by these same contextual factors particularly discomfort, embarrassment and lack of good advice and support.

How did the women relate to their mothers' experiences? Were memories, beliefs and experiences 'handed down'? How were generational changes conceptualized by the women?

Hally *et al.*, believed that mother/daughter relationships were significant in infant feeding choices. Their study, conducted in Newcastle, the same city as mine, discovered that women 'who live in close proximity to their own mother are more likely to bottle feed than breast feed' (Hally *et al.* 1981: 69). This did not of course mean that grandmothers necessarily advise bottle feeding. Rather Hally *et al.* suggest that 'the proximity of the mother to the maternal grandmother is characteristic of a particular culture where bottle feeding is the popular choice for mothers' (ibid: 69). Their methodology did not allow for qualitative exploration of mother/daughter relationships and their influence on infant feeding. I was able to ask each woman about the part her mother played in her infant feeding experiences and to explore their relationship in more detail. In addition some of the women were grandmothers themselves and I was thus able to gather data about another aspect of generational interaction.

For most women in this study, despite their generational differences, breast-feeding is part of their cultural history in the sense that twenty of them had themselves been breast-fed. Many were able to remember their mother breast-feeding younger siblings. Only four women in the study did not know whether they were breast-fed. One woman, Tessa Rowe, had in the 1920s been fed by an aunt. Her mother wasn't able to feed her and her aunt 'had great beautiful milk she couldn't get rid of' because her own baby was 'weakly' and wouldn't feed properly. Only two women knew that they had been bottle fed. Despite this solid background in breast-feeding there were limitations on most of the women's ability to discuss it with their mothers. There appeared to be no shared language with which to discuss many aspects of reproduction and sexuality, despite very intimate households where mothers often had several children born at home. Beatrice Callender (in 1968) describes talking to her mother about childbirth, 'I had to be dead inventive finding alternative words'. In fact discussions between mothers and daughters often separated out advice about child rearing from discussions about those aspects of reproduction which involved discussing the woman's body. It was rare for women to have ever talked to their mothers about bodies in so far as such discussions might have any possible sexual aspects.

In answering my questions about what their mothers talked with them about it was clear that many women placed breast-feeding in the same category as sex and menstruation; something that shouldn't be discussed. Many women had received no information about menstruation from their mothers and sexual advice was minimal and to the point; 'keep away from boys'. It may be that since mothers were confident about discussing child rearing, but not breasts, with their daughters, bottle feeding provided a medium through which this helping relationship could be conducted without straying on to uncomfortable areas.

Women across the generational range then saw breast-feeding as part of a history of tough living conditions, large families and as having a draining effects on mothers. Where their mothers had breast-fed a number of children, women thought they 'had done enough' or lacked time for feeding younger siblings. Breast-feeding was for many women part of a cultural history of motherhood which was certainly not romantic and serene. 'Natural mothering' carries a less attractive image for these women than some of the infant feeding literature tries to convey.

Generation and social class have often some together in social policy in ways which are inherently conservative and frequently victim blaming. Many attempts have been made to explain poor health and poverty in particular localities through concepts such as 'culture' of poverty or 'transmitted deprivation' or 'underclass' (see Rutter and Madge, 1977; Oppenheim, 1990a; and Alcock, 1993, for discussion of these). Attempts are constantly made to show that it is the attitudes and behaviour of poor people passed down through generations which perpetuate poverty. In relation to health these attitudes are seen to be characterised by fatalism and the low value placed on health maintenance and prevention. Hally *et al.* (1981) perhaps unintentionally reinforce this tendency, through specifying the close proximity of mothers and daughters as connected with the 'problem' of poor breast-feeding rates.

Although the idea of cultural habits as the link between poor health and poverty has particularly firm roots in the USA, it has played a part, and continues to feature, in British social policy. The belief that working class or black people don't take measures to protect health and that they pass on to their off-spring negative attitudes about health professionals dies hard, despite the lack of convincing evidence (see Blaxter, 1990 for discussion of lifestyle and health and Blackburn, 1991 for explorations of health and poverty). Older women, as mothers and grandmothers, are often implicated in this thinking, using and reinforcing the negative connotations of the expression 'old wives tales'. Mothers are assumed to give their daughters home spun advice (usually bad) and influence them away from health professionals. Cosslett (1994) describes the repression of these 'old wives tales' within both the male dominated medical narrative and the parallel natural childbirth discourse. Blaxter and Paterson's inter-generational study of mothers and daughters in Scotland set out to explore this. They tested the hypothesis that: 'perceptions of health experience might, in poor socioeconomic circumstances, create attitudes of apathy towards health care and conflict with health professionals, and that these attitudes might be transmitted through generations, especially among the female members of the family' (Blaxter and Paterson, 1982: 3).

They found that, although there were sometimes similarities between the generations in terms of low expectations of health professionals, these similarities often arose directly from the women's own experiences rather than being 'passed on'. There was little evidence in their study that grandmothers actually did pass on advice to their daughters; instead they 'left it to them'. The study therefore found little continuity in health related behaviour. Where there were similarities between mothers and daughters it appeared to relate to underlying structural factors, such as low or irregular income rather than through attitudes being 'transmitted'. Blaxter and Paterson explored breast and bottle feeding amongst the two generations, the grandmothers having given birth between 1950 and 1953. As in my study many grandmothers gave up bottle feeding soon after leaving hospital where they had been 'made' to breast-feed. In the younger generation even fewer women breast-fed. Their impression was of a change in the approach hospitals take so that, although breast-feeding was still official policy for the younger generation, it was rarely 'pushed'. Many of the younger women were against breast-feeding because they found it repulsive and embarrassing. Grandmothers did not push breast-feeding with their daughters. These findings resemble mine in several ways: authoritarian hospital practices particularly in the past; ambivalence about breast-feeding going back a long way; growing resistance to breast-feeding due to embarrassment; and no evidence that grandmothers directly influenced their daughters' feeding choice.

In my study those women who were grandmothers themselves placed a particular value on 'not interfering' with their daughter's choices in infant feeding. They were more concerned with their daughters' and grandchildrens' health and well being than with breast-feeding per se. Lucy Cooper for example (1930) said to her daughter who bottle fed, 'do what you want, I won't interfere'. Maureen Watson (1941) told me her daughter, 'bottle fed because she was going back to work, I don't interfere'. Jean Richards (1949) had four grandchildren; all were bottle fed. Jean said, of her daughters and daughters-in-law, 'You can advise, but if they don't want to take notice, it's a convenience thing and they're figure conscious'. Audrey Soulsby (1951) had been particularly keen on breast-feeding and had done so herself. She was disappointed that her daughter had not been able to do the same. However her daughter's health was accepted as the explanation, 'Valerie wanted to breast-feed but couldn't because of having a caesarian'. Eleanor Kershaw (1930) saw her daughter as inheriting breast-feeding problems from her, 'my daughter's the same as me, she's got no nipples, all hers were on the bottle'. Amongst women whose daughters were not yet old enough to have children of their own this same feeling of it being 'up to them' was common. For example, Carol Cook (1973) said, 'I'd tell her my experience but I'd leave it to her, dictating to someone doesn't help'. Gina Godfrey (1969) had a slightly different approach however because she regretted not breast-feeding, 'I would certainly tell them my experience and say they'd be missing a lot if they didn't breast-feed'.

It is interesting that working class grandmothers are seen as something of a problem in terms of breast-feeding promotion but that the notion of 'doula' appears popular since it is linked specifically to breast-feeding (Kitzinger, 1979). In the same study as Hally *et al.* point to what they see as a negative association between mother/daughter proximity and bottle feeding they extol the virtues of the doula:

> all mothers desiring to breast feed should be introduced to an experienced person who would provide practical help, and support the mother at times of anxiety and emotional distress. Such a person sometimes known as a doula may be a relative, friend, or a voluntary worker from an organisation like the National Childbirth Trust. (Hally *et al.*, 1981: 8)

Mothers then are seen as in need of support to fulfill their breast-feeding roles, not in their own right to care for their babies in whatever way seems right to them. Jelliffe and Jelliffe also suggest that it is 'the small, mobile nuclear family with little contact with older generations' (1978: 200) which is particularly connected with a low prevalence of breast-feeding. Clearly older generations are approved of when they deliver a message which accords with that of the policy makers. It is alarming that negative views about grandmothers are repeated in an otherwise informative book on breasts and health (McConville, 1994). Here the Hally research is misquoted to indicate the malicious influence of ignorant grandmothers on breast-feeding rates.

DIFFERENT MEMORIES: ASIAN WOMEN'S STORIES

During the period covered by the study, Asian women became an important part of the population of the inner west end of Newcastle, as of other British cities. As noted in chapter one, concern has been expressed about the fact that Asian women in Britain appear to adopt the bottle feeding habits of the indigenous population despite the fact that they come from countries where breast-feeding is much more common than it is in Britain (Jones *et al.*, 1977; Goel *et al.*, 1978; Treuherz *et al.*, 1982; Shahjahan, 1991; Costello *et al.*, 1992). These worries about the feeding habits of immigrant and minority ethnic groups are echoed in other industrialized countries (Ryan *et al.*, 1991; Rossiter, 1993). Hence the feeding habits of black mothers attract particular attention. Phoenix

(1990) has questioned the tendency in health policy to focus on black women as fundamentally different from white,
usually in ways which invite pathologising attention to the
lives of black women. For example she regards the focus on
the higher mortality rates of babies whose mothers were born
in the Indian sub-continent as over-generalized and overplayed. She notes that in any case the differences between
the infant mortality rates amongst black and white women
are decreasing. In addition there are regional variations in
the infant mortality rates amongst Asian women. Hence,
Phoenix argues, to categorize all black women as 'at risk' is
oversimplistic and reinforces the tendency to see 'blackness'
in itself as the problem. Efforts to address higher infant
mortality rates are often based on racist thinking and assumptions about cultural pathology (Bryan *et al.*, 1985;
Rocheron, 1988). The concerns of black women themselves,
that they experience ethnocentricity and racial discrimination in the delivery of health services, have been far less
central to the concerns of policy makers. For example, ob-
stetricians and midwives are particularly likely to be white
and this leads to discriminatory attitudes and services in
maternity care (Phoenix, 1990). Hence although mortality
and morbidity rates amongst black people are a cause for
concern, affected as they are both by their social class position and also by racism (Grimsley and Bhat, 1988), these
concerns have not been translated into a coherent anti racist
policy within the NHS (McNaught, 1988; Ahmad, 1993).
Instead 'difference' is treated in essentialist ways identified
as a product of culture. Infant feeding policies and practices are no exception to this broader picture.

It was in this context of racism in health provision, and a
tendency to pathologize the cultures of black people, particularly black mothers, that I sought the infant feeding
experiences of Asian women. I expected to find both similarities and differences between them and white women but
did not have pre-conceived notions as to what these might
be. Phoenix shows that even some fairly well intentioned
assumptions about Asian cultures neglect the similarities
between white women and Asian women in their experience of maternity care. For example, both groups sometimes
have problems understanding medical terminology and pro-

cedures, and some women in both groups object to male doctors, while others do not (Phoenix, 1990). Modesty and communication problems are frequently perceived as problems to do with Asian culture. All Asian women for example are assumed to be more 'modest' than white whereas there is considerable complexity in these feelings amongst both groups. In Phoenix's view this 'special needs' approach fails to take account of racism and discrimination in the delivery of maternity services. I was therefore cautious about anticipating cultural or other differences in advance of the study. The task is to look at the infant feeding experiences of Asian women and at the ways in which they were similar to, or different from, white women in the study. The small numbers mean that, to a greater extent than for the study as a whole, the ideas presented here are tentative.

Three of the four Asian women I interviewed were born in Pakistan and one in India. All had come here to marry when they were in their teens. All were living in extended family households at the time of the birth. Rajina Mondal was different from the other three since her mother-in-law came over from India in order to help with the birth and then stayed for several years. The others came to this country to join husbands and in-laws who were already established here. Two of the women breast-fed, one for three months, and one for five. Two bottle fed; one because she planned to, and one (Rajina Mondal) because she couldn't establish breast-feeding after a caesarean. In other words three had wished to breast-feed. Two of these expressed firm 'cultural' beliefs about breast-feeding. They felt that in their culture it was very important to breast-feed and that a child who was breast-fed was especially close to the mother, whereas a child who had not been breast-fed was somehow 'different'. Rajina Mondal (1977) was particularly distressed that she had not breast-fed and still had not managed to tell her daughter this even though she was by then nine years old. Her daughter apparently talked positively of having been given her mother's milk and her mother was too 'ashamed' to disillusion her. Rajina's mother-in-law had been very angry with her for not breast-feeding. Rajina herself was still very distressed about this during the interview and considered it a major failure and source of shame.

Naheed Akhtar, who I described earlier, also talked of the importance in her culture of breast-feeding. However she experienced discomfort in breast-feeding both physically (she didn't like the feeling and had a breast abscess at some stage) and socially (she found it embarrassing). Hence although she breast-fed for three months it was not a positive experience.

I discussed these 'cultural' beliefs with Parveen a woman of Pakistani origin who both helped me contact the women and acted as interpreter where necessary. At that time she herself was unmarried and had no children. As she thought about what they had said she recognized aspects of her own memories and experiences which connected with this. For example, she told me that in Indian films a common insult is to say that a man would be more of a man if he had his mother's milk. Although this seemed to have particular application to men, the important link between mothers and their children which breast-feeding represents also applied to mothers and daughters.

Fildes (1988) and Khatib-Chahidi (1992) describe breast-milk as highly significant in social relations within Muslim socities. One example is 'milk kinship' the idea that women become related to children through giving them their milk even if they had not given birth to the child. The Koran emphasizes the importance of breast-feeding although it supports wet nursing where necessary. In fact the Koran appears to be less adamant regarding breast-feeding than some interpretations of it suggest (Maher, 1992). Raphael (1985) reported that in the Indian village which was part of her study, men were particularly keen that women breast-feed, thus following the teachings of the Koran, as they interpreted it. Women were more ambivalent, since it was they who experienced the exhaustion of frequent childbirth and breast-feeding. Although cultural beliefs about breast-feeding might thus be traced to the Koran it is important to note that in my study Rajina Mondal, the woman who expressed the strongest feelings about this, was actually Hindu and none of the others mentioned the religious basis for the beliefs. Clearly individual interpretations of 'culture' are highly complex. What is more, these beliefs were not expressed by two of the women, one who breast-fed and one who did not. Both accounted for their practices in much the same way as the white women did. Rukhsana Rehman (1980) thought breast-feeding was good for the baby and it seemed to work well, despite some embarrassment. The other woman, Nasreen Malik (1979), bottle fed from the start thinking breast-feeding too embarrassing and therefore inconvenient. It is clearly all too easy to resort to 'cultural' interpretations of the habits of women from minority ethnic groups. The common linkage between the madonna and breast-feeding in Christian thinking is regarded as less of a fascinating novelty than muslim beliefs in the same way that whiteness generally is not problematised (Frankenberg, 1993).

Apart from these cultural beliefs, clearly far from monolithic and deterministic, how did the Asian women differ from the white women? Perhaps the most significant way is that all of them had recent memories of a country where breast-feeding is common and they related this to their feelings of embarrassment here – there you would breast-feed amongst lots of women who were doing so, you would not be alone. Those features which go to make a breast-feeding community and those which shape a bottle feeding community are clearly complex. It is certainly not as simple as suggesting that it relates to whether women had seen breast-feeding, whether they know it's better, or even simply that women believe that it's more modern to bottle feed as has been suggested (Treuherz *et al.*, 1982). A recent small scale study of the same area within which mine took place looked specifically at Bangladeshi women (Shahjahan, 1991; Costello *et al.*, 1993). Alarm was expressed that women were not being as 'good' in England as they had been in Bangladesh: 'There was a remarkable reduction in the incidence and duration of breast feeding on arrival in the UK. 42% of the infants born in the UK (last child) were breast fed at birth, but only 20% continued beyond 3 months in comparison to 92% for those born in Bangladesh from the same mother' (Shahjahan, summary of study).

When the male author of this study discussed this in a seminar where Bangladeshi women were present he put it to them that they would breast-feed their children for maybe two years in Bangladesh. They made it clear to him that they had no intention of doing such a thing when there was a choice. What is missing in most studies of Asian women's breast-feeding habits in Britain is the recognition that breast-feeding in their countries of origin is part of an entirely different set of social arrangements surrounding the whole pregnancy and childbirth process. From Raphael's study (1985) and from comments made to Shahjahan (1991), we can suggest that these different social arrangements are likely to include, at least in rural areas: less medicalization of childbirth and infant feeding; greater support for breast-feeding often out of necessity; more knowledge about breast-feeding in women's own families; less sexualization of breasts; possibly greater separation between the sexes in terms of physical space, in other words, more 'women's space'. Instead of focussing on these factors, the studies I have referred to here concentrate on women's attitudes.

CONCLUSIONS

We have then a locality where, during the period covered by the study, breast-feeding was no longer perceived as the most obvious way to feed babies. It had little popular appeal in the sense that mothers themselves and others in the community went to great efforts to make sure that support for it existed. Whilst some women wished to breast-feed and some of these did so successfully, there was considerable ambivalence about it in the face of other demands and pressures. This ambivalence appears to cut across generational and ethnic differences. It has been suggested that such a culture develops when women have not seen anyone breast-feed (Hally *et al.*, 1981; Jones, 1987; DHSS, 1988). This does not appear to be the case here as indicated earlier; many of the women had memories of their own mother breast-feeding, and the Asian women particularly had been part of cultures where breast-feeding was very common. It has also been suggested that women, particularly in situations like that of Asian women moving to Britain, come to believe that bottle feeding is modern and of higher social status (Jelliffe and Jelliffe, 1978; Treuherz *et al.*, 1982; Van Esterik, 1989). This seems at best a very partial explanation since Asian women in this community have retained 'cultural' beliefs about the importance of breast-feeding. There was no evidence that they thought of bottle feeding as higher status, rather that bottle feeding for some of them emerged from circumstances which were similar to those of white women. Raphael suggests that in situations where a poorer woman appears to be following the example of more affluent women this is 'not out of admiration or blind ignorance but because she saw a feeding pattern that worked and suited her own situation' (1985: 19). Similarly where support is not available for breast-feeding as such, and where there are many barriers to its achievement, bottle feeding represents a successful and appropriate alternative.

What do these women have in common? I had decided that I would look at women in this particular community because it was one which has been identified as having low rates of breast-feeding. It is also an old community which has had ups and downs in its economic fortunes (Benwell Community Project, 1981; City of Newcastle upon Tyne, 1988). It has retained some characteristics of a traditional working class community which has many families who remain and live close to one another. It has not for the most part been gentrified. Housing designs and schemes have come and gone but housing has remained as a social problem for many people over several generations in the sense of housing which is below the standards elsewhere in the city. In such a community women often do not have lives which lend themselves to decision making, control and planning. They are however particularly subject to the control of others and to poorer health and fewer resources (Blaxter and Paterson, 1982; Graham, 1984; Blackburn, 1991). Bottle feeding may then represent an avoidance of control by others, perhaps not deliberately chosen much of the time, but arising out of attempts at retaining some control given the competing demands. Gieve (1987) writes of mothering as being characterised by a struggle for control, something that she sees as inevitably a losing battle. Poorer material resources add an extra dimension to this lack of control.

This does not mean that poverty and deprivation dominated women's accounts. Despite the fact that this area is recognized as one which has experienced long term deprivation (Benwell Community Project, 1981; Townsend *et al.*,

1988) only a few women remember the period of their early mothering as being difficult and they clearly had exceptionally and persistently poor circumstances. Perhaps one of the reasons why women did not talk in negative terms of their lives is that these women, like many other people, see poverty, implicitly at least, as partly the fault of the individual (see Oppenheim, 1990a for discussion of changes in these attitudes). So to acknowledge one's own money difficulties might be to suggest that you were not a good manager, or that you squandered the money by 'going out'. One particular way in which many of the women accounted for their relatively easy circumstances was that they claimed that their husband's were 'very good' and readily handed over the money, keeping nothing for themselves. This appeared to be a claim partly of good luck and partly of good management. In this case proper husband management, part of the work of an effective wife.

It is also the case that baby care has made increasing consumer demands. There is now a vast industry producing 'essential' baby equipment which certainly was not the case for women in the earlier parts of this study. For example, when Child Poverty Action Group (CPAG) estimated the cost of maternity and baby equipment based on a Mothercare catalogue in 1990 they estimated that it cost £1050 (Oppenheim, 1990b). Hence, when women claimed they 'didn't want for anything', there literally was less to 'want for' at least in the earlier generations. Women's economic circumstances as they emerge in this study represent the broader pattern of women's dependence; on husbands who are 'good'; on relatives who are 'kind'; and, even less reliably, on the state which sometimes fills the gaps.

Certain facets of life in this community suggest that women's lack of control over their lives in the sense of being unable to think too far ahead and to plan and use their personal space militates against breast-feeding when it is no longer the 'only' method of feeding. Other chapters will explore the interaction between this culture, itself in part a product of the material realities of housing, work and income, and the fact that breast-feeding involves women's bodies in a way that bottle feeding does not.

It is important that we recognize the complexities of class

and culture in relation to breast-feeding. The Newsons investigated class differences in breast-feeding in the early 1960s (Newson and Newson, 1963). Their explanation of the apparent contradiction whereby poorer women are less likely to 'save money' by breast-feeding has some limitations. They suggest that middle class women see breast-feeding as a duty and, since they are less prudish than working class women, are more likely to do it regardless of whether they enjoy it or not. Working class women, in their view, are more prudish and their overcrowded housing conditions mean that breast-feeding might be affected by the incest taboo. They also believe that working class women simply reject health advice in this respect, 'working class women feel free to suit themselves in the matter of infant feeding' (Newson and Newson, 1963: 175). This view of working class culture and its relationship to breast-feeding is problematic in a number of respects. First, the concept of incest taboo needs to be contextualised. Why should the sight of women's breasts provoke fears of incest in working class Nottingham but not in rural Africa or Pakistan? It is important that something as culturally specific as feelings about bare breasts are not explained by reference to pseudo-natural phenomena like incest taboos. In fact Hally *et al.* found no class differences in those who were embarrassed about breast-feeding (1981). Second, the Newson's suggestion that working class women do not take health advice seriously does not recognize the complex structural and material reasons why women might take health advice seriously but not follow it. Graham (1976, 1993), for example, in her study of smoking in pregnancy found that smokers were not unaware of health education messages. One of the reasons they might nevertheless ignore these messages was connected with the ways in which women achieve autonomy: 'For smokers it was cigarettes that served as identity markers, the symbolic props by which particular times of the day were carved out for the establishment of adult, self-directed, non-domestic relationships' (Graham, 1976: 404). Other recent studies have also suggested that poorer women are often very aware of health advice (Blackburn, 1991).

Third, the Newsons appear to conceptualize women as 'objects' rather than 'subjects' in relation to their culture.

They deal with working class women who do not breast-feed, and middle class women who do, rather than recognizing that all women make decisions within complex cultural situations which are linked to social class, but not determined by it in any straightforward way. For example many women in my study saw breast-feeding as an ideal and did not reject it in the rather crude way suggested by the Newsons.

There is no one answer to why some women breast-feed and some do not, However better resources, more support and good health provide a sounder, less stressful basis for breast-feeding. A recent qualitative and feminist study of infant feeding supports this evidence that having greater control over one's circumstances is associated with succesful breast-feeding (Dyball, 1992). Despite differences and similarities within this group of women infant feeding is structured and patterned, as it is for all women, through material circumstances, health, familial relationships and feelings about bodies. For some women a particular combination of these circumstances, or way of handling them, results in breast-feeding. For others, their particular combination results in bottle feeding. A number of themes and questions arising from this picture are addressed in other chapters.

First, control over physical space emerges in many studies, including mine and that of the Newsons (1963), as important in infant feeding and perhaps is a major difference between working class and middle class women. The meaning of bodies in physical space and why some bodies should appear problematic in some space is explored in the next chapter.

Second, the meaning, and potential, of sexual discourses around breast-feeding, and the changing nature of these, need further examination. Women have few ways of talking with each other about bodies, sexuality and reproduction and in some respects therefore about breast-feeding. There is some apparent change here with women wanting to be more open with their daughters and thinking that their daughters should be better prepared for adult sexuality and reproduction. These issues are explored in chapter five.

Third, there has been a change from apparently authoritarian practice on the part of health professionals to a more laissez faire one, although the promotion of breast-feeding has received greater emphasis at a policy level in recent years, as indicated in chapter one. The context of infant feeding experiences remains however at least in part a medical one. This will be explored in chapter six.

Fourth, women appear to be engaged in a struggle to keep some control over their lives. This is not a one dimensional or always conscious struggle. It often involves fending off demands and balancing one expectation against another – passive, rather than active, struggle. Chapter seven explores the ways in which we might conceptualize this and how infant feeding practices might be located in this process.

The question of whether feminists should endorse pro breast-feeding policies, as well as why and how, can only be addressed after these issues have been more fully explored. This will be a central theme in the final chapter.

4 Public Space and Private Bodies

The question of where, in different cultures, it is thought appropriate to breast-feed, and how this might be explained was an important part of my motivation for undertaking this work. Studies of breast-feeding in Britain frequently refer to the difficulties of breast-feeding in public (Bacon and Wylie, 1976; Jones and Belsey, 1977; Hally *et al.*, 1981; Martin and White, 1988). In this chapter I explore the meanings of public and private in relation to infant feeding. This particularly concerns the question of how breast-feeding became a 'private' activity in the industrialised world in the sense of being conducted 'out of sight'. The need for modesty, identified as an important dimension of women's experience in the previous chapter, is a product of the discourses of femininity which construct women as always 'really' part of the private world. But infant feeding is also private in another sense: it is undertaken in women's own, that is their private, time. This too requires exploration.

MANAGING WOMEN'S BODIES

Analyzing the construction and maintenance of separate private and public spheres, as well as the complex and changing relationships between them, has been of enormous importance in feminist scholarship (Oakley, 1974; Rosaldo, 1974; Oakley, 1976a; Hartmann, 1981, Gamarnikow *et al.*, 1983; Turnaturi, 1987). The notion of public and private has been understood as fundamental to patriarchal social relations (Walby, 1990). As Dominelli has described it: 'defining womanhood in terms of domestic labour confines women to the private arena while men dominate the public one where acknowledged power and authority reside. Keeping the two spheres separate is essential in maintaining relations of subordination and domination (Dominelli, 1991: 267). How-

106

ever the boundaries between the two arenas are far from
static. For example, women in most industrialized countries
are no longer simply confined to the private domestic sphere.
Walby (1990) suggests that during this century we have moved
from a system of private patriarchy, where women were excluded from public spheres, to a system of public patriarchy
where women are segregated and subordinated within public spheres. Despite the changing boundaries of private and
public, and the changing location of women, we are still
left with a situation where 'what men do is valued above
what women do even if both men and women do the same
things in the same places at the same time' (Imray and
Middleton, 1983: 14). They refer to the treatment of public
breast-feeding as an example of the marking of boundaries
between private and public:

> If pregnancy is out of place in the House of Commons,
> the more so is breastfeeding; to breastfeed openly is a
> flagrant admission of womanhood. The knowledge that a
> woman member is breastfeeding provokes sniggers from
> some men and overt and covert hostility from some women
> members who fear that in being associated with someone
> who is breastfeeding they will be identified as 'women'
> and therefore 'out of place' in this male club . . . Preg-
> nancy, breastfeeding and child-care taking place within
> the House of Commons may be seen as the most private
> part of the private sphere moving into the most public
> part of the public; a rejection of and a challenge to the
> validity of boundaries. (Imray and Middleton, 1983: 20)

My study suggests that even 'private' space is not simply an
arena where 'anything goes': breast-feeding is not a neutral
activity in the private world either. In the household, as we
shall see below, women have to negotiate what to do, where
to do it, and in whose presence, and with whose approval,
it can be done. Households are a complex mixture of private and public space, although they are often characterized as if they were *the* private world. For women the
household is also the public world, in effect the workplace
(Little *et al.*, 1988; Doyal, 1990). As the public world has
altered, through the changing structure of the labour market,

to include more women, it has through this process become more (hetero)sexualized (Walby, 1990). This has also happened in the private world; a linked process of public/private merging combined with sexualization has taken place at home through the reinforcement of heterosexual couple relationships as central to people's lives. In relation to infant feeding practices, women have to negotiate their way through sets of expectations about what kind of activity is appropriate in which bit of the household. There is rarely much of the household space which they control. Smaller households and the increased merging of women's and men's social worlds have reduced women's space. The distinction between home and neighbourhood is also not a clearcut one; the public and private operate in both of them. Again, however, the relationship between the two is not static. Paradoxically then, although women are seen to 'belong' in the private world their privacy in the home is frequently limited. During the period covered by this study the very idea of privacy at home was elaborated. For example Crow said of the 1950s: 'It is also in this period that the modern domestic ideal of an affluent nuclear family living in a home of their own and enjoying the benefits of leisurely home life took shape with emphasis placed on the privacy of the individual household rather than the wider community' (Crow, 1989: 20). For many women in my study an actual home of their own was not available particularly at this early stage in their married life. It is however possible, even with a small sample such as this, to discern individual versions of a transition from a more neighbourhood based life to a more private nuclear family one, where there is less space for women to be together.

The language of what should be private and what public dominated these women's accounts of infant feeding. Although these 'rules' were, for the most part, accepted by the women they were clearly somewhat restrictive: 'You never exposed yourself because you had blouses that opened down the front. But if the child wanted a feed, you had to do it even if you were on the car and the child was crying. I've done that and I've nearly smothered her [laughs]' (Bertha Combe, 1922). I attempted to pin Lucy Cooper (1930) down a little further when she said, 'I never fed her in front of

anyone'. I suggested that she must have fed at least in front
of her husband in her six weeks of breast-feeding. As she
hesitated in giving the answer I suggested that perhaps she
was not keen on feeding in front of him. She agreed that
she had been uncomfortable and that this was very inconvenient.

Jane Harrison (1936) breast-fed for only three weeks, and
the restrictions about who she felt comfortable with, and
where, played a major part in her experience of this. She
felt embarrassed about feeding even in front of her husband, and when I asked whether he felt the same, she said,
'Well he didn't say nothing but when I put her on the bottle
I think he felt we could take her more places. And being
thirty years of age I think I felt it more being amongst stran-
gers . . . it gave that much more freedom'. Her control over
household space also depended on her dad's sensitivity, 'Me
father was a very modest man, very, very nice and if he thought
I was embarrassed he'd go into another room'.

Monica Andrews (1951), who only breast-fed for four weeks,
made the distinction, as did many of the other women, between feeding in front of women and feeding in mixed
company. For Audrey Soulsby (1951) however, even though
she breast-fed for eight months, absolute privacy was crucial;
feeding in front of her mother and father or even a woman
friend was unthinkable, 'I remember at my Mum and Dad's
house going into the bedroom'. This was related to Audrey's
perception of the right way to run a household stressing
privacy between the sexes; 'you didn't even mix your washing
with your brothers'. Ada Brown (1959), in a similar period
but in something of a contrast to this, had distinct memories
of a neighbourhood where several women breast-fed together,
keeping a shawl handy in case 'the coalman came for his
money'. Gina Godfrey's (1969) short feeding experience had
been very restrictive. She put this down to her youth and to
the fact that it wasn't 'socially acceptable then'. Naheed Akhtar
(1970) was clear that she had needed to be in a different
room for breast-feeding if any man was present. I asked about
her husband in this context, and she laughingly said that
he was always working, even at night. Rukhsana Rehman
(1980) also felt less than happy about feeding in front of
her husband. At night, the only time he was present, she

'usually did it with the light out when he was asleep'.

For most of the women then breast-feeding was a major restriction even in their own home. Seen through the eyes of these women 'breast-feeders', the home was not a place where you were free to be yourself, if that self was one that might provoke some embarrassment or discomfort even for an activity such as this, which might be seen as 'essential'. Going 'upstairs' or to the bedroom clearly excludes women from all sorts of activity and from any notion of 'public' life in the household. The household was certainly not arranged with their needs in mind, even though it might have been seen as their rightful place. The public world beyond the household was even more 'out of bounds' for women when they were breast-feeding. Several women admitted that they discovered the benefits of 'going out' when they gave up breast-feeding, even though they didn't identify the wish to go out as a reason for their giving it up: to do so would perhaps appear selfish!

There were glimpses in this study of other ways of organizing space. Eleanor Kershaw, who gave birth in 1940, was particularly informative about how she perceived that things had changed during her lifetime. 'I would only do it on my own. Mind you, when I was young, twenty or twenty one (about 1931/2), I've seen women just pulling their breasts out, feeding children in front of everyone. I didn't think anything of it then . . . it was nothing then to see a woman feeding her baby'. I asked if this was 'in public' and she said, 'Well I don't know about public, but in houses'. She felt that she had somehow become more modest, 'I used to like to try and cover myself. But I had aunties. I've many times seen me aunty when I was 14 or 15 feed the baby in front of everybody'. She was herself surprised at rediscovering this memory and went on to say more, 'I remember my grandmother and she had four daughters. They all had big families and all the mothers collected together. I remember my aunty sitting talking and just giving the baby the breast.' She agreed that people seem to have become more modest and was puzzled about why this should be. In other words, Eleanor Kershaw had memories of 'women's space' albeit in the household rather than in the streets or other public places. Ada Brown had similar memories although at an entirely different period, in 1959. Her community, like that described by Eleanor, was characterized by large families and women's space:

> I'm racking my brains trying to picture the community as a whole, well two or three streets in particular and the baby clinic we went to once a week. No-one ever had any hang ups about breast-feeding in public. We'd lived there a long time and most people had children of comparable ages – it was nothing to go into a room and find three or four women together breast-feeding babies.

As noted above Ada's experiences contrasted with those of Audrey Soulsby, although Audrey's first child was born in 1951, eight years earlier than Ada's. As we have seen, Audrey laid particular value on privacy in her life. This applied to many experiences: 'They're moments that are just so yours and to share them with anyone else – no. They're a woman's own private business, there's not much private these days – it's what a woman does best. It's best to keep it for her, I've done it all myself.' Ada and Audrey's very different experiences partly arose from their contrasting living situations. Ada lived, at the time her first child was born, in a very overcrowded shared household in a neighbourhood where people popped in and out. Audrey lived in a household with just her husband and child and didn't have people 'popping in'. These different living situations appeared then to concern both physical space and also different values in relation to family, motherhood and appropriate feminine behaviour. The different effects on these two women's bodily practices in the 'public' world is important even though they were both 'breast-feeders'. Ada was able to continue an active social life in the neighbourhood. Audrey, on the other hand, had acquired both the physical reality of nuclear family life and the values that went with it. She thought it extremely important to maintain the privacy of the domestic boundary. Her breast-feeding entailed considerable separation from other adults.

As noted in previous chapters, some of the Asian women felt that feeding would have been different if they had had their babies in Pakistan or India. Nasreen Malik (1979) said,

'In Pakistan all my family, all the women I know, breast-feed, so I wouldn't have felt so alone'. Many of the women in the study, white women and Asian women, held the idea that there is, or was, a time and place where one might feel comfortable about feeding; other countries, or the distant past, or perhaps a time more recent than one's own breast-feeding experience. Some women said that had they been older or younger at the time, they might have been able to cope better with the difficult experiences of negotiation which breast-feeding brought them. For most of the women though, the reality which they experienced was of household and neighbourhood space where they had to keep out of sight as breast-feeding mothers. Household space emerges from these discussions as fraught with complexity in terms of how it might be used. No one dismissed lightly the questions about where breast-feeding could safely be done.

Although there was some basic consistency in what constitutes privacy, no men for example, there were also differences: the front room; the bedroom; the bus; the park; the street; all might be seen as public. Sometimes body management had to be achieved by careful adjustment of clothing rather than through use of public space. The language which is used to distinguish between the public and the private concerns modesty, shyness and discretion:

> People were modest then, I'm told I'm old fashioned. (Lucy Cooper, 1930)

> I wouldn't have liked to do it in front of strangers. You were so prim and proper in those days. (Polly Williams, 1932)

Mary Moreland (1936) stressed the need for modesty and that clothing was the way to achieve this:

> I was very discreet, no-one could see. If men were there, you always had to have a blouse so you were well covered. Mother was very strict about that.

Feeding in public, beyond the front door, didn't arise for Mary because she said she didn't go out. There were also variations in what actually constituted modesty; sometimes your dad being there would be immodest and sometimes not. Women have to try to establish what behaviour is appropriate where by being sensitive to feelings, their own and others, particularly shyness and embarrassment.

> I was quite shy at that time. I didn't like the idea of it at all, to be honest. (Patricia Poole, 1965)

> I would have felt okay in front of my mother and my sister but not my dad. My Dad's a bit of a prude and sometimes I'd be embarrassed and he'd be embarrassed. If I had a baby now I couldn't do it in front of you I'd be embarrassed. (Margaret Pearson, 1975)

> I would do it nicely. [demonstrates discretion] Sometimes shame, some people not ashamed, but I would feel ashamed, a shy feeling. (Rajina Mondal, 1977)

Women's bodies are managed through a set of discursive practices concerned with their responsibility for modesty and appropriate privacy. There is no clear set of rules, rather women have to achieve modesty through careful 'reading' of individual situations, taking into account their own confidence. This can be seen as a version of what Doyal has described as 'emotional housework' (1990: 507), where women are expected to manage social relationships within the household. Maher (1992) relates this deep seated discomfort about public breast-feeding to the challenges to various power relationships which it involves: 'That a woman should breast-feed at work or in public is a violation of cultural categories, of the deep-seated taboos which sustain a power structure.' (Maher, 1992: 20) This is a very different view from that of the Stanways, authors of the very popular *Breast is Best*, about how women manage the embarrassment of breast-feeding: 'Little do they know that a hormonally induced change takes place in breast feeding mothers that enables them to feed in public with equanimity' (Stanway and Stanway, 1978: 183).

Hally *et al.* (1981) discovered that women who lived in more crowded households were less likely to breast-feed and suggested that this may be due to lack of privacy. My study suggests greater complexity in the sense that, as noted above, some women could recall periods when women's shared space in the neighbourhood or household meant that breast-feeding was more feasible. This should not however be simply envisaged as a lost 'better world' where women had greater freedom. In Rosaldo's discussion of the ways in which gender inequality is embedded in public/private dichotomies she identifies those societies with particularly sharp divisions between men's and women's worlds as ones where women can at times create their own sets of meanings through relationships with each other. These are also however societies where gender inequality is particularly great, and these separate women's spaces are heavily influenced by male authority and patriarchal definition (Rosaldo, 1974). On the other hand losing women's space cannot be equated with greater freedom and gender equality, as we have seen. There was considerable individual difference then in women's experience, depending on relationships in the household, the sensitivity of others, and how much 'women's space' there was. What remained consistent was women's responsibility for being modest and discreet and checking out the implications of breast-feeding in each particular setting.

Discourses of class and sexuality are also bound up with appropriate levels of privacy. I commented in the previous chapter on the discussion of breast-feeding and social class in the Newsons' study. They talked about embarrassment in relation to breast-feeding as connected with 'general prudishness about nudity' and suggested that 'overcrowding and lack of privacy in most working class environments arouse deep fears that incest taboos may too easily be violated' (Newson and Newson, 1963: 175). This comment must be seen in the context of 'official' professional beliefs over a long period of time that incest (which might now be termed child sexual abuse) is a working class phenomena (Gordon, 1989). This belief has served two purposes. First, it has disguised similar abuse in middle class households which is only now, partly as a result of feminist informed action, becoming visible (Campbell, 1988; Macleod and Saraga, 1988, 1991). Second, in emphasizing social class, even 'sympathetically' by pointing the finger at overcrowding, gender is overlooked. Working class women are held responsible for moderating the supposedly more dangerous sexuality of their men. One can see the same discourse at work in relation to breast-feeding. The women in this study were aware of their responsibility for modesty and secrecy about certain bodily functions. Embarrassment about breast-feeding is frequently seen as a product of working class culture rather than as having a more pervasive gendered dimension. For example, in a recent large scale study of attitudes to breast feeding, the author concluded: 'The belief that breasts are symbols of sexuality and attractiveness . . . seems to be present among working class men as well as their wives' (Jones, 1987:83).

This perception is related to discourses about class and incest which affect not only the infant feeding literature, the unchallenged view of the Newsons being the prime example, but to some extent the experiences of women in that it is seen as their responsibility to 'keep away from boys' as a number of women in this study were told by their mothers. In other words their sexual safety was dependent on their personal behaviour. Audrey Soulsby (1951) described the way her mother had passed on ideas about strict separation between the sexes within the household based on her own experience: 'She came from a pit village. They only had two rooms and a big family. They had a tin bath. Everything had to be boys and girls separate. It was the only privacy they had. My mother was the same with us.' This was in a social context where as Audrey describes, 'men were the be all and end all and women were their slaves', in other words where gender inequality was particularly marked. Audrey had clearly acquired some of her own anxiety about privacy from her mother. Keeping out of sight while breast-feeding can be seen as a dimension of this discourse of the dangers of working class sexuality in overcrowded households. The working class home is perceived as potentially dangerous unless properly managed by women.

SEXUALIZING PUBLIC AND PRIVATE SPACE

The processes through which infant feeding has become part of the private world can be analyzed in terms of the broader separation of home and work. The development of capitalism and the processes of industrialisation, which took place over several centuries in the Western world, produced a gendered separation of workplace and home: men and work, women and home. As well as relating to physical locations in actual space this arrangement is, most importantly, also ideological in that it is accompanied by beliefs about where both genders 'ought' to be even when they are not, perhaps for long periods of time. As Maher describes it: 'the spatial categories imply categories of relationship whereby relations of emotional and physical intimacy are confined to the private sphere, and impersonal work, political or social relationships characterise the public sphere' (Maher, 1992: 19–20). The belief that women's 'natural' place is in the home along with all sorts of nurturing and caring activities is very deeply rooted in the gendered discourse of public and private. Maher goes on to say that within societies where this spatial and ideological separation has not taken place, where women farm together for example, there is no need for breast-feeding to be conducted in a separate sphere.

An understanding of the way in which gender has become so deeply embedded in public and private divisions is useful then in understanding the experience of infant feeding. It is also illuminating to examine the discourses which have accompanied the construction of private and public spheres and the boundaries between them. It is through these discourses that breast-feeding has come to be seen as an activity which should be conducted in private, both in terms of time as well as place.

During the Victorian period public and private worlds became particularly dichotomised and also gendered. Discourses concerning bodies, and particularly the sexuality of bodies, were important in this. Davidoff (1983) writes of the processes which produced a 'world view' with divisions between masculine and feminine; between working class and middle class; between urban and rural; and also separated bodily functions, particularly those seen as sexual, from the public gaze. Those groups of people who were linked to the devalued parts of these hierarchical divisions became associated with the body, or certain parts of it. Davidoff draws attention to the work of Victorian sociologist Herbert Spencer who used a body metaphor in his descriptions of society. Within this language adult middle class males were the 'head', the thinkers, whilst workers were sometimes literally referred to as 'hands', doers. Middle class women represented the emotions or sometimes the soul. The 'nether regions' of the body and society were represented by criminals, prostitutes, paupers, beggars, the 'work-shy'; very much out of sight, but certainly not out of mind. These nether regions then were separated from 'the body politic', the important part of the social world. Women, children, servants and all black people were deemed to be closer to nature than adult white men. Sexuality, as a part of nature, was identified as an animal drive which must be tamed. Davidoff uses Weber's words to express the links between these different divisions and their effect: 'the more rationalised the rest of society becomes, the more eroticised sexuality becomes' (Weber, 1968: 603).

Amongst women this production and taming of sexuality operated in part through divisions between 'ladies' and 'women', a discourse which in any case was already available within Christianity: Madonnas and Magdalens. As I have outlined in earlier chapters, breast-feeding has frequently symbolised women's connectedness to nature, usually, although not necessarily, representing virtue. During the Victorian period this growing discourse about the naturalness and sexuality of women, and their disquieting presence in the public world, took many forms. Women were increasingly seen as disturbing the public world especially if they were viewed as less than respectable. In the 1860s the numbers of women in prison for public order offences (such as public drunkenness, using obscene language) reached a peak. Increasingly, however, the management of women was achieved through forms of regulation which came less from external surveillance than from the internalized controls of discourses of femininity and respectability. In order to achieve this it was necessary to produce myriad ways of categorizing women and their behaviour in relation to respectability. Infant feeding provides a particularly interesting example of this. Although during the nineteenth century wet nurses were frequently used in upper class English households they were viewed in much the same way as prostitutes, in being seen as performing an essential 'function', but being simultaneously despised at all levels of society and hence subject to personal scrutiny (Wickes, 1953). The growing expectation from the eighteenth century onwards, referred to in earlier chapters, that mothers ought to breast-feed their own babies represented the fixing of this activity as part of nature but also as requiring control.

I have already referred in chapter two to the belief that high rates of infant mortality were a product of women's failure to breast-feed, due to their paid work outside the home. As well as a moral panic about motherhood debates surrounding the Factory Acts in the 1840s were also preoccupied with women's bodies and sexuality. A major concern about working conditions in the mines was that men and women working together might engage in immoral behaviour. Walby indicates the obsession of the Commissioners with the state of undress of many women and young girls commenting: 'The Commissioners themselves seemed more concerned with the sexual implications of the chains with which women and girls dragged coal carts than with the severity of the labour they implied' (Walby, 1986: 116).

Thus the bodies of women, black people, children and the 'lower' classes were eroticised. As well as identifying these groups as close to nature, the discourses which constructed this eroticism also categorized them on moral grounds, those who were dangerous and irresponsible, as against those who could be trusted to control themselves and others; respectable white working class women, for example. Those parts of the public world which are most significant in political and economic terms have most apparent distance from the worlds of nature, bodies and sex. Foucault's work has revealed the paradoxical nature of this apparent absence of sex in that, in many institutions, an assumed lack of sexuality is accompanied by a preoccupation with it (Foucault, 1981). Hence women's very absence from many workplaces and other parts of the 'public world' served to reinforce them as sexual beings. Hearn and Parkin suggest that these assumptions were rewritten to form the basis of organizational theories in the early part of this century. Scientific management (Taylorism or classical organisation theory) based on the machine metaphor, characterised the manager as mind, the worker as a 'mindless' cog, and the woman as body. Women's bodies became inherently sexualised and associated with the private world. It was as sexual bodies that women re-entered the public world during this century. This sexualisation remains basic to a discourse which is able to be reworked to accommodate the changing involvement of women in the labour market.

Hearn and Parkin (1987) and other organization theorists, following the direction of Foucault's work, have suggested that workplaces are actually permeated with sexuality. This leads to a reframing of conventional notions of the private and the public. Recognising that sex and work cannot be separated from each other problematises the supposed separation of public and the private. Gender hierarchies are created through the discourses which suggest that these separations are real, possible and desirable. Women's bodies, which signify sexuality, are controlled within all kinds of space, most often through an expectation that they will control themselves through appropriate behaviour and presentation. Some space, however, particularly represents masculinity and power. There are clearly settings which women are simply not permitted to enter, but, even in space where they are 'allowed', but which is not 'theirs', their gender is inherently problematic if attention is drawn to it. Imray and Middleton's comment (1983) on breast-feeding in the House of Commons illustrates the way in which unequal gender relations are maintained by struggles over the place of supposedly private (female) behaviour in space which is seen to be significant in the public (male) world. What appears to be disturbing is the very particular form of 'sexuality' which is observed when breast-feeding takes place in public places. Current dominant discourses of active heterosexuality, identified in chapter two, *expect* women's bodies to be sexualized – but in ways which signal heterosexual availability or involvement. Many other workplaces would be similarly ruffled by breast-feeding (a colleague told me that her breast-feeding in a polytechnic office was widely commented on) but would accept all sorts of other 'sexual' practices – soft porn calendars, flirting, affairs, low cut dresses, short skirts, tight trousers.

Breast-feeding disappeared from the public world as part of the physical, ideological and gendered split between home

and work, described above. Hearn and Parkin refer specifically to breast-feeding as an example of the supposed separation of sexuality and work which actually reinforces the
sexuality of women's bodily practices and experiences. Possibilities for resistance to this sexualization are also evident
within this same discursive construction however:

> The frequent practice of breast feeding in the mills and
> factories of the industrial revolution represented a response
> to economic exigency *and* an introduction of the 'sexual'
> into the public arena. More recently the second world
> war brought on a more ordered version of such practices
> with the mushrooming of workplace nurseries. Now
> workplace nurseries are much less common and where
> they do exist they usually only take children after wean-
> ing from two and a half or three. The separation of sexu-
> ality is reaffirmed. Against that, some women have been
> partially successful in their attempts to either desexualize
> breast feeding in its practice in public places or, in doing
> so, to promote the sexual in public. While this may be
> more usual in cafes, restaurants, and other public places,
> in paid work organisations it remains very unusual. (Hearn
> and Parkin, 1987: 10)

Although, as we have seen in this study, there were variations for different women in the meaning of 'private' in
relation to breast-feeding, all of the women acknowledged
the need for such considerations. Paradoxically despite the
problematic nature of 'public' breast-feeding, breasts themselves, in certain packages and of certain types, have become far less private. The Newsons suggest that this
sexualization of breasts took place from about the 1930s
(Newson and Newson, 1963). Although I noted in chapter
two that the link between breasts and sexuality is not new,
there have been shifts in the connections between breasts
and sex in popular culture, as part of changing discourses
of sexuality. Breasts have in some ways come to represent
public sexual pleasure, often with a 'fun' connotation. (Page
three, topless bathing, fashion, 'boob-tubes'). In other words
breasts have become sexualized in our culture in particular
ways, with certain rules about who should see them, when,

what they should look like, who should suck them and where. This suggests that there are a number of complex, even contradictory, discourses of female sexuality operating in relation to private/public boundaries especially as regards breasts. Women, apparently, are expected to be actively heterosexual but to avoid drawing attention to sexuality where this is connected with reproduction.

TIME, SPACE AND WOMEN'S WORK

Combining infant feeding with paid work did not arise for the women in my study. Despite their different generations, the two periods of their life, having babies, and going out to work, barely coincided. Even when they were in paid work women still arranged their working life around their domestic responsibilities. They expected, and were expected, to do so. Several women spontaneously told me who looked after the child while they were working, anticipating that such an explanation is expected. Women did not have a 'career path' or long term approach to work; they took what came and often filled in or took short term jobs. None of the women had planned breaks or maternity leave; even those who went back after a short period were often 'filling in'. There was often no sharp distinction between being employed and being unemployed; memories about when they went back to work were far less clear than information about childbirth and pregnancy. This does not mean that women think of work as less important than men do, but that work and home responsibilities are linked for women in complex ways. For many women their work, since they became mothers, centred on the home to an extent where they had trouble describing what they did as work; childminding and fostering which several of the women did, or had done in the past, fell into this category. This question of what actually constituted work for women was a very complex one. For example, I was aware that many women were very active in their local communities in various ways; in fact that's how I came to meet some of them. These activities though did not feature as work in these discussions, even though some of it involved considerable time and responsibility.

The Asian women in the study were slightly different from the white women with regard to work, although not completely so. Rajina Mondal (1977) for example, was different from many of the other women, both black and white, in that she returned to sewing factory work very quickly after giving birth. The other Asian women, who had not yet worked outside the home, have probably had little opportunity to do so, given patterns of discrimination and employment segregation as well as home commitments which often include shared responsibility for family businesses.

Whatever variations there were in their working patterns, infant feeding took place in their 'private' time as well as space. For this group of women having to return to paid work played no part in their feeding decisions. This context, where infant feeding takes place as part of unpaid domestic labour, does have an impact on women's experience of it, however. It might have been the case that women valued the privacy and 'time out' which breast-feeding involved. That women in this study did not value time out might be partly understood as an outcome of the conditions of privacy; sitting on your own in a cold bedroom, away from everyone else, doesn't exactly sound attractive. Looking at the occasions when breast-feeding can operate as useful 'time out' for women gives us a greater level of understanding of the particular public/private divisions which structure infant feeding. For example, in certain circumstances breast-feeding can be used by women to get 'time out' from work. Talking of black women's experience of slavery, Bryan, Dadzie and Scafe suggest that breast-feeding offered women some means of control:

> The African tradition of breast feeding through infancy was just one of the many ways in which Black women succeeded in disrupting the slavers' attempts to extract and exploit our labour. As an effective (though unreliable) form of natural contraception, it successfully disrupted many a slaveowner's efforts to force his women slaves to breed; and because feeding a child is both frequent and time consuming, nursing mothers were often able to reduce the number of hours they worked in a day. Above all, it was an activity difficult to punish, and as such it was a

particularly effective form of passive resistance (Bryan *et al.*, 1986: 126).

Other writers have suggested that certain taboos on women's bodily functions can also sometimes be used by women to get time away from work. 'Backstage' areas like women's toilets and washrooms can be used for all sorts of activities. Martin notes: 'The double-edged nature of the shame of women's bodily functions here works in their favour: if private places must be provided to take care of what is shameful and disgusting, then those private places can be used in subversive ways' (Martin, 1989: 95).

During the period covered by this study there were, as we have seen, fewer private collective women's spaces which might be used in this way. Sayers (1982) also observes the usefulness of having to take time out because of what might be seen as negative aspects of women's bodies. Like Bryan *et al.*, cited above, she relates this to women's position within production rather than reproduction, and also highlights the difference between working class and middle class women in this respect. In discussing the way middle class women have tended to play down the effects of menstruation she suggests that: 'the claim that women are unhampered by menstruation and menstrual distress should be resolved through drug treatment has, in the case of working-class occupations, not served the interests of women' (Sayers, 1982: 182). This, she says, is because claiming menstrual distress can sometimes be used to improve working conditions by demands for rest periods and paid leave. But for middle class women this would have brought identification of their differences from male colleagues, which may not have served their interests. Hence, where women are part of production, and have little individual control over, or ultimate responsibility for, work, the need for privacy and time out can work to women's advantage. The need for privacy and time out are not always disadvantageous for women. The complex, often competing, demands for labour and for feminine behaviour have different implications for working class and middle class women and tend to be resisted in different ways according to relevant circumstances.

These examples of women being able to 'use' their biology

to gain greater control over their time are all situations where women are either in paid labour or, in relation to slavery, where time spent in breast-feeding is time 'taken' from those in control of women's time and bodies. In my study, the need for privacy was not seen as welcome time out because it excluded women from social activities, from 'going out' rather than from work. For some women breast-feeding was seen as too restrictive in this respect, 'I didn't want to breast-feed, I wanted to be out' (Carol Cook, 1973). Although many of the women claimed not to go out of the house very often we have already seen that breast-feeding prevented them joining in household life. This sometimes meant isolation from other women as well as from men. What appears more important however is that since their work took place in the household these women would still have to complete domestic tasks even if they took time out for breast-feeding. As noted in chapter three several women commented on the length of time breast-feeding takes and that they could not get other work, that is housework, done. Many women lived in shared households, but, as noted in chapter three, this did not always mean that help from others was forth-coming. Somewhat surprisingly quite a number of women who bottle-fed got help with this aspect of domestic labour:

Oh yes, anyone fed him, even the men. It happened a lot. (Elizabeth White, 1939)

Mother fed her regularly. (Maureen Watson, 1941)

Mother fed the baby during the day quite a lot. (Florence Hope, 1943)

My mam used to, my brothers used to, quite often. (Jean Richards, 1949)

My husband did it sometimes when he wasn't at work. He took his turn. (Monica Andrews, 1951)

My mam, dad and Jack used to sometimes. Jack used to give him his feed at night. (Evelyn Moore, 1965)

My husband helped at night. (Patricia Poole, 1965)

John sometimes fed him, very occasionally my mother-in-law. (Beatrice Callender, 1968)

My mother-in-law did it sometimes. (Naheed Akhtar, 1970)

We had a big family, yes, everyone helped. My husband often gave her her evening feed and took turns through the night. (Mandy Scott, 1970)

It was the oddest thing. My brother-in-law was only thirteen at the time and he used to feed her a lot. (Carol Cook, 1973)

My sister-in-law did it sometimes. (Rajina Mondal, 1977)

Women appeared to get more help with bottle feeding than with other household duties, and from a wider range of people. Whilst we might expect housework to have taken less time in the later period covered by the study since conditions were less harsh (improved sanitation and heating, for example) in practice time spent on housework is not a constant demand since it relates to the standards of housewifery expected. For example, Turnaturi has argued that, during the 1950s, as homemaking began to be seen as a job in its own right, for all women not just the bourgeoisie, 'domestic activities began to take up more rather than less time' (Turnaturi, 1987: 273). Doyal (1990) also identifies the rising demands and increasing expectations as regards household work. What is more, as we saw in chapter two, expectations of mothering, particularly for psychological and emotional care have also risen (Riley, 1983; Walkerdine and Lucey, 1989). Forman and Sowton (1989) have argued that the time required for reproduction does not fit well with time as conceptualized in the industrialized world. Control of reproduction was not only achieved through separating it from the public world but also through controlling the time it required by specifying how long it might take and in 'whose' time it should take place. Working class women in Tyneside, where there have been relatively low rates of paid female employment, have themselves borne the full cost of infant feeding since it was always conducted in their already demanding domestic time. Davies (1990) notes from her research on time in women's lives, that their relationship to both public and private spheres means that they do not get 'time out' as men do, since their work and responsibilities cut across dominant notions of the boundaries between work time and leisure time. Kahn (1989) suggests that patriarchal and capitalist structuring of time needs to be replaced by time which allows unrestricted breast-feeding involving what she describes as the 'mixed zoning' (Kahn, 1989: 31) of private and public. These ideas will be pursued further in the final chapter.

The dominant way of seeing breast-feeding as part of women's natural capacities means that it is not identified as work. This process, whereby breast-feeding is devalued and not seen as involving labour has been commented on in relation to attempts to construct a feminist economics: 'Every time I see a mother with an infant, I know I am seeing a woman at work. I know that work is not leisure and it is not sleep and it may well be enjoyable. I know that money payment is not necessary for work to be done' (Waring, 1988: 25). Waring also notes that 'breasts and breastmilk operate as a microcosmic example of all the forms of enslavement present in the concept of reproduction' (ibid: 206). This devaluing of women's work, its reduction to a 'natural' capacity which costs nothing, and its firm separation from production, is crucial to feminist economic analyses. This is overlooked by the pro breast-feeding lobby. Instead women's position as consumers of infant formula is somehow explained psychologically. For example, the idea that women easily fall sway to advertizing and 'propaganda' partially motivates the WHO/UNICEF code (1979). In chapter three I described the way in which women from minority ethnic groups were seen as victims of the false belief that bottle feeding is more modern. What is evident is the extent to which responsibility for this aspect of reproduction, like so many others, falls on to women so that they have to juggle their own resources to accommodate it. Using the meagre resources which have sometimes been provided by the state in the form of baby milk, or purchasing infant formula when they can afford it, seems entirely rational in this context. With these means someone else may feed the baby, they might find it takes less time, or they might be free to go out without people staring at them. Just as women in this community can be seen as making rational decisions with regard to utilising available resources for feeding their babies Maher makes a similar observation about women in Morocco:

> it is clear that formula feeding makes inroads on *male cash income* (since women get cash from men for milk powder) and not on female bodily resources. Women, in bottle-feeding, give up the impossible task of compensating with their own bodies for the shortcomings of a social and material environment which is hostile to women and children, and attempt to offload some of the burden of parenting and food production onto men. (Maher, 1992: 8 [emphasis in original])

Sharing the burden of feeding can sometimes be achieved through bottle feeding.

RETHINKING PRIVATE/PUBLIC BOUNDARIES: THE CONCEPT OF FEMININITY

The concept of femininity is a useful means of exploring this complex interconnectedness of public and private worlds. For example, breast-feeding did not in itself exclude the women in this study from the world of paid work. Their position as mothers first, and workers last (if at all), was established through many customs, beliefs and social arrangements. Most particularly this was achieved through a range of practices which ensure that women are recognized as women, and that, even if they become part of the public world in a physical sense, they remain ideologically part of the private world. Women are expected to remain feminine and to conduct themselves according to the complex demands which this brings. For women there are many private and public worlds. As we have seen it was not the world of work from which women in this study were excluded through breast-feeding. The relevant public world was often much more immediate; household life; the streets; the buses. This 'exclusion' from these public worlds involved two somewhat contradictory strands. First, the notion that respectable women did not breast-feed in public – to do so was to invite categorisation as 'a bit raw' (Tessa Rowe, 1944) or 'in their element doing it, they've even done it on breakfast TV' (Elizabeth White, 1939). Second, since women were supposed to enjoy privacy and not to want to go out, few women, especially those in the early part of the period, planned their infant feeding to openly fit in with the goal of 'going out'. Women as private people, whose place in public was always conditional, was reinforced.

The memories of women's space of some kind, where breast-feeding might have been less hazardous and restrictive in terms of social contacts, suggests that public and private worlds have become increasingly integrated and that there is an expectation that there will be less physical segregation of the sexes. The discourse concerning the appearance of breasts in public seems to operate through a number of dichotomies. First, women are divided into those who observe the rules of respectability and those who do not. This division has close parallels with other hierarchies: class (rough and respectable working class); race (black women as closer to nature and therefore seen as less 'civilised'); generation (some older women believed that younger ones 'expose theirselves all day every day now' Elizabeth White); and urban versus rural ('they haven't got a lot of morals in the country' Tessa Rowe). Second, heterosexual availability is separated from child bearing. Breasts are acceptable in public if they are presented (clothed or not) in ways which correspond to non reproductive (hetero)sexuality. Links between motherhood and sexual breasts are clearly disturbing unless firmly held within a discourse of mothering in a 'private' place. These dichotomies intersect with each other so that women's bodies are constantly scrutinized, by themselves, and others, to make sure that they neither deny sexuality, nor flaunt it. It is through the daily construction of femininity that women's bodily experiences are mediated.

The opening paragraph of de Beauvoir's book, *The Second Sex*, where she argues that 'one is not born but rather becomes a woman' (1953: 8) still provides the starting point for much contemporary exploration of the construction of women as feminine. Although she has been criticized for generalizing too far from the experiences of white bourgeois women in contemporary France, she nevertheless produced a set of questions and methods of analysis which have been very fruitful in looking at the myriad ways in which women are produced, maintained and 'policed' as women. Her examination of these processes concerned the minutiae of bodily and behavioural practices which produce women. The work of Foucault has added to this approach a greater consciousness of the construction of sexuality as a discursive process, often self imposed, acting on and through subjectivity; not simply through the intervention of someone else. The idea of femininity as a set of discourses concerning women, produced through a range of regulatory practices, and in different sites, has been an important way of investigating how patriarchy can both change and yet be maintained. For the survival of patriarchy, women must remain recognizably and visibly women in all settings, in order that the values and meanings attached to the different genders be maintained. Crucial to this process of the construction of femininity is the link with the idea of the natural. Femininity is assumed to be natural, but must at the same time be worked at. This provides both a method of control; you're never quite 'real' or natural enough; but also a space in which a woman can 'play' with gender, where she can have space in which to construct 'herself' as 'woman'. This 'space', often arising from contradictory notions of femininity, gives the possibility of resistance. Detailed studies of the construction of feminine bodies and feminine appearance and behaviour (Brownmiller, 1984; Bartky, 1988) have, of necessity, a high degree of cultural and historical specificity. However there is continuity in the contribution which the endless reproduction of femininity, albeit in varied and changing forms, makes to the maintenance of gender inequality and patriarchal social relations. Most particularly femininity is a never completed project: 'Femininity always demands more. It must constantly reassure its audience by a willing demonstration of difference, even when one does not exist in nature, or it must seize and embrace a natural variation and compose a rhapsodic symphony upon the notes'

(Brownmiller, 1984: 3). What is more, to fail at some aspect of femininity is to fail as a woman, again in Brownmiller's words, 'a failure in core self identity' (ibid: 3). It is important then to understand the complex bodily practices of infant feeding as connected to the discursive production of femininity, the 'real' woman.

Breast-feeding is a supposedly natural activity but, through the historical processes described here, has become a highly problematic endeavor. Breast-feeding, like other bodily activities on behalf of women, is judged according to 'unwritten', and often contradictory, rules concerning how women ought to behave and where they ought to be. All the women in my study, and others who are contemplating breast-feeding, know that their bodies are potentially disturbing. They have to discover where and to whom, and to decide how this 'disturbance' might be handled. Women are expected to be modest, to take notice of other's embarrassment, and often to be shy themselves. These expectations relate to those discourses of femininity which divide women into those who were respectable and those who weren't. But, as will be explored further in the next chapter, even keeping out of sight as women is no longer the answer. Revealed breasts are not in themselves simply a sign of debauchery. There are many situations when the right kind of breasts can be highlighted as a sign of womanhood. Breast-feeding is especially paradoxical in relation to femininity. As Brownmiller suggests, many aspects of femininity are constructed on the basis of the most minute biological differences. Breast-feeding in public, in the House of Commons or in other workplaces, appears to disturb because it shows that women *are* different from men. There are probably many reasons for this apparent contradiction but one important dimension is that such responses reveal the inconsistencies in discourses of femininity. For example, discourses of good natural mothering may conflict with notions of femininity which stress women's appearance and (hetero)sexuality. As well as producing difficulties for women, these inconsistencies also provide room for women's resistance.

It appears that there are many different versions of private and public space. The difficulty for women is that their bodies, which signify varied sexual meanings, are seen as potentially problematic in each one of these. What is more the relegation of breast-feeding to the private sphere does not simply concern modesty and embarrassment. It also involves the placing of infant feeding in the private sphere in the sense that it has become women's own responsibility to fit it into their other unpaid and economically unvalued domestic duties. However, as we have noted in chapter two, breast-feeding has not simply been left to mothers; it is a public issue in that surveillance of women is frequently conducted as a means of supposedly promoting breast-feeding. The 'working conditions' of infant feeding crucially involve a notion of breast-feeding as a private 'duty', arising from women's natural capacities and therefore requiring no financial, or other, resources. Breast-feeding developed this aspect of its place within private and public discourses as part of alarm, in the last century, and in the early part of this, about infant mortality rates. Breast-feeding mothers had to stay at home and do their duty in private, but feeding itself became a public issue, subject to professional surveillance.

Femininity, as it has been conceptualized in this chapter, appears highly problematic for women. This thinking echoes de Beauvoir's work in viewing the experience of being feminine as largely negative. However, other feminists are critical of the extent to which de Beauvoir envisaged that women's emancipation would be achieved through women adopting 'male habits and values' (Evans, 1985: xi). Young (1990b) suggests that we should not overlook the special experiences, such as pregnancy, childbirth and breast-feeding, which arise from women's unique female biology. She sees de Beauvoir's account, including for example her views on pregnancy and childbirth, as far too negative about women's bodies and experiences. She describes it as a 'revolt against femininity' based on a wish for sexual differences to be transcended (Young, 1990b: 74). In her view this way of thinking has been superceded in recent few years by what she describes as 'gynocentrism' which 'defines women's oppression as the devaluation and repression of women's experience by a masculinist culture that exalts violence and individualism' (ibid: 73). In this view, breast-feeding might contribute to a different set of values than those of the dominant, masculine, culture. Young herself argues that valuing some dimensions of women's differences from men is more useful than de Beauvoir's approach. However she suggests that, rather than adopt one or the other, we should find ways of avoiding this dichotomy. The possibility that being feminine might have positive, as well as negative, dimensions for women provides a useful way of approaching the discussion about women's feelings about their bodies and about breast-feeding in the next chapter.

5 Breast-feeding, Sex and Bodies

In the previous chapter I examined the discourses and processes through which women's bodies are perceived as always problematic in private space as well as that designated as public. This chapter focuses on women's own experiences of their bodies and analyzes these in relation to discourses concerning female sexuality. At the end of the previous chapter I suggested that it is important to examine the extent to which the experience of being feminine is a negative one for women, or whether it is useful to see femininity as potentially positive. This question is explored in this chapter.

The central question of the chapter is whether breast-feeding provides a challenge to phallocentric modes of thinking about the body. Feminist writers such as Adrienne Rich put their faith in fundamental social change emerging through women taking control of their bodies:

> The repossession by women of our bodies will bring far more essential change to human society than the seizing of the means of production by workers ... We need to imagine a world in which every woman is the presiding genius of her own body. In such a world women will truly create new life, bringing forth not only children (if and when we choose) but the visions, and the thinking, necessary to sustain, console, and alter human existence–a new relationship to the universe. (Rich, 1979: 285–6)

Rich's intention is to redefine sexuality through invoking a repressed womanliness which contains the potential for a transformed relationship between women, their bodies and their sexuality, thereby challenging other social relations (Rich, 1980, 1984). Other feminists see this way of thinking as dangerously close to patriarchal representations of femininity in that women's bodies are depicted within both as

133

pervaded by sexuality (Segal, 1987; Young, 1990b). But Rich is not speaking of a female sexuality which has been defined for us by men. Her strategy is an attempt to overcome the mind-body dichotomy which lies at the heart of Western thinking so that, as she describes it, women can 'think' with their bodies as well as with their minds. Women who are active in promoting breast-feeding frequently deploy similar language to Rich in seeing breast-feeding as an expression of women's power (Kitzinger, 1979; Palmer, 1993; McConville, 1994).

A central dilemma for feminists lies in whether to identify breast-feeding as a unique and important aspect of female sexuality. In a sense there is an inherent contradiction in focusing on the sexual aspects of breast-feeding while trying to rid ourselves of patriarchal notions that women are ruled by their biology and their sexuality. Introducing a collection of feminist research on the social control of girls Cain wrote of a similar irony: 'in spite of . . . our resentment that girls are seen only in terms of their sex, this book is in large part and paradoxically . . . about the sexuality of girls' (Cain, 1989: 4). Cain justifies this contradictory preoccupation by seeing the task as deconstruction (analysis of the discourse of sex which is used to control) and reconstruction (to try to imagine an alternative to the discourse). She describes this as a 'hazardous process' (ibid: 5). It is this same hazardous process of deconstruction and tentative reconstruction in relation to breasts, breast-feeding and sexuality which I embark upon in this chapter.

I will argue that women have had to understand their breast-feeding experiences within an increasingly sexualized discourse. This growing sexualization has accompanied an expectation of a more prominent role for men in early infant care: their presence at birth, for example, is now routine. This has contributed to breast-feeding being redefined within a framework of active heterosexuality and nuclear family life. In the first part of this chapter the increasing sexualization of the breast-feeding literature is explored. This is followed by consideration of how women themselves deal with the sexuality of breast-feeding. The final part of the chapter addresses the question of whether feminism provides a different discursive location for breast-feeding.

SEXUALITY IN THE BREAST-FEEDING LITERATURE

The written texts of breast-feeding are almost constantly troubled by the demon of sexuality. Various strategic devices to manage this interloper have been adopted. One is to studiously ignore it. A second is to treat the idea that breast-feeding is sexual as a false Western idea. A third is to appropriate breast-feeding as a heterosexual activity.

i. Literature in which Sexuality is Ignored.

The World Health Organization's (WHO, 1981c) comparative study of infant feeding and social conditions in Chile, Ethiopia, Guatemala, India, Nigeria, the Phillipines, Zaire, Hungary and Sweden contains virtually no mention of sexuality as a dimension. Sexuality is not addressed in the objectives for the study nor in the questionnaires used. There is no reference to sexuality except for a very brief question about whether women need privacy to breast-feed their babies, an issue which receives no exploration. In their 1988 study of breast-feeding promotion programmes Jelliffe and Jelliffe do not apparently view sexuality as a significant dimension. In their chapter on developments in the design of promotion programmes the possibility of anything to do with sexuality being influential is dismissed. Loss of 'figure' is listed as an influence on maternal anxiety but is not discussed. 'Taboo on breastfeeding in public (possibly decreasing)' (Jelliffe and Jelliffe, 1988: 439) is listed as a 'common Western misconception' but receives no discussion.

Apple (1987) in her interesting study of the medicalization of infant feeding pays no attention to sexuality. Similarly, Sussman's study (1982) of the rise and decline of wet nursing in France does not consider sexuality as a dimension.

ii. Texts which See Links between Breast-feeding and Sexuality as Important but Based on False Beliefs

In some respects this theme is a variant of the first category in that it rests on a similar view of the relationship between sex and breast-feeding; which is that there is no 'real' connection. Literature in this category acknowledges that beliefs in breasts as sexual have an influence on breast-feeding but suggests that these are misconceptions resulting from 'civilisation' or 'Hollywood'. Hence, in the view of such literature, policies must either ignore such myths or attempt to dissuade women from their irrational views. An example of this arises in a study of the attitudes of mothers to infant feeding which was conducted at Newcastle General Hospital in 1975: 'Some said the idea of suckling a baby was repugnant to them and a few regarded it as primitive. These feelings may perhaps arise from the esteem of the breast in modern Western culture as a sex symbol rather than as a functional organ (Bacon and Wylie, 1976: 309). As noted in the previous chapter, there is a strong social class dimension to this theme in that middle class women (and men) are assumed to be less susceptible to such irrationality. The Newson's study, discussed earlier, provides the best known and most influential example of this.

iii. Literature which Regards Breast-feeding as a Sexual Activity in Itself

There are three important strands in this literature. First, breast-feeding is seen as physiologically sexual in that breasts are 'erogenous zones'. This view arises from sexology, the science of sexuality, referred to in chapter two, which is based on examining and recording the range of human sexual responses. As a discipline sexology takes a positivist stance, is physiologically based and, in the spirit of that philosophy, frequently ignores its own implicit value base. Some contemporary pro breast-feeding literature written for health workers recognizes the sexuality of breast-feeding within this physiological paradigm and treats it accordingly:

> The milk-ejection reflex is closely connected with the sexual reflexes. Sexual stimulation may cause oxytocin to be secreted from the posterior pituitary, and so make milk flow. The connection works in the opposite direction, too, and many women have sexual sensations while they nurse. This makes some women feel guilty and anxious instead of just accepting the sensation for what it is: nature's way of making breast-feeding pleasant, and of helping the survival of the

species. Most women accept this when they learn that it is common and normal. (Helsing and Savage King, 1982: 31)

The second important strand within the literature which recognizes the links between sexuality and breast-feeding concerns the relationship between heterosexuality and breast-feeding. This literature is also constructed from the discourse of sexology. There is a preoccupation with the place of breasts and breast-feeding in the overall map of sexuality. Although Kinsey *et al.* (1953) did not address pregnancy and breast-feeding as potentially sexual experiences, others have been concerned to explore the question of whether breast-feeding is an asset or a problem with regard to sexual intercourse. For example, Masters and Johnson (1966) claimed that breast-feeding women were more eager than other women to have sexual intercourse in the post natal period. Goldfarb and Tibbets (1980) point out that, although this finding has been often quoted, Masters and Johnson's other comments have been ignored. For example, many of the women in their study admitted that their early return to sexual relations was motivated by their guilt and 'concern' for their husbands' suffering, rather than suggesting simply that breast-feeding made them feel more sexy. Kitzinger (1979) points out that in 1960s America when these studies were done there were so few women who were breast-feeding that they could hardly be seen as a random sample of the population. In contrast to Masters and Johnson, Goldfarb and Tibbets, in a breast-feeding advice manual for health workers note that most clinical reports on lactating women describe 'a diminished libido during early lactation' (1980: 176).

Some pro breast-feeding literature has remained with the Masters and Johnson approach in a pre-occupation with how breast-feeding can accommodate what are assumed to be normal heterosexual relations. The Stanway's popular book *Breast is Best* is the most prominent example of this. They repeat the Masters and Johnson view that breast-feeding women return to intercourse more quickly than other women:

Certainly the breast feeding woman returns to normal more quickly physically but it's also more likely that the repeated feelings of sexual arousal (however minimal they are) also make her more receptive to sex. Some studies show that a substantial number of women are more sexually active when breast feeding than at any other time. This is good news for fathers who often feel left out at this time! (Stanway and Stanway, 1978: 182)

The Stanways convey a vivid picture of what they see as 'normal' heterosexual marital relations. They are deeply concerned that a woman's pleasure in her baby should not detract from her relationship with her husband and give advice about how women can manage this. They suggest that husbands may resent breast-feeding because 'until now his wife's breasts have 'belonged' to him' (ibid: 183). According to the Stanways a woman should handle this by making sure she reassures her husband that he can retain ownership of her breasts despite this temporary intrusion: 'Don't let him feel that because the baby's feeding that's all you see your breasts as doing. Let your husband play with your breasts as he did before' (ibid: 183).

Whilst the Stanways see breasts as important visual symbols of female sexuality they suggest that their meaning is significantly different for men and women: 'Men look at beautiful girls because they get a simple animal pleasure from them – women look at them to see what other women have got that they haven't. And usually it's breasts they're comparing (ibid: 183). This text clearly contains firm views about male and female sexuality and understands breast-feeding within this model. The sexuality of breast-feeding for them is physiological but relates to heterosexuality through a set of organizing principles concerned with sexual intercourse and male sexuality as over-riding 'needs'. Women's needs are not examined. Instead women are portrayed as ministering to their husbands' needs, when they are not fully occupied with baby care, and as relating to other women only as objects of comparison and jealousy. An American text (Eiger and Olds, 1972) is almost a replica of this influential advice book by the Stanways.

Jordan (1986), in an article entitled 'Breastfeeding as a Risk Factor for Fathers' is, like the Stanways, concerned about ways in which the threat to men of breast-feeding can be reduced. She sees this threat as arising from womb and breast envy and because: 'From conception, most men realise their wife's body is not solely "theirs" ' (1986: 95). Although this view could give rise to a feminist reading Jordan is keen to squash this threat to heterosexuality. She suggests that such difficulties can be anticipated and dealt with by health professionals through enhancing communication between fathers and mothers, enabling fathers' involvement in childcare, and nurturing the marital relationship. This model, like the Stanways, appears to be based on a strategy of reassuring husbands that their wives' breasts belong to them 'really'.

The third approach which links breast-feeding and sexuality sees breast-feeding as a very special part of a unique female sexuality. Sheila Kitzinger, a prominent activist, writer and educator on childbirth and breast-feeding compares aspects of female sexuality with heterosexual intercourse: 'Birth is an intense and dramatic psychosexual experience, quite as much or even more so than love-making and intercourse. In the same way breastfeeding is psychosexual too, involving as it does a giving of the woman's body, release to let the milk flow, and relations between bodies, her own and the baby's' (Kitzinger, 1979: 14). The roots of this approach in sexology become clear when we read Havelock Ellis's similar comparison of breast-feeding with sexual intercourse: 'The complete mutual satisfaction, physical and psychic, of mother and child, in the transfer from one to another of a precise organicised fluid, is the one true physiological analogy of the relationship of a man and a woman at the climax of the sexual act' (Ellis, 1903: 229).

Kitzinger suggests that most discussions about sexuality start from male perspectives and leave out the wide range of sensual and erotic experiences, including breast-feeding which are part of women's experiences of their bodies. Oakley also notes that: 'the sexual satisfaction of childbirth and lactation is played down, while the pleasures of heterosexual (marital) intercourse are emphasized as the correct outlet for female sexual desire' (Oakley, 1980: 248).

One writer, Palmer (1988), suggests that breast-feeding, as an exclusively female sexuality, is particularly threatening to men, and that this accounts for their embarrassment and discomfort about breast-feeding when they show no such uneasiness at the wide display of bared breasts in advertising and pornography: 'if one colleague breastfed a child during a business meeting the embarrassment would be too overwhelming. The poor dears must be protected from such pressure' (Palmer, 1988: 95). Palmer sees this threat as resulting from a demonstration of a power that is exclusively female. She gives an example of a man describing a female colleague whom he disliked, as breast-feeding 'aggressively'.

Links between sexuality and breast-feeding are thus conceptualized in a number of ways in this literature: from ignoring any possible links; through attempting to fit it into a framework dominated by heterosexual marital intercourse; to seeing it as a demonstration of both female sexuality and power. I will return to more explicitly feminist versions of this last category in the final section of this chapter.

WOMEN'S EXPERIENCES OF THEIR BODIES

In my own study I explored breast-feeding as a bodily activity in a number of ways. In the last chapter I focused particularly on the need for privacy and modest behaviour. In this chapter I look at more intimate feelings about bodies in relation to breast-feeding. I began by asking about the kinds of feelings which women had about feeding their babies whether or not they breast-fed.

Some women were puzzled about being asked how they felt. Perhaps it had not occurred to them to think about their own feelings, or perhaps they had no words in which to express themselves. This is in some ways unsurprising since, as Oakley noted in her study of childbirth: 'Few people have thought to ask women what it feels like to be pregnant, to give birth to a baby and to breast feed' (Oakley, 1980: 78). Young (1990c) expresses surprise that, in the explosion of feminist literature in recent years, so little has been written about women's feelings about their breasts. When she told women that she was writing about 'the breasted experience' they had much to say. This reluctance to talk about breasts may well be beginning to break down particularly because of the all too common experience of breast cancer and the recognition that treatment regimes have for too long been left to male medics (McConville, 1994).

For the women in my study breast-feeding evoked stronger and often more equivocal feelings than bottle feeding. For some women bottle feeding was merely functional, 'I had no special feelings, very often I thought, get this down, it was a job to be done'(Evelyn Moore, 1965); 'With the bottle? oh yes, the bottle would disappear' (Monica Andrews, 1951). For other women, however, bottle feeding was recalled positively as a 'very motherly feeling' (Patricia Poole, 1965); 'I used to like to feed him with the bottle, I enjoyed the closeness' (Beatrice Callender, 1968); 'I used to enjoy feeding him with the bottle 'cos he was enjoying it, I could see he was' (Eleanor Kershaw, 1940). Bottle feeding seems straightforwardly to do with feelings about successful mothering, the pleasure of doing the job properly, and providing evidence of this through an empty bottle. Such feelings were related to something they could control. Shirley Hill (1973), for example, experienced bottle feeding positively especially when she was on her own, 'he's mine and I'm looking after him, sounds daft you know, I used to talk to him. I used to like it better on my own, 'cos they'd [relatives] try to take over'.

Breast-feeding experiences had much more potential to arouse strong feelings. Sometimes these feelings were entirely negative, and, for some women, such feelings had stopped them from considering breast-feeding in the first place. Positive feelings were sometimes 'motherly' and occasionally sensual, although it is an overstatement to suggest a clearcut distinction between the two. Jane Harrison's positive feelings, when asked if she enjoyed breast-feeding appear to relate to motherliness, 'Yes [hesitantly] it didn't bother us. I thought it was marvellous. I thought for a long time that natural was best' (1936). Similar language was used by Audrey Soulsby (1951), 'I was giving him the best that life could offer, a good start, giving him the best, I loved feeding my babies'. Only a few women were able to express sensuality in positive terms. Ada Brown was open about this and it seemed straightforward for her: 'It was a lovely feeling, a very close feeling, so warm, a cuddly feeling, makes you one person again rather than two separate beings' (1959). Beatrice Callender, who gave up breast-feeding after one week, was slightly puzzled by, and interested in, her own feelings, when asked if she enjoyed it: 'Yes, I did. It was pleasurable, yes pleasurable. Am I a pervert do you think? [laughs]. When I was on my own doing it I could know my own feelings, I wasn't that screwed up, on my own it felt pleasurable and easy and I could acknowledge that' (1968).

Jean Richards recognized the potentially sensual/sexual nature of breast-feeding describing herself as having 'no hang ups', but her positive feelings related much more to mother-liness, 'it was just an automatic thing, something that was good for the baby'. Other women expressed strong dislike of the physical experience of breast-feeding, although often they could not find the words to describe their feelings:

> No, I didn't, no, no. Oh no, no. I don't know it just seemed to draw. I couldn't say I enjoyed it. I was glad it was over, I can't describe it. I didn't enjoy it. (Monica Andrews, 1951)

> No, it was a tickly feeling. (Naheed Akhtar, 1970)

> I don't like the itching. (Rajina Mondal, 1978)

The feelings expressed here, motherly duty and/or pleasure on the one hand, or sensual/sexual and perhaps therefore uncomfortable on the other, suggest that the language of motherliness offers a more straightforward language for women's pleasure than sensuality. This can conveniently be applied to both breast and bottle feeding.

As a means of getting into discussions about women's bodies without asking what might seem crudely inappropriate questions I showed the women a health education book containing fairly 'explicit' photographs of childbirth. Their responses to these photographs are interesting and were rather surprising to me at first. The book is a 'guide to becoming pregnant, being pregnant and caring for your new born baby' (Health Education Council, 1984: front cover). It is very carefully produced with advice from a range of health professionals and social researchers, and is partly based on research with parents. In fact the OPCS survey of 1985 (Martin and White, 1988) notes that most mothers routinely received a copy of this book. It is attractively presented, clearly written with, in my view, beautiful photographs and drawings.

A wide range of people are photographed, not simply the white middle class attractive young mothers of some similar literature. Before my research I simply saw the pictures as pictures, accurate in some self evident sense, useful in giving reasonably realistic information. I was initially rather surprised by the strong negative reactions of some of the women in my study. Analyzing these reactions has helped me to understand something of the politics of looking and being looked at even in Health Education literature.

At first I found it frustrating that women did not see what I saw in the photographs. They did not see the 'obvious' content which I perceived. Instead a number of them were shocked at seeing the woman's body uncovered; I had seen this as 'obviously' a part of childbirth:

> They expose you more now even at the birth of your baby. (Lucy Cooper, 1930)

> Terrible, really isn't it, we were all shaved, not naked. (Polly Williams, 1932)

> You're exposed terrible, I wouldn't have fancied that. (Eleanor Kershaw, 1940)

> I wouldn't have liked to be photographed. (Florence Hope, 1943)

> Fancy being photographed in that position. What do you think? (Beatrice Callender, 1968)

A number of the women were clearly preoccupied with the social scene which the photograph depicted, and with the taking of the photograph. It had not occurred to me to question the taking of photographs in such situations. In fact it has become fashionable amongst middle class parents, especially those concerned with 'natural' childbirth, to take their own photographs of birth scenes. An insight into such responses can be achieved through the work of the critical feminist photographer, Spence (1986; Coward and Spence, 1987). Her work explores the way in which what is presented as natural within photography, in 'family albums' for example or 'medical' literature, is actually carefully constructed, albeit without conscious intention, to convey particular images and values. Despite my efforts to denaturalize childbirth and breast-feeding, I had been initially unable to recognize the process of socially constructing these photographs to depict the supposed naturalness of women's bodies in childbirth. One barrier to understanding this had come from my inability to recognize the limitations and construction of my own 'gaze', as well as the messages which the photographs conveyed to me. I was obviously comfortable with my position as onlooker. A number of the women in the study could not identify themselves as a suitable onlooker and in fact forcefully rejected that position. Elizabeth White (1939), for example, asked 'is it from the man's point of view?' suggesting that the usual gaze in relation to women's bodies is expected to be male. Even the 'medical gaze' was suspect for some of these women when it involved unnecessary exposure. For example:

> My midwife used to throw the sheet over you, she didn't even expose you to herself and she was over 70. (Lucy Cooper, 1930)

> I refused to let a male student be in the room when I had a baby. You're exposed terrible. I couldn't have fancied that. (Eleanor Kershaw, 1940)

> I never like to show myself in front of anyone and I never would have let the doctor examine me week after week. (Jane Harrison, 1936)

Petchesky has pointed out the origins of photography in 'late nineteenth-century Europe's cult of science . . . linked inextricably with positivism' (1987: 62). Like Sontag (1979), Petchesky describes the powerful influence of this on Western culture in the sense that photographs are seen to represent objective truth and rationality. Through asking questions about what is included in the photograph and what is not, and from which (or whose) perspective the scene is witnessed we can search out its implicit messages. For some of the women in my study, the photographic scene clearly jarred with their feelings. They fixed on the position of woman as object and questioned the suitability of the camera's gaze. Their discomfort in relation to her exposure and her pain emerged from their feelings about their own childbirth experiences, together with what had been important to them in managing the process. Practices concerning the visual display of childbirth have undergone a major change, particularly since the late 1970s in that, whereas none of the women in my study had given birth in the presence of the baby's father, this has now become commonplace. Beatrice Callender talked about not wanting her husband there when her children were born. She had been fearful of the birth but had found a way to manage it, surprised by her own strength. But she hadn't wanted her experiences to be on display:

> I didn't want him there at all and he was glad to go, he was quite squeamish then. He didn't want to see it and I didn't want him to see it. It probably sounds strange but I didn't want him to see us in all me glory and gunge. I just hadn't reached the stage where I could let him see everything I had in broad daylight with people around. I just couldn't have done it (Beatrice Callender, 1968).

For Beatrice her husband's presence generated worries about 'being seen'. Whilst Petchesky rejects the view of some feminists that 'visualisation and objectification as privileged ways of knowing are *specifically masculine* (man the viewer, woman the spectacle)' (Petchesky, 1987: 68) she suggests that visual aspects of reproduction carry different meanings for men and women. An example of these gendered differences occurred in a study by Prendergast and Prout (1990). This concerned the impact on boys and girls of a health education film about childbirth. Girls were particularly concerned that the film revealed the mother's pain but seemed not to do so from her point of view. They were left, rather like the women in my study, feeling uneasy rather than reassured. Prendergast and Prout suggest that, whilst supposedly depicting the 'reality' of childbirth, the film actually shows the scene from the point of view of the medical staff, with the woman's body as object of medical attention and as 'a naked vulnerable and passive thing' (ibid: 142). Cosslett (1994), in her discussion of women's experiences of childbirth, talks of her own discomfort with photographs depicting childbirth since they always objectify the woman, looking at her from the position of audience. This supposedly objective representation, the photograph, carries messages which, for women, sit uneasily with their own view of the world. Looking again at the pictures I used and which have become familiar in literature about childbirth I can see that the position of the camera is in line with the medical staff's view of the woman. The prominence of the father in all the shots, which I had previously overlooked, now seems striking. The book has clearly tried to take a multi-cultural approach in depicting women from different ethnic groups but has overlooked 'cultural' messages concerning women, specifically how their experience is managed. The format of the photograph suggests that the women's experiences are being managed by the medical staff, and by their husbands.

Not all the women rejected the photographs. A number were interested in them: Gina Godfrey (1969) thought them 'lovely pictures'; Shirley Hill (1973) said, 'I like it. The books I had were just diagrams'; Margaret Pearson (1975) also thought they were lovely, 'I cry when I see births on television'. Other women responded to them as fairly neutral rather than emotional: 'They don't revolt me at all, to me they're natural'(Evelyn Moore, 1965); 'If someone had given it to me it wouldn't have bothered us in the least' (Ada Brown, 1959). But these views contrasted with what these women thought about their potential usefulness if you were about to have a baby. A number of women thought that they would have been 'put off' had they seen them at the time: 'It would have terrified the life out of me' (Beatrice Callender, 1968); 'I might have been a bit shocked . . . nothing can prepare you for how it's going to feel' (Gina Godfrey, 1969); 'It might have put us off' (Mandy Scott, 1970); Evelyn Moore said that she wasn't shocked now but 'if I'd seen these prior to the birth I might not have wanted to go through with it' (1965).

Although not entirely clearcut, these views had a generational dimension. For the most part it was the older women who were shocked at the sight of the picture, although the woman who was most shocked was Nargis Ahmed (1970) who refused even to look at them properly, having had one glance. But this shock was complex and often related to the actual photograph rather than the event itself. For example, Lucy Cooper (1930) forcefully rejected the photographs but said 'I would be upset at this picture but I've seen babies born because I've been with my friends and it's a beautiful sight to see a baby born. Beautiful'. Some of the women thought that women did need more information but rejected this kind of representation as a medium for conveying this. Mary Moreland (1936) said, 'It's a good thing that young girls know more these days but I don't agree with this book'. Amongst the 'younger' women similar ambivalence was expressed about the usefulness of these photographs. Beatrice Callender (1968) said, 'when something like that's going to happen to you . . . well I think most people . . . you try to get as much information as possible' but she disliked the photographs, 'No I don't like them . . . ooh I think it's the pain on her face, it brings it all back, it is painful'. Other women thought that whilst their daughters were more knowledgeable than they had been, they too disliked such photography.

The photographs then do not simply represent 'knowledge'. For some of the women in this study they carried with them signs and messages which were not simply about useful information. Although Petchesky's caution about the dangers of essentialism in relation to the idea that 'looking' is male and being 'looked at' is female is worth noting, the reactions of women in this study can be placed beside common modes of visual representation of women's bodies, and the discomfort generated by being on display. Berger's classic comment on women's place in visual representation does not seem an exaggeration of women's experiences during childbirth and while breast-feeding:

> from earliest childhood she has been taught and persuaded to survey herself continually . . . And so she comes to consider the surveyor and the surveyed within her as the distinct elements of her identity as a woman. She has to survey everything she is and everything she does because how she appears to others, and ultimately how she appears to

men, is of crucial importance for what she normally thought of as the success of her life, her own sense of being appreciated as herself by another. (Berger, 1972: 46)

This suggests that Beatrice Callender's feelings (noted above) about her husband's presence at the birth must be placed in this context of gendered patterns of the visual. It also echoes de Beauvoir's thesis concerning how women learn to become women which was referred to in the previous chapter. Both de Beauvoir and Berger suggest that women learn to watch themselves being watched, seeing their bodies as objects and thus being unable to be active subjects. Young (1990c) argues that women's feelings about their breasts are powerfully shaped by their being such an important visual symbol of female sexuality, although she suggests that this nevertheless leaves room for other, sometimes more positive, breasted experiences. Perhaps we can see women's reaction to these photographs as potentially a form of resistance to this 'object' position.

This material suggests that sexuality for these women is inevitably connected with the ways in which their bodies are routinely talked about, looked at, examined and represented. The contradictions which they express, and the ambivalence which they show, however suggests though that there is more to this than a simple rejection of sexuality as 'nasty and dirty'. There are 'places', 'times', 'situations' when women 'enjoy' aspects of child bearing and breast-feeding and their own and other women's bodies, although it is often difficult for them to find a language in which to express this. There are inherent difficulties with language and forms of representation within which to express these experiences. Perhaps Jean Richards' (1949) comment suggests the complexity of how women experience their own and other women's bodies, both associating aspects of reproduction with pleasure but finding representations of women's sexuality potentially problematic: 'My daughter was there when her daughter had a baby and enjoyed it. I was there when my daughter had hers, I got into it, [the pictures are] very lifelike, but I wouldn't have liked it then. It's just a woman having a baby but some would look on it as a dirty picture.'

BREASTS AND DISCOURSES OF SEXUALITY

Breasts have then come into their own as important sexual equipment within the developing discourses of active heterosexuality and sexual pleasure which have accompanied the movement from private to public patriarchy. Expectations regarding femininity have been transformed in that women are now expected to be visibly and actively (hetero)-sexual rather than simply shy and modest. Breasts now signify female gender perhaps more than any other part of the body. Having the 'right' shape and size of breasts is a metaphor for being the right sort of woman. Too small and you're a frump, too big and you're a tart (McConville, 1994). In this context the 'right' sort of woman is sexually active and desirable but not too much so. Young notes that a woman 'often feels herself judged and evaluated according to the size and contours of her breasts, and indeed she often is' (1990c: 189). But expectations about breasts are not static. Brownmiller notes how her breasts went from being 'wrong' (too small) to 'right' within a decade: 'By the mid 1960s when I put away my bra and girdle in response to a newer model of the feminine body, I found that without one iota of change in my physical dimensions, my breasts were suddenly not too small' (Brownmiller, 1986: 11).

Sexual politics are often conducted around breasts. The apocryphal tale of the start of the women's liberation movement involved bra burning at a beauty queen contest. The words 'page three' divide Britain into two camps, those 'lasciviously' in favour and those 'puritanically' against. This is in large part a gendered division, with women being most significantly 'against' (Short *et al.*, 1991). And breasts are not just there to be looked at. Feeling, sucking, stroking breasts is part of 'light' petting, an essential bit of 'foreplay'. Breasts then are fun, not serious: light petting, 'above the waist', soft porn. Baring them on the beach is a good way to get an all over tan – and adds to the scenery. Breasts get serious as a result of cancer – 'loss' of a breast being seen in popular imagination as more tragic than possible death (Lorde, 1980; Young, 1990c; McConville, 1994). Breasts then are highly symbolic of those processes which make up the construction of femininity. How women manage their breasts is a major indicator to themselves and others of how they manage their sexuality.

As I noted earlier feminism has had, and still has, a complex and contradictory relationship to sexuality. In chapter two I referred to changes in sexual politics during this century, particularly the shift from seeing women, especially bourgeois women, as pure and sexless to actively sexual (Jeffreys, 1985; Mort, 1987; Weeks, 1989a; Roiphe, 1994). These issues are still live ones within feminist politics (Coveney *et al.*, 1984; Hunt, 1990). Whether and how pornography could or should be controlled is one of ain arenas for these debates at present (Betterton, 1987; Chester and Dickey, 1988; Assiter, 1989; Segal and Mcintosh 1992; MacKinnon, 1994). A major difficulty for feminism is that of finding any 'independent' discourses about sexuality, a concern I will return to later in this chapter. But first a number of points arise from how women in my study talked about breasts, sexuality and bodies.

Most women found it difficult to name and evaluate the sensations that arose from breast-feeding. Attempts to explain them were a sometimes uncomfortable mixture of feelings that 'belong' to mothering and feelings that 'belong' to sex. There were hints from Beatrice Callender that it is only when you are alone and in control that you can know for yourself what 'feelings' mean. A number of women found breast-feeding extremely distasteful and looked for ways to avoid it. For example, Elizabeth White (1939) gave up breast-feeding after two weeks ostensibly because she thought the baby wasn't getting enough milk. But underlying this reason she, like some other women, had strong negative feelings about breast-feeding, 'I didn't like it and I didn't want to do it'.

One important dimension of women's experience involved a set of dynamics concerned with the belief that women's bodies are there to be looked at. This being 'looked at' is usually done by men and it is women's responsibility to manage their 'object' position. In the earlier period covered by this study women were expected to avoid the 'gaze' falling on 'sexual' parts of their body in order to maintain privacy and respectability. In the latter part of the period there had been some change in this, in that women were to be looked at as sexual beings, but this sexuality was that of (hetero)sexual participant. Hence modesty and privacy had different meanings for the different generations, although it is important not to make too sharp a division, in that breasts have not simply become sexual, after an assexual past. Discourses of modesty gradually and unevenly gave way to, or merged with, expectations regarding attractive appearance.

Although women's bodies are 'looked at' all the time, representations of women's bodies add a particular dimension to this. There was a strong link for women in this study between photographs which exposed women's bodies in whatever context and pornography, 'dirty pictures'. It was also possible, on the other hand, for some women to relate positively to photographs of women in childbirth, to see visual beauty in both the image and the reality. Despite this effort by the women to explore their reactions to the photographs and to relate them to their own experiences of witnessing birth, strong and ambivalent feelings were expressed about the process of the photograph being taken. It conveyed to many women layers of vulnerability (to exposure, to sexualization, to lack of control, to pain) which they found profoundly uncomfortable.

Some of the women were deeply ambivalent about sexual 'knowledge', often mistrusting both its form and its purpose. Some women felt they were ignorant, and wanted to be less so, but were uneasy about how this might be achieved and what the costs would be. Some felt at odds with dominant expectations of sexuality describing themselves as 'prudes' or 'old fashioned'. They disliked current sexual 'talk' seeing it as too open and failing to maintain privacy. They had their own language though, colourful expressions which do not convey simple prudery; 'we wouldn't know our mothers were expecting until we could see the bump they were cutting the bread on'. I found group interviews with these women difficult to manage in part because of the level of joking. Several times I heard an apocryphal story about being on the bus with a toddler who refused the breast. The standard reply was, 'If you don't have it, I'll give it to the man over there', accompanied by much hilarity. This is not the language of the shy, modest women which they aspired to be. Douglas suggests that a joke is mildly subversive of the accepted

order without disrupting it, 'a temporary suspension of the
social structure, or rather it makes a little disturbance in
which the particular structuring of society becomes less relevant than another' (1975: 107). Their language then suggests that the practices surrounding femininity are powerful
but not monolithic. There is some room for women to 'play'
with femininity. In contrast with this joking some women
indicated that they found even the 'educational' discourse
about sexuality uncomfortable. Jane Harrison (1936) said
in a very puzzled voice: 'If they'd given the book to me I'd
have refused it. And yet I was ignorant and now people are
educated.'

So how might we summarize the discursive practices which
surround breasts? During the period covered by this study
they appear to have been on the move, whilst at the same
time retaining some crucial elements of continuity. The
movement concerns the increasingly explicit construction
of breasts as sites of sexual pleasure. Breasts are now *required*
to be sexual as a part of the discourse of sexual enjoyment
and happiness for women increasingly evident since the 1930s
(Wilson, 1977; Coveney *et al.*, 1984; Mort, 1987; Young, 1990c).
As this discourse has moved from the language of happy
married love to one of heterosexual 'liberation' breasts have
been used as signs of involvement in the right kind of sexuality. The discourse of heterosexuality contained in popular
breast-feeding advice books confirms this. Continuity has been
achieved in at least two connected ways. First, breasts have
been constantly scrutinized, looked at and examined. Their
inadequacy for feeding babies has preoccupied the medical
profession as well as midwives and health visitors, as indicated in earlier chapters. Possible and actual malignancy has
kept them well in the medical gaze (Spence, 1986; Young,
1990c: McConville, 1994). They have come to be the constant object of the male gaze, the sine qua non of female
attractiveness and therefore approval. We are surrounded
by representations of breasts, decoration in many workplaces,
titillation over the morning tea.

The second aspect of continuity concerns the responsibility which women have to keep their breasts respectable –
but also 'attractive'. This means that women have to manage the gaze of others. To be respectable – a good girl –

means having your breasts looked at to order, at the right time, by an appropriate person, and for the correct purposes. Managing the scrutiny of your breasts is even more complex than simply about time, place and viewer, however. It also involves questions about what different breasts mean. This involves not just size and shape, which have been referred to earlier, but also class and race. Black breasts carry with them a language of female sexuality which is different from discourses of white female sexuality, a language which has historically constructed black women as 'always available' in order to justify sexual abuse by white men (Jordan, 1974; hooks, 1982; Miles, 1989). The bodies of poorer working class women are particularly likely to attract attention as signs of a lack of respectability. I recall a woman who received the constant attention of social workers for her inadequate mothering. One of the most commented upon aspects of her appearance, in case conferences for example, was that she frequently left her breasts exposed. Expert discourse understood this as an act of incredibly alarming deviance. Mary Moreland (1936) in this study also understood this very well: 'I still don't like to see women breast-feeding. Class makes a difference. You've got to think of a different class of people. Some just don't care. People with a couldn't care less attitude, not particular what they say and do in front of people.'

A woman must be attractive and desirable and even, in the liberal discourse of active heterosexuality, desir*ing* of men. But she must also be respectable, for which read, controlled, so that she is not so desirable and desiring as to break free from the control of particular males. She must not take her sex into her own hands. In the context of infant feeding, though, she must also be a good mother as well as a lively and attractive sexual partner. Her children must be nourished and nurtured, as well as her man's sexual needs being met. Medical knowledge and regulatory mechanisms can be called upon to ensure she uses her breasts responsibly for nurturing her children, as we will see in the next chapter. These two sets of expectations, mothering and sexuality, are to a large extent in conflict with one another. The experience of women, as this study indicates, is then constructed through and around these often conflicting discourses.

CREATING ALTERNATIVE DISCOURSES OF SEXUALITY

There appears to be an increasing separation between discourses of sexuality and those surrounding motherhood. This separation arises in part from the development and availability of contraception and the shaping of female sexuality as potentially independent and active. Reproduction and sexuality remain linked however through the disciplinary discourses of femininity and heterosexuality. Good girls and women must tread carefully along the thorny path of respectable wife, accommodating (desirable) lover and responsible mother. These discursive practices are conducted through various attentions to women's bodies. I have suggested above that breasts are specifically involved here as a site of both visual and tactile pleasure for men and nurturance for babies, with all the potential contradictions which this brings. Breasts provide a bodily focus for the policing of women through the dichotomising discourse of the whore and the Madonna.

Feminist theory and practice has been particularly preoccupied with challenging such 'uses' of women's bodies and this is now a major area of conflict between feminists. In some respects this ambivalence resonates with the experience of women in this study. Among them, there is a wish for better knowledge, and greater freedom, but considerable reservations about whether the forms of knowledge and freedom now offered really have brought benefits. A major difficulty is in finding a language and knowledge of sexuality which is not already coded as patriarchal. As indicated earlier Rich and other 'cultural' feminists have attempted to provide a female way of 'knowing' about our sexuality, which she sees as significantly connected to practices surrounding mothering. She separates the 'institution' of motherhood from the experiences. The institution she describes thus:

> Rape and its aftermath; marriage as economic dependence, as the guarantee to a man of 'his' children; the theft of childbirth from women; the concept of the 'illegitimacy' of a child born out of wedlock; the laws regulating contraception and abortion; the cavalier marketing of danger-

ous birth control devices; the denial that work done by
women at home is a part of 'production'; the chaining of
women in links of love and guilt; the absence of social
benefits for mothers; the inadequacy of child care facilities in most parts of the world; the unequal pay women
receive as wage earners, forcing them into dependence
on man; the solitary confinement of 'full-time motherhood';
the token nature of fatherhood, which gives a man rights
and privileges over children toward whom he assumes
minimal responsibility; the psychoanalytic castigation of
the mother; the pediatric assumption that the mother is
inadequate and ignorant; the burden of emotional work
borne by women in the family – all these are the con-
necting fibres of the institution. (Rich, 1977: 276)

Despite the negative influences of this institution it is Rich's
view that women's experiences of mothering are frequently
positive. She suggests that the lives of all women are shaped
and controlled through the institution of motherhood. This
applies whether or not women have children; she believes
in any case that the dichotomy between the mother and
the childless woman is a false, male devised one. Women
cannot in other words escape the discourse through which
their lives are viewed, examined, judged and controlled. As
noted at the beginning of this chapter Rich's 'solution' is
for women to repossess their bodies and thus to change
human existence, although she does not equate this process with 'natural childbirth'. If we took her perspective breast-
feeding might well be seen as part of the power and sensuality
of mothering which has been lost to women through the
institution of motherhood and might be repossessed as part
of a new way for women to relate to their bodies. We might
add to the description of the institution of motherhood 'the
control of breast-feeding by baby milk manufacturers to increase their profits; the exploitation of women's breasts
through pornography'. Sichtermann (1983) argues that it
is important to create a culture where women could recapture the lost eroticism of the breasts and breast-feeding, as
an 'expression of female sexuality' in 'the art of love'
(Sichtermann 1983: 64). This she considers an important
feminist project, one that focuses on pleasure rather than

duty. Young (1990c) suggests in her essay, 'Breasted Experience', that there are spaces within our culture where women get pleasurable experiences through submerged aspects of the hidden sexuality of their breasts, despite their construction through the patriarchal gaze. According to Young, breast-feeding can, at times, for some women, provide just such an experience.

The difficulty with Rich's approach, and that of other gynocentric and cultural feminists, as Young herself acknowledges (1990b), is that they partially replicate the assumption that there is a female 'nature' located within the female body which pre-exists culture, much the same culture/nature dichotomy as within patriarchal ideologies. Rich attempts to provide an alternative discourse of women's sexuality through her poetic language, but in so doing offers perhaps a one dimensional view of what women 'really' are underneath, thus inviting the criticism of essentialism. She does however attempt to deconstruct dominant discourses which tie women to their male defined sexuality and to begin the reconstruction of female sexuality.

It has been suggested that we might have to risk the dangers of essentialism in order to explore the deeply hidden possibilities of women's sexuality. Fuss suggests that the dichotomy between essentialism and constructionism might well be a false one:

> If we are to intervene effectively in the impasse created by the essentialist/constructionist divide, it might be necessary to begin questioning the *constructionist* assumption that nature and fixity go together (naturally) just as sociality and change go together (naturally). In other words it may be time to ask whether essences can change and whether constructions can be normative. (Fuss, 1990: 6)

Fuss goes on to argue that it might be strategically or politically useful to 'deploy' or 'activate' essentialism. The conservatism of essentialism, she argues, depends on '*who* is utilising it, *how* it is deployed, and *where* its effects are concentrated' (ibid: 20) [emphasis in original]. This argument is based on the notion that 'essence' is a 'sign' and we should not act as if 'essentialism had an essence'(ibid: 21). In this way we can view Rich as deploying essentialism to make visible, and then rupture, the dominant discourse of male defined female sexuality. An example of this might be that it is important to recognize that breasts have been coded as sexual and to work with this, rather than ignore it or treat it simply as a 'false Western belief' as some of the infant feeding literature does. Although the many texts on infant feeding which see the sexualization of breasts as a product of 'artificial' Western culture are in a sense making use of social constructionist thinking, theirs is an approach which is essentialist in its effect, in that it simply asserts that breasts are not 'really' sexual since they are 'really' there to provide milk for babies. In this way ignoring the sexualizing of breasts tries to defeat constructionism through a 'superior' assertion of what is essential. This denies women's experiences (they might see their breasts as not 'really' either simply sexual or for feeding babies) and also reduces the possibility of using breasts as a 'sign' of another kind of female sexuality in order to disrupt and explore the discourse.

We can ask whether or not it is useful to see breast-feeding as containing some 'essential', but hidden, female sexuality. If this is the case we can then ask whether or not the more widespread practice of breast-feeding is a goal for feminism, in order to release this sexual potential and challenge male defined sexuality. It might be possible to argue that breast-feeding and childbirth can be expressions of female sexuality/sensuality, and that breast-feeding may disrupt male views of the sexuality of breasts. We might see the beginnings, or fragments, of sexuality in the comments of Beatrice Callender that when she was alone she could know her own feelings, or in Ada Brown's feeling that 'it makes you one person again rather than two separate beings'. Similarly Mary Moreland talked unselfconsciously of her delivery in ways that were clearly sensual, a feeling expressed in her tone as well as in her words: 'My mothers friend stayed with me – she had a big family. She kept squeezing me to her – she said, oh Mary you smell lovely, I'll never forget it (1936).

Breast-feeding and childbirth, as important female experiences, might be seen as potentially the locations of uniquely female languages of sexuality and sensuality. However, current infant feeding knowledge and policies which see breast-feeding as what real women 'do', mean that such an approach would fit all too easily into the ready made discourse of 'natural' women. As described in chapter two breast-feeding is identified as the natural responsibility of 'real' women as mothers. Feminists who suggest that breast-feeding is also some kind of natural 'right' for women, a way of expressing their true sexuality fall all too readily into these dominant modes of thinking which have helped to construct femininity through setting up ways to check on whether women use their breasts 'properly', that is naturally. Women are simultaneously deprived of resources for the 'work' of breast-feeding (and other aspects of reproduction). It is also particularly important to be cautious about endorsing breast-feeding as inevitably a source of female power given the class and ethnic differences in breast-feeding patterns across the western world. The rights and wrongs of breast-feeding behaviour would be all too familiar.

Breasts and breast-feeding are surrounded by discursive practices which control women through specifying what they should feel and when, how they and their breasts should be looked at, and by whom, in short by providing all practices involving breasts with ready made meanings. As we saw earlier in this chapter, seeing breasts as sexual can simply be fitted into heterosexual norms and expectations. Altering these discursive practices through the construction of feminist alternatives involves addressing and changing the power relations which they involve. It is this process of changing the power to give meaning to our bodies which needs to be the focus of feminist practice, rather than simply wishing to increase breast-feeding. We do not know whether breast-feeding has an intrinsic meaning, beyond the social relations and contexts in which it takes place. In our wish to avoid closing off the social constructionist/essentialist debate this can, and should, remain an open question. Mary Nelis, describing her life in Northern Ireland (Fairweather *et al.*, 1984), suggests that breast-feeding can be connected with women's power:

> the only women who fed their babies in front of anyone especially their men-folk would be made fun of. But I carried on regardless. And you know breast-feeding gave

me a sense of my own power – would you believe that? I
came from as puritanical a background as anyone else
here, but when I gave birth and fed my first baby, I felt
the most intense emotion, and sense of happiness and
pride, that I'd ever felt in my life. I didn't care what anyone said: this was beautiful and this was *right*. (Fairweather
et al., 1984: 162 [emphasis in original])

We do not know the sources of the feelings expressed here,
except that for this woman breast-feeding did operate in a
way which challenged heterosexual norms. Her feelings were
clearly part of resistance to dominant social relations and
practices. It does not present a 'soft' and romantic picture
of breast-feeding, rather a woman finding a way to understand, describe, and experience her body, outside dominant
discourses. It is also about a woman developing confidence
in her body despite the meanings offered by discourses of
femininity, meanings which often destroy confidence. Female bodies are never 'good enough'. This increased confidence is extremely important, as de Beauvoir noted in her
discussion of the way women become women, 'Not to have
confidence in one's body is to lose confidence in oneself'
(1953: 65). Such confidence does not arise only from the
act of breast-feeding but through the social relations, contexts and language which give it meaning, and through
women's resistance to dominant meanings. Breast-feeding
as a social practice should be located in feminist efforts to
develop its own discourses and practices concerning women's
bodies. Since breasts cannot be separated from other aspects of bodies, and sexuality cannot be separated from
sensuality in mothering, so breast-feeding is a part of other
feminist projects concerned with bodies and sex. The current deep divisions in feminist theory and practice concerning
languages and representations of the body, in pornography
for example, are indicative of the real difficulties in such
projects.

The women in this study, along with many others around
the world, represent the necessity of finding languages and
knowledges to explore our experiences of our bodies. They
also reveal the major pitfalls in attempting to do so – women
are deeply divided, their experiences too contradictory to

begin to talk. For many women there is no language which can accommodate their experience apart from labels (the self applied term 'prude' which a number of the women used, for example) which close off possibility. But there are also signs of resistance and change. There is considerable anger about the display of breasts on Page Three (Short *et al.*, 1991); there are reports of women's outrage at being asked to leave cafes and other public places when breast-feeding (e.g. *Guardian*, 6.2.90; Joint Breastfeeding Initiative, 1990). Such resistances though, readily disappear in the ready made differences and divisions between women of age, generation, class, race. For example, we need to ask which women use spaces in department stores and restaurants where breast-feeding facilities might be provided. We are likely to find a social class difference in this aspect of public space, as in others. Forms of resistance which convey an asexual or 'pure' image of women can also fuel conservative anti-feminist views about women's sexuality, providing new forms of censorship and control; the revolt against Page Three might easily fall into this trap.

In the next chapter I explore the surveillance of another aspect of femininity – mothering – within which breast-feeding plays an important part. For many women breast-feeding as an expression of female sexuality, and breast-feeding as an aspect of good mothering, are in contradiction with each other. Young (1990c) sees this as a product of the patriarchal control of the mothering/sexuality boundary. She believes it is important for feminists to disrupt this dichotomy. How women manage these contradictions will be examined in chapter seven, and the question of whether some kind of deployment of essentialism can overcome the gender neutrality versus difference debate as it relates to breast-feeding will be addressed in the final chapter.

6 'She Said the Baby Belonged to the State': Health Professionals and Mothering

Infant feeding habits have been scrutinized, from the eighteenth century onwards, through mechanisms developed for the control of both the quantity and 'quality' of the population. Mothers, often through the interventions of health professionals, have been specifically targeted in these processes. Foucault places breast-feeding in this context involving what he describes as the changing form of power, from the power of death to the power over life:

> What is interesting in the eighteenth century is . . . one finds all sorts of new types of knowledge being applied: the emergence of demography, observations regarding the spread of epidemics, enquiries into nurses and the conditions of breast feeding . . . The establishment of apparatuses of power making possible not only observation but also direct intervention and manipulation in all these areas. (Foucault in Gordon, 1980: 226)

Although infant feeding has become part of the 'private' domestic world through the construction of women as natural mothers, it has remained symbolic of a 'public' concern with mothering. In this chapter I examine the interventions of health professionals into infant feeding practices. These interventions took place within the broader context of changes in routines surrounding childbirth and infant care. These changes include: the whole process of childbirth and infant care moving from the informal to the professional; from home delivery to hospital care; the development of ante natal care; the increased use of drugs and other childbirth technology and management techniques; and the consolidation

161

of obstetrics and the curtailment of midwifery (Oakley, 1976b; Oakley, 1980; Doyal, 1983; Oakley, 1984; Doyal, 1985; Doyal, 1987; Oakley, 1987; Stanworth, 1987; Lewis, 1990).

Many of these changes have been viewed as a process of medicalization: of childbirth in particular; and of reproduction in general (Ehrenreich and English, 1979; Oakley, 1980; Chamberlain, 1981; Reissman, 1983; Oakley, 1984; Homans, 1985; Oleson and Lewin, 1985; Martin, 1989; Miles 1991). The processes of medicalization have been woven into the state's increasing control over women's lives through the interventions of health and sometimes other welfare professionals (Wilson, 1977; Hutter and Williams, 1981; Dale and Foster, 1986; Abbott and Sapsford, 1990). In this chapter I examine Apple's description of the medicalisation of infant feeding as a process through which 'mothers lost their singular position; babies regularly were bottle-fed under medical supervision' (1987: 3).

PROFESSIONAL INTERVENTIONS IN INFANT FEEDING

There is some evidence that between the 1930s and the 1960s hospitals evolved less authoritarian infant feeding regimes. Blaxter and Paterson observed that hospitals in the 1960s and 1970s no longer appeared to 'push' breast-feeding in the way they had done in the 1950s for example (Blaxter and Paterson, 1982). In fact it has long been recognised that hospitals have a somewhat contradictory relationship to breast-feeding. Concern that hospital practices actually discourage breast-feeding, even when they seek to actively promote it, have been expressed since at least 1943 when it was noted that: 'Study of the figures leads us to estimate that about 80 per cent of babies leave hospital wholly breast fed, and that 95 per cent of the babies born on the district are wholly breast fed when the midwife leave (MoH, 1943: 2).

This report suggested that, whilst a larger number of 'artificially fed' infants might have been anticipated amongst those born in hospital, since women admitted to hospital included those with more health problems, there was still a proportion of babies who were being 'unnecessarily' bottle fed (ibid: 3). This report had a number of criticisms of

hospital practices, including the fact that breast-feeding itself was often 'regimented, over scientific and unnatural'
(ibid: 4). Examples of this included babies being brought
to their mothers to be fed, and then taken away again, and
being too frequently weighed. Somewhat paradoxically, despite enthusiastic breast-feeding promotion there was a rapid
resort to bottle feeding if any problems occurred. Increasing hospitalization for childbirth at this period brought breast-
feeding regimes which were frequently counterproductive.
What appears to have altered between the 1930s and the
1960s is the level of authoritarianism in hospital practices.
The symbolic commitment to breast-feeding has remained,
although in both periods, the more authoritarian 1940s, and
the more liberal 1960s, actual practices frequently resulted
in bottle feeding. My study provides evidence of pressure to
breast-feed prior to the 1960s:

> In those days you had to breast-feed them in hospital.
> (Florence Hope, 1943)

> No one bottle fed in hospital. There were no bottles.
> (Audrey Soulsby, 1951)

Ada Brown (1959) had particularly negative experiences of
an authoritarian, but supposedly pro breast-feeding regime,
in a maternity home:

> She was a sleepy baby, and there was this sister who wanted
> everyone to breast-feed anyway, probably for all the right
> reasons. What a dreadful attitude. You didn't feed the baby
> for the first 24 hours because you didn't have any milk
> and I didn't know about colostrum then. The first feed
> she fed a little bit but not very well and this horrible dragon
> actually pinched the back of her neck and toes. They al-
> ways called you mother and she'd be saying 'come on
> mother, you're not doing it right'. For five days we fought
> like that every single feed, we fed them strictly every four
> hours. I had a temperature and they said 'Your blood
> pressure is up, is something bothering you?' I said 'I'm
> having trouble feeding her' and they very patronisingly
> said 'all new mothers have this problem'. This nurse came

and I said, 'look I can't feed her, I'm going to have to put her on the bottle'. She said 'nonsense, you're just not trying. I said "how did you manage with yours?'. She said 'I haven't got any children'. That was it Pam, I just ignored her from then on. I was so incensed this woman was telling me and she didn't have any kids.

Other examples support the view that during the 1960s and 1970s, although a nominal pro-breast-feeding policy remained in place, there was little pereceived coercion from hospital staff:

I was asked how I wanted to feed him and when I said bottle, no one said anything else. (Evelyn Moore, 1965)

They just gave me tablets and told me to bottle feed. (Patricia Poole, 1965)

They didn't persuade you. Only one woman in my ward breast-fed. (Shirley Hill, 1973)

There was never any pressurisation. I tried putting her to the breast but it wasn't very successful. You were never forced into anything. (Carol Cook, 1973)

I say no, doctor please, operation painful better to stop. He said OK. (Rajina Mondal, 1977)

I wanted to bottle feed and no-one said anything. (Nasreen Malik, 1979)

This lack of persuasion about breast-feeding can in part be accounted for by the fact that real concerns about the negative effects of bottle feeding only began to be redis-covered and then firmly expressed in the 1970s. Pro-breast-feeding messages are likely not to have filtered through to health professionals until somewhat later. These more laissez-faire practices appear to have made for more comfortable relationships between hospital staff and women. This absence of pressure was most appreciated by those who had already decided against breast-feeding, and who said so from the start. But for those who expressed an interest in breast-feeding, hospital staff were sometimes experienced as unhelpful. Mandy Scott, even though she wanted to breast-feed, described hospital practices as authoritarian and intrusive even in 1970: 'You were made to try. You were told you had to carry on trying. One day I had one nurse with the baby's head and one with my boob, trying to force her. I lost my temper then and thought that's it. I was worried she wasn't getting fed. I refused to try after that. It wasn't a nice experience.'

Hospital settings are clearly difficult places in which to establish the supportive stress free atmosphere which is conducive to breast-feeding. There appears to be something of a contradiction in a pro-breast-feeding policy in the context of policies which have increasingly hospitalized women for childbirth. Sharp evidence of the conflict between these policies is indicated within the OPCS studies of infant feeding. For example: 'The steepest drop in the prevalence of breast feeding is in the first week of life, so the period in hospital is particularly important' (Martin and White, 1988: 30). That this occurs in a situation where, as Martin and White acknowledge, most babies are delivered in hospital, poses a major problem for the implementation of breast-feeding policies. Recent official support for home births may begin to have some influence on this (DOH, 1993). There have in fact been changes in those specific hospital practices which had been identified as making breast-feeding difficult. For example, in the more recent OPCS studies fewer mothers reported having to feed at set times, or not having their babies beside their beds. Breast-feeding was also being initiated more quickly after birth. Important as these practices might be they are not necessarily solutions to more major underlying difficulties in hospital settings. Ironically for mothers in my study relations with health professionals progressed more smoothly once women were placed within the bottle feeding category.

What was most striking about health professionals outside the hospital setting is that none of the women in my study perceived them to have played a positive role in their feeding experiences. For many women their contact with health professionals appeared to have played a minor role. This was perceived to be entirely appropriate; it was something of a source of pride to have managed without 'help' from such people:

> I never had anything like that. You just had to look after your own child. (Bertha Combe, 1922)

> I used my own judgement. I was a shy person, very independent. (Lucy Cooper, 1930)

> I just did what my sisters had done. (Mary Moreland, 1936)

> I've never been in a clinic in my life. I just used my own discretion. I never had a health visitor, nobody ever came and looked at her. I just let her grow up naturally. (Jane Harrison, 1936)

> The old mothers' advice is best, I couldn't afford the doctors bills. (Elizabeth White, 1939)

A somewhat greater level of intervention was observable in later years but some women continued to see it as a source of pride that they ignored this:

> About every two months if you didn't go to the welfare the health visitor would call. What could they tell you, they weren't married? (Florence Hope, 1943)

> When you've been brought up with seven kids, you used to think I know more than you. (Jean Richards, 1949)

> I wouldn't have dreamed of asking the health visitor. (Ada Brown, 1959)

More openly negative comments were made by women who had babies in more recent years:

> I used to resent them calling. I felt they were interfering. (Evelyn Moore, 1965)

> I didn't like the way they took over . . . at the time I think they did that and I resented it. I didn't care for that at all. I couldn't see the point of her. (Patricia Poole, 1965)

I felt then and I think now, sometimes you have to take what health visitors say with a pinch of salt. I used to make my own mind up, they have to say something to cover themselves. (Beatrice Callender, 1968)

I used to use them to get the baby weighed and that was it. My mother gave me more help than they did. (Gina Godfrey, 1969)

They just come to check you've got the right equipment for the baby. (Mandy Scott, 1970)

I chased her out... 'you're not here to tell me what to do'... I didn't see her again after that. (Mandy Scott, 1970)

Particularly conflictual encounters between health professionals and mothers involved weaning, rather than breast-feeding itself, although there is certainly a connection between these two concerns. Bottle feeding mothers are often perceived as starting the baby on 'solids' too early (DHSS, 1988: 27). Blaxter and Paterson note about early weaning: 'These decisions were, however, one of the greatest sources of conflict with health visitors and clinic doctors. The health visitors' notes were full of criticism about overfeeding, adding extra milk powder, giving full-cream milk or cows milk too early, feeding cereal or other solids at a few weeks, (Blaxter and Paterson, 1982: 135).

Early weaning led to conflictual relationships with health professionals in my study: 'I gave him Farleys' rusk in his bottle at one month. I used to get wrong off the health visitor. She was alright, she didn't think it was right feeding him off a spoon, but he was taking it alright. He was my bairn, I'll do what I like' (Shirley Hill, 1973). This conflict about early introduction of solids to some extent rests on questionable notions of quite what 'natural' feeding is. As described in chapter three there is a very common assumption that 'natural feeding' involves *exclusive* breast-feeding for several months. Raphael's anthropological study of several communities where breast-feeding is still the norm provides strong evidence, conflicting with this view, that mothers give babies all sorts of foods from an early age even when they are breast-feeding (Raphael, 1985). In this country, as with bottle feeding, there is social class dimension to early weaning. Blackburn (1991) suggests that poorer women wean their babies early in order to cope with too many demands; trying to soothe a crying baby by adding cereal to its bottle may at least apparently alleviate these.

Weaning practices, perhaps because they occur later in babies lives than questions about whether to breast-feed or not, seem to involve more assertion by the mother of baby care as her responsibility as in Shirley's comment above: 'he was my bairn'. The question of who the baby belonged to was also of great significance to Carol Cook in 1973. The baby was on Cow and Gate, but the 'milk wasn't filling her' so she gave her rusks at two and a half months which the health visitor disapproved of: 'I've no good things to say about her – she was a pain in the backside. I told her not to come back and she told me the baby belonged to the state. I told her where to get off. They sent for me from the clinic. I agreed to go to the clinic if I needed to. I don't agree with health visitors.' Overall then many of the women, in Beatrice Callender's words, took what most health professionals said, 'with a pinch of salt' and some women became very angry indeed if health visitors in particular tried to go beyond this marginal place.

An exception to this conflictual, or at best somewhat cool, relationship between mothers and health professionals, was that a number of the women valued baby clinics as a social space and means of meeting people:

The clinic was very good, they looked after the babies, we had this club. (Monica Andrews, 1951)

I used to go to Diana Street clinic for social reasons and to get the baby weighed. I didn't get advice from anyone. (Audrey Soulsby, 1951)

I went to Malvern Street clinic. It was more of a social thing really, with a huge coal fire and a circle of wooden chairs. The MPs wife used to dole out the milk and if you asked to see the health visitor she asked one to come the next week, but I wouldn't have dreamed of asking the health visitor. (Ada Brown, 1959)

I got National Dried Milk from the clinic. It was also a social thing, a lot of us had babies together and stayed friends. (Evelyn Moore, 1965)

Shirley Hill who dealt with the health visitor very assertively found the clinic, 'fairly helpful' (1973). That women find clinics helpful has often been noted. Dame Janet Campbell, in the introduction to the Women's Health Enquiry of 1939, acknowledged the importance of clinics as meeting places for mothers: 'The success of the Infant Welfare Centre is in some degree attributable to the pleasure the mother finds in spending an afternoon away from home and in meeting kindly doctors and nurses as well as other women with whom she can talk' (Spring Rice, 1981: xv).

Campbell also noted appreciation of health personnel 'particularly of the women officers, lay or medical' (ibid: 54) as well as of clinics. It is important to remember, however, that until the 1948 National Health Service women had few rights to medical care except during pregnancy and whilst nursing. This provided a significantly different context for relationships between mothers and health professionals than that which developed later. Lewis (1984) suggests that infant welfare clinics, which were run by local authorities, were more acceptable to working class women in the 1920s and 1930s than the 'schools for mothers' (run by volunteers) which preceded them. The 'schools for mothers' taught women breast-feeding, but also required them to follow strict feeding routines. In contrast to the findings of the Women's Health Enquiry, Lewis cites evidence for the unpopularity of state employed visitors, such as health visitors. Lewis notes that for working class women, health professionals 'often served to increase their burdens by exacting higher standards of child care and housekeeping' (Lewis, 1984: 39).

Another exception to the negative comments about health professionals in my study is that the Asian women made few negative comments and appear to have been much less assertive. The particular position of Asian women in relation to health services in general and in those in this city in particular provides at least a partial explanation for this. There have been few attempts to provide services in a sensitive and appropriate way (Grimsley and Bhat, 1988; McNaught,

1988) through, for example, making sure that, 'the professional staff delivering those services reflect the racial mixture of the communities which they serve, and are encouraged by that service to make sure its help is appropriate for and accepted by ethnic minorities' (Hillman, 1989: 87). Even if we take only the most obvious criteria of communication between health professionals and their clients, all the Asian women in this study would have been limited by their lack of English and the health professionals lack of Punjabi or Urdu. It is also unsurprising that they came to expect little, and made few demands, since they had no experience of more culturally appropriate services. It may have also been that they were reluctant to make negative comments to me, a white woman.

As I noted in chapter two there have been some small scale investigations into the feeding habits of women from some of the ethnic minority communities in Newcastle (Lin, 1991; Shahjahan, 1991; Costello *et al.*, 1992). These studies recommended that mothers in these communities (Chinese, Bangladeshi and Pakistani) should be targeted for extra attention with regard to their feeding habits in a number of ways: pamphlets in local languages; being advised that bottle feeding is not the current trend for white women in this country; videos on breast-feeding advice in local languages; explaining weight charts so that mothers can plot the growth of their babies; the production of halal baby food; women's groups; even readings from the Koran to support breastfeeding. The concerns of the medical profession here triumphed over those of the women themselves; these were not even on the agenda. The doctors (male) who were involved in the research conducted individual interviews with women in their homes, with assistance from female interpreters. Their findings were then presented at a community health project in the west end of Newcastle to an audience of about forty health professionals, using various diagrams and statistics, plus a 'shock-horror' slide show consisting of 'a Chinese baby being bottle fed', 'a Bangladeshi baby being bottle fed', 'cans of formula and packet food found in the homes of Chinese, Bangladeshi and Pakistani babies'. In contrast to this moral panic, local black women community workers had conducted group interviews with women from these communities and had heard accounts of the ways in which, for example, breast-feeding in Pakistan is built into all kinds of support systems, such as other people doing the housework whilst the mother has time to establish breast-feeding, as well as lots of advice from informal midwives. This insight into totally different feeding contexts was ignored, and instead it was concluded overall that the women were merely ignorant, taken in by what they see as the fashionable habits of white women. That they clearly do not adopt other 'white' habits with regard to dress and food was ignored. Also overlooked were any concerns that the women themselves had about their own or their babies health. Instead breast-feeding, rather than broader health concerns, remained the target.

Not all the women were dismissive of health professionals to begin with. Some women had wanted advice about specific problems but felt they hadn't received it. Some of course had so little faith in health visitors that they did not ask for help even when they needed it. Evelyn Moore (1965) for example, who was otherwise disparaging of health visitors, felt she had wanted more advice about colic and had to turn to her own mother instead. Gina Godfrey's son also suffered from colic and she too relied on her mother's support because, 'I didn't know if I could say to the health visitor, he screams all the time, I thought it was my fault' (1969).

What emerges from these data is a picture of women 'managing' the interventions of health workers in relation to infant feeding. These workers, particularly health visitors, were seen by these mothers as serving some kind of 'surveillance' role which can usually be handled through ignoring their advice or, if needs be, rejecting it completely. The relationship is one in which the professional is seen as an 'official' carrying out an essentially 'policing' role; 'they said they were paid to see the baby'. Health visitors and community midwives are most often seen in this role since they are the ones who are thought to be entering homes 'uninvited'. Paradoxically, although this interaction is clearly negative for the workers, it can perhaps be seen as positive for the women. Women expressed confidence in themselves or other people in their community, through rejecting the experts. Although health professionals were recognized as being in favour of breast-feeding, they tended to be valued if they did not push it too hard. On the other hand, for those who wanted to breast-feed, particularly in more recent years, there were strong and negative memories of extremely inadequate help and support. Authoritarian pro breast-feeding practices do not seem, from this evidence, to have been replaced by positive and encouraging regimes. Clinics, however, seem to have been valued, particularly because they provided social space for mothers and because, it seems, women could go there on their own terms and without the inference of 'policing' which home visiting entails. As noted earlier, attention seems to have shifted from the question of whether women breast-feed to concerns about age at weaning. As well as negative comments based on irritation with the policing role, there was disappointment from some women that health professionals failed to give useful advice on the odd occasion they were asked for it.

One major difference between British and American experience of early mothering is that in the UK women professionals play a larger part. From a feminist perspective one rather sad, although perhaps not unexpected, indication from these data is that women professionals were described in much more negative terms than male. This forms a central theme in the next section.

FEMININITY AND THE SEMI-PROFESSIONS

Some feminist thinking about practice in health and social welfare, particularly in social work, suggests that women professionals may have something positive to offer to women clients because of their shared life experience, although it is also recognized that class and other power differences must be acknowledged (Dale and Foster, 1986; Webb, 1986; Hanmer and Statham, 1988; Dominelli and McLeod, 1989). What emerges in my study is that women professionals were judged much more harshly by these mothers than were male. All the women professionals were part of the so called semi professions of midwifery, nursing, and health visiting, whereas all the male professionals were doctors. Gender power and professional status differences were closely interwoven. Doctors were much more likely to be talked about in positive terms and their advice was more likely to be listened to. Some women described the doctor in almost hero like terms, perhaps unsurprisingly given the particular role they had played. Polly Williams (1932) had been extremely ill with a septic breast and remembered that her doctor was there whenever she woke from the anesthetic, 'day or night'. Similarly Monica Andrews (1951) had had several miscarriages and a neonatal death. She described the 'miraculous' birth of her son following this history as due to the consultant Mr S. a 'marvellous man'. In Jane Harrison's case (1936) the doctor was treated as someone with great authority and the midwife as someone with more intuitive knowledge:

> When I saw Dr Tiplady the second time he said, don't be surprised if you can't feed her because of your age. Therefore I don't want you to eat anymore. Just try, when you think she's not getting enough, put her on artificial feeds. The midwife was very good . . . she says I think you should put her on the bottle. I said do you think so? She said yes, I don't think she's getting enough to eat. I said how can you tell? She said I don't know but we people can just tell.

Later on both Jane and the midwife received endorsement from Dr Tiplady: 'I told him I'd put her on the bottle. I though he'd play war but he didn't. He said I think you've done the right thing. I told him Mrs D. advised it. He said well if she advised it, that's alright you haven't done it because you couldn't be bothered. I says, no, far from it.'

Having been found 'not guilty' of selfishness both Jane and her husband felt they benefitted from the greater freedom bottle feeding gave them. She remembered her married life, with one child, very positively and clearly enjoyed 'going out'. Eleanor Kershaw (1940) was also advised against breast-feeding by the 'doctor at the welfare' who found her nipples were too small, 'well, they know best'. Naheed Akhtar (1970) also sought the doctors authority to change to bottle feeding because the baby wasn't putting on enough weight, even though she had been persuaded to breast-feed in hospital. Carol Cook (1973), one of the most assertive women

I talked to, summed up her experiences, 'My doctor was good, but the midwife and health visitor were rubbish'. In Rajina Mondal's case (1977) the doctor supported her in not breast-feeding in the face of considerable opposition from her mother-in-law, and therefore earned her respect.

A major contrast between the way in which the women talked about their doctors and their attitudes to women health professionals concerned the way in which the authority of women professionals was judged on the basis of their personal lives, particularly whether they were themselves mothers. I have already described Ada Brown's experience (1959). She dismissed the nurse's advice immediately once she discovered that the woman had no children. Similarly Florence Hope (1943) discounted the advice of women professionals on this basis. She didn't ask the health visitors anything, 'what could they tell you, they weren't married'. Similarly Jean Richards (1949) thought she knew more than them because of her personal experience. Gina Godfrey (1969) rated her mother's knowledge more positively than the health visitor, 'she's had three, she knows more or less what she's doing'. Where women professionals did receive positive comments it was because of their ordinariness, or dedication and hard work. Although Bertha Combe (1922) thought she was harshly treated by the nurse while she was in labour, this was forgiven because, 'nurses worked hard in those days'. There was much more acceptance of midwives who were well known in the local area. Again ordinariness, in the form of familiarity, was important and several were recalled by name and described (affectionately) as a 'dragon' or a 'bully'. For women, being too 'professional' was a negative if this meant being 'outside' of the local culture, and of motherhood. Male professionals did not appear to be judged by these women on the same basis. Women were judged on private, that is 'personal' criteria, whereas men had a much more easily understood and assured position in the public world.

Oakley (1981b) notes that, in studies of working class communities in the 1950s (Rees 1950; Dennis *et al.*, 1956; Young and Willmott, 1957; Kerr, 1958), health visitors were talked of more positively than other health professionals since they were 'either mothers themselves or could be talked to like mothers' (Oakley, 1981b: 103). This has similarities with my findings in relation to the acceptability of women health professionals whose knowledge and expertise was seen to be rooted in shared experience. For women in my study, the main support was expected to come from their own mothers, rather than from outsiders. Other studies have indicated that it is mothers who have little support from their own families and friends who most appreciate health visitors (Mayall and Foster, 1989). However, even in such situations, women express disappointment that health visitors do not seem to them to take their worries very seriously (Urwin, 1985).

It is perhaps unsurprising that health visitors are talked of in the negative terms they were here. They are at the forefront of policies which focus on the mother. Abbott and Sapsford note that whilst health visitors may not see themselves as having these 'policing' intentions they: 'can be seen as targeting the mother, working with definitions of 'good' and 'bad' mothering and attempting to shape mothers in particular directions' (Abbott and Sapsford, 1990: 120). In relation to infant feeding, although 'good mothering' does not necessarily any longer require breast-feeding as such, feeding habits more generally remain a focus of intervention. A major difficulty for health visitors, and one which is evident here, is the lack of a clear and shared idea of their role and of their knowledge base. What was common to these women was that health visitors were perceived as there to 'keep an eye on you', meaning the woman as a mother. Abbott and Sapsford note that health visitors see themselves as health educators but 'work with a set of ideas about the family and child development which are patriarchal and middle class' (1990: 120). The women in this study seemed very capable of dismissing the content of the health visitors' educational message, unless it could be used to justify their own behaviour.

This does not mean however that health visitors were insignificant. The women were in fact being very astute in recognizing that what was important was that they came at all, or might do so. In some respects the significance of the health visitor's role can be seen as a symbolic one. It symbolizes the state's concern with mothering, the fact that mothers need to be watched. Even though individual health visitors may not have intended to be seen in this way, the fact that their role is conducted through individualistic modes of interaction reinforces a model of health which holds individual women responsible for their baby, whatever the social context of their mothering.

In fact, it is around the question of who is responsible that much of the conflict occurs. Many of the women were very clear that they were responsible for the baby, it was what they were there 'for'. Being judged as a mother was of vital importance for self identity, and the idea that someone might challenge this sphere of influence was the cause of some of these angry encounters. This sense of individual responsibility on behalf of mothers seems to contradict in some respects with what might be seen as a 'collective' responsibility by the state being enacted through the visits of health visitors. Health vistors constitute a particularly sharp example of the contradictions between collectivism and authoritarianism in state welfare policies (Dingwall, 1977; Dale and Foster, 1986). As Oakley notes, the education of mothers which has been so central to health policy, has not meant education by other mothers within the community but by those of 'superordinate social status' (1984: 259). Although some of the women recognized that health visitors were there to protect children, 'I know that they're there to check that everything is alright in the home' (Margaret Pearson, 1973), by implication the gaze of the health visitor implies there 'might' be something wrong with your mothering. As Worrall notes of women magistrates and social workers, they are part of a range of women professionals who, 'stand between the demands of the patriarchal state and the mass of women on whom these demands are made, translating 'expert knowledge' into 'common sense' for the consumption of the always-already failing woman' (Worrall, 1987: 108). The visit of the health visitor symbolizes the 'always-already failing' mother in terms of infant care. Hence, whether they recommend breast-feeding, late introduction of solid food, or slimmer babies, the relationship is already structured in many working class communities as one where the 'gaze' of the state is in itself as significant as the actual knowledge imparted.

Urwin suggests that one of the difficulties of communica-

tion between mothers and health visitors arises from the
fact that the health visitor's role is to identify problems which
may lead to 'later deviance or pathology' (1985: 176). Thus
the health visitors role is in relation to regulatory mechanisms which separate adequate from inadequate mothering.
For the health visitor, if the mothering appears adequate,
as evidenced by babies 'normal' development, she need not
concern herself with problems identified by the mother. The
health visitor's responsibility is to check on whether a woman
is a responsible mother: women's own experience of mothering is not necessarily central to this. So long as a problem
expressed by the mother is 'normal' in the eyes of the health
visitor, it is not really significant, whatever it might feel like
to mothers themselves.

It is interesting that the clinic was seen as much more
neutral and was sometimes valued. The image conveyed is
of a place where women had a considerable amount of control, they took the baby to get weighed or to meet friends.
The clinic seems capable of being seen as a resource and
one which does not carry the message of potential individual failure to the same extent. Other studies have suggested that clinics carry less connotations of 'policing' than
do home visits (Mayall and Foster, 1989). My findings are
in some ways in contrast with a study of 'wives of semi skilled
workers' by Orr (1980a). She found that most of them valued home visits more than the clinic although she acknowledged that some of them were just 'appeasing' the health
visitor. Where her study did produce similar findings to mine
was in the fact that a significant number felt that the ideal
health visitor should be married with children. The tendency for women to have negative views about childless health
visitors has been observed in other studies (Field *et al.*, 1982;
Miles, 1991).

Women as patients speak of women as professionals within
the same discourse of femininity and good mothering which
forms the basis of the relationship. In some ways then this
is a two way process, but also serves to reinforce the situation as one where women watch each other and watch themselves. The role of health visitors is partly symbolic, but is
also one aspect of a wider set of practices of 'women watching women'. That health visitors are an often unwitting part

of an already established mechanism of control of women was recognized by Abbott and Sapsford: 'they are not themselves aware of the way they police the family: they accept as "truth" the discourses that inform their practice and therefore fail to recognize the ways in which they are used to shape the behaviour of their clients' (1990: 148).

I have suggested here that the inability of health visitors to recognize this stems in part from the fact that their 'actual' advice is frequently rejected; they do not feel they are imposing their views on mothers. Their real importance is as part of a set of social relations in which women are always suspect and must watch themselves and each other. Paradoxically health visitors are themselves watched, not least by the women themselves, who know how to judge a woman and know that being married and a mother plays a major part in this.

I have described health visiting and midwifery as semi-professions and this is clearly not an unproblematic term. I do not propose to explore the term itself here however. Its use in this context refers to the lower status of these professional groups in relation to medicine, which is often seen as the archetypal profession. What is more, health visiting and midwifery are often under the control of doctors themselves (Hearn, 1985, 1987). Within my study, the higher status and greater power of doctors in the eyes of the women was readily discerned. One of the real distinctions however is not simply in terms of relative status, but in the discourses which structure the relationship between women clients and women professionals. Both are in the business of judging whether the other is a 'proper woman'. On this basis it is difficult to imagine how women professionals might realistically claim the same professional status as men. The language, image, practices and social relations of professionalism are patriarchal (Hearn, 1985, 1987; Turner, 1987; Abbott and Wallace, 1990). What is more, it is questionable whether increased status without some radical re-thinking of the role of all professions in relation to mothering is desirable. Perhaps, though, the use of the discourses of femininity by women in their judgement of health professionals should not be seen as totally negative. It is possible that women were seeking a way of their experiences and knowledge being valued through commonality with women professionals. I will return to these questions in the final section of this chapter.

MEDICALIZATION AND INFANT FEEDING EXPERIENCES

I noted, at the beginning of this chapter, Apple's thesis that infant feeding has been medicalized as it moved from the control of women to be conducted under the supervision of the medical profession, and that through this process bottle feeding, rather than breast-feeding, has been promoted. She suggests that: 'The shift from breast feeding to doctor-supervised bottle feeding resulted in large part, from the self conscious promotion of applied science in American life' (Apple, 1987: 182). Bottle feeding was readily promoted as more 'scientific' and requiring expert intervention since calculations had to be made, chemicals were required for sterilization, and the whole process had a more medicinal character. Indeed the term infant *formula* was deliberately adopted by baby milk manufacturers to convey the idea of something scientific which had to be calculated (Jelliffe and Jelliffe, 1978: 187). I have suggested in chapter two, however, that it is not simply bottle feeding which represents the process of medicalization. Breast-feeding too has been subject to scientific investigation, control and endorsement. The whole process of infant feeding, whether by bottle or breast, has instead come under medical scrutiny. It is not only the use of 'technology', in this case bottles and 'artificial' formula, which constitutes medicalization, it is a whole set of social relations. Reissman defines medicalization in terms of two interrelated social processes: 'First, certain behaviors and conditions are given medical meaning-that is, defined in terms of health and illness. Secondly medical practice becomes a vehicle for eliminating and controlling problematic experiences that are defined as deviant, for the purpose of securing adherence to social norms (Reissman, 1983: 4). With regard to infant feeding, medical meaning has undoubtedly developed. Breast-feeding has become symbolic of an abundance of healthy qualities. The vehicle of medical practice has, as I have suggested in the last section, been used not to support either breast or bottle feeding in any particularly clearcut way. Rather, it has been used as a window into mothering itself, not looked through for the most part by doctors themselves, but by the women (mainly) who have been cast in the role of their handmaidens, health visitors and sometimes midwives.

Both breast and bottle feeding have been medicalized in different ways. Bottle feeding can be seen as more 'scientific', with weighing and sterilizing. Indeed one difficulty for feminism in relation to infant feeding has been that bottle feeding can be equated with technology. And technology has in itself been thought problematic by some feminists (see Arditti *et al.*, 1985; Corea *et al.*, 1985; Stanworth, 1987 for explorations of feminism and technology). But for some women breast-feeding allowed far greater levels of supervision including physical intrusion. Mandy Scott's description of 'one nurse with the baby's head and one with my boob' and Ada Brown's comment about 'this horrible dragon actually pinched the back of her neck and toes' suggest breast-feeding as deeply intrusive and embarrassing. Bottle feeding, at least when breast-feeding is not seriously pushed, involves no risks of such intervention. It appears far less subject to supervision. For some women, once bottle feeding decisions were accepted things eased up considerably. Carol Cook's description, from her perspective as a convinced bottle feeder, of the pro breast-feeding culture in the hospital conveys an atmosphere of stress, difficulty and medical scrutiny:

'A lot were breast-feeding on the ward. The staff made more effort when they were struggling, closed the curtains and had a talk to them. One young one was very depressed' (1973). Both the setting and the social relations of breast-feeding have become medicalized, as part of the medicalization of childbirth. Childbirth takes place in hospital, with significant technological intervention. But initiation of feeding appears remarkably crude and untechnical, as in the cases of Ada Brown and Mandy Scott. So an odd discourse of 'natural' appears. For a number of women, childbirth was extremely 'unnatural' and afterwards, some, at least in the earlier period were seemingly almost coerced into 'natural feeding', in a highly medicalized hospital setting. In this way women chose 'unnatural feeding' in order to defend themselves from the 'unnatural' hospital intrusions and relations.

Reissman makes two other points regarding medicalization which are significant here. First, she suggests that women have themselves, for a complex set of reasons, contributed to redefining certain experiences into medical categories. Women, she suggests, sometimes collaborate in the process of medicalization because of their own needs and interests. As I suggested in chapter two women's reproductive capacities give them a different relationship to collective provision and governmental forms of intervention. For example, women's experience of childbirth has made them particularly susceptible to medicalization. Although pregnancy is an ordinary life event, and usually has a healthy outcome, women have been all too aware for many centuries that this is not always the case.

It is not surprising, as Reissman (1983) suggests, that in the nineteenth and twentieth centuries, women wanted some freedom from pain, exhaustion and possible death for themselves and their children. As Lewis notes: 'Early twentieth century women's groups were content to exchange their power to determine the meaning of childbirth as a domestic event in return for increased safety and pain-relief' (Lewis, 1990: 26). Although we are now aware that medicalization was something of a mixed blessing at best, it is easy to see how women might have been ready to believe, or hope, that it would bring improvement. In any case, as Lewis also points out, hospitalization did not at first mean the degree of technological intervention which has now become fairly routine. For some women, as well as a promise of safety, being in hospital to have a baby also provided some respite from household work. For example, Bertha Combe in my study had her baby in hospital in 1922 (only 15% of mothers had babies in hospital in 1927, Stanworth 1987). She had saved thirty shillings to go to a maternity hospital. This was because she knew the work involved in having a baby at home, having tended her aunts in childbirth. As she said, 'I went to the hospital because I had no-one to look after me, I had plenty of aunts but they never offered'. Both her parents were dead, and she lived in poor housing, a tenement with no running water. It is not difficult to see how bottle feeding might hold out the same kind of promise of respite for some women, as I have suggested in earlier chapters.

The second point which Reissman makes is that, although medicalization theory highlights the importance of professional power, it minimizes the impact of social class. She suggests that, at least in the United States, middle and upper class women colluded with physicians in the process of medicalization in different ways than working class women. In relation to childbirth, for example, upper class women, according to Reissman, invited anesthesia and relief from pain believing themselves more susceptible to pain than lower class women and thought that, with 'twighlight sleep', childbirth would once again become natural. They believed that this would decrease women's oppression, and, because they could afford to pay, this became a lucrative market. Reissman goes on to suggest that similar professional/class alliances have been produced by more recent feminist critiques of 'unnatural' childbirth. These critiques, she argues, have been incorporated into a new kind of medicalization: 'Even when "natural": childbirth occurs in birthing rooms, birth is still defined medically, is still under the control of physicians, and still occurs in hospitals' (Reissman, 1983: 8). The class specific nature of this new form of medicalization can also be discerned in the British context. It is undoubtedly a set of practices most actively demanded by middle class women, if the social class make up of the National Childbirth Trust is any indication (Kitzinger, 1990). It is perhaps middle class women who are more likely to have the social confidence and control over their environment to make such demands, as well as the kind of nuclear family arrangement required by this new form of parenting which often relies on father's presence and involvement at the birth.

Similar points can be made about infant feeding. In chapter three I described common memories of infant feeding which these women gleaned from their mothers' experience. They saw breast-feeding as exhausting and demanding, a symbol of poverty. One apocryphal story I heard several times was of a woman who was so poor that once her child had started school she had had to breast-feed him in the school yard at dinner time. It is not surprising then that they were particularly likely to experience bottle feeding as desirable. In chapter two I suggested that breast-feeding became a some-what nominal policy and baby milk was sometimes traded by the state for women's continued commitment to keeping up the birth rate. It is interesting in the accounts of the women in this study that health professionals similarly seem to have made increasingly nominal recommendations to breast-feed. In that way they retained their role of watching mothers without direct conflict. This may of course be a negative way of describing the ambivalence of health professionals about pushing breast-feeding. It could equally be that they have a broader commitment to women's health than to see breast-feeding as more important than other issues. Some health visiting literature certainly recognizes the need for sensitivity about feeding (Robertson, 1988).

CURRENT PROFESSIONAL THINKING

It is useful to examine the apparent gap between policy and practice with regard to the promotion of breast-feeding, where breast-feeding is strongly advocated but not 'pushed' with individual women. There are a number of ways of explaining this, leading to different suggested courses of action. There appear to be three possible forms of explanation and resultant practice, all of which play some part in the literature of health professionals: research reports, journals, textbooks, discussion papers and the like.

The first explanation suggests that the gap between policy and practice is a problem of poor implementation, in a somewhat technical sense. In this approach, health professionals are seen as needing tighter guidelines, a more consistent set of systems, greater coherence in the advice of different professionals. The most prominent example of this is the Joint Breast-feeding Initiative which was launched, with government support, in October 1988, after lobbying by the Royal College of Midwives and the Health Visitors Association, along with the National Childbirth Trust, the La Leche League and the Association of Breast-feeding Mothers (DoH, 1988; Henschel, 1989). The intention of this is to recover the lost 25% of mothers who begin breast-feeding but give up in the early stages. This has resulted in a number of health authorities launching their own initiatives through arranging local symposia to up-date staff and encourage them to be more committed to the promotion of breast-feeding. This initiative has a similar philosophy to the joint WHO/ UNICEF statement, 'Ten Steps to Successful Breast-Feeding' (WHO/UNICEF, 1989). This emphasizes staff training and communication, as well as hospital practices such as informing all women about the benefits of breast-feeding, encouraging breast-feeding on demand, not giving any dummies (pacifiers) to breast-fed infants, and establishing breast-feeding support groups.

The Royal College of Midwives has taken this approach further and issued a 'Ten Point Policy and Practice Checklist' for midwives, so that they can assess the 'quality' of their practice (McDowall, 1991). This is in the form of a list of statements, written in the first person singular, so that midwives can check for themselves that they have done all they possibly can to follow the 'rules' of successful breast-feeding, including having read government guidelines, advice from their professional body and local policy statements.

This approach is in line with the philosophy of target-setting in health policy exemplified in the *Health of the Nation* (Secretary of State for Health, 1992). While a more consistent approach is clearly desirable, since the confusions of current practice have been well documented (e.g. Garforth and Garcia, 1989), this is unlikely to tackle the more fundamental aspects of how breast-feeding fits with women's lives. The Royal College of Midwives apparently recognizes that the professional task is rather more complex than can be accommodated through following a ten point plan. For example, point number three of their plan says: 'I am careful not to cause anxiety or distress to a mother who is unable to breast-feed or has made a firm and informed decision against breast-feeding' (McDowall, 1991: 361).

We have seen in earlier chapters that being 'unable to breast-feed' is a far from clearcut technical category; indeed it is sometimes assumed that all mothers can breast-feed. One might also ask how a mother might demonstrate that her decision not to breast-feed is 'informed'. This set of 'commandments' for midwives might also be seen as a regulatory mechanism as far as their own professional judgements and skills are concerned. While one would not wish to detract from the intention to offer better support to those wanting to breast-feed this approach can at its best be seen as a technical one, and perhaps therefore of somewhat limited value. At worst it might be a mechanism of control in relation to women as mothers, and as professionals.

A second explanation for the policy/practice gap recognizes that there are more profound difficulties for many women in breast-feeding than might be addressed through this technical, professional-centred approach. This is perhaps suggested by the above statement which recognizes that some women have made a firm and clear decision against breast-feeding, and that there is therefore no point in attempting to change this. The result of this thinking appears, from the literature, to involve targeting those who want to breast-feed and offering greater levels of support to them. For example, one piece of research which has been widely quoted shows that, for some groups of women, more support from a consistent and sympathetic person can lengthen the period of breast-feeding (Jenner, 1988). The group referred to in this research was composed of 'white, working class (according to the Registrar General's criterion) women aged between 19 and 32 years, either married or cohabiting, and all very keen to breast feed' (ibid: 321). A similar approach is built into one health visiting textbook. Robertson (1988) suggests that in relation to breast-feeding, mothers in Social Class 1 manage well enough without support, whilst those in Social Classes 11, 111 and 1V benefit from support. Those in Social Class V are not mentioned. While from the professional point of view targeting those who can benefit from one's services seems entirely sensible, there are questions to be asked about supposedly universal services which find they have no role to play with those living in the worst socio-economic conditions. The statement from the Royal College of Midwives about not making bottle feeders feel guilty, noted above, is also, because of the social class distribution of reluctant breast-feeders, likely to result in no particular attention to those from poorer backgrounds as well as to those who are young and single. One would not of course wish to argue for greater pressure to be put on these women, or a return to the more authoritarian practices which some of the women in this study experienced. However there is clearly room for more thinking about women who are more 'difficult' as far as breast-feeding promotion is concerned, not to find better ways to make them breast-feed, but to think in greater depth about their needs. For example, in a recent study on the infant feeding practice of women at risk of low birth weight delivery, Rajan and Oakley (1990) suggest that hospitals should not adopt policies which, either implicitly or explicitly, suggest that low birth weight babies 'should' be bottle fed. Targeting those mothers who are in the 'right' category for breast-feeding would tend to adopt this approach by default. Rajan and Oakley also suggest that all mothers need attention to their emotional as well as their physical well-being, having their feelings and opinions respected. To simply make breast-feeding the goal, and target those mothers likely to succeed, would not achieve this.

A third explanation for the policy and practice gap is at present less fully articulated than the first two. This involves a recognition that breast-feeding promotion simply does not fit with the needs of many women. However, rather than simply exclude them from any kind of service, this approach involves more profound re-thinking of the professional role. For example, within some health visiting literature, questions are raised about how the profession can re-examine its body of knowledge, in terms of how far this has been constructed on the basis of normative views about women as mothers, neglecting the needs of women in their own right (eg. Orr, 1980b; Luker and Orr, 1985; Orr, 1986; Mayall and Foster, 1989). A particular feature of this thinking is the recognition that professionals need to re-think the models of education which they bring to their involvement with women (Mayall and Foster, 1989; Foster and Mayall, 1990; Beattie, 1991). For example, in Mayall and Foster's study of the perceptions of both mothers and health visitors of the health visiting role, they found that mothers 'did not accept that health visitors had a right to give unsolicited advice' (Mayall and Foster, 1989: 69). They also found, however, that many health visitors adopted a 'top-down', or directive, but covert, model of health education, which was resented by the women in their study. One major difficulty is that many of the health visitors in their research took the view that their knowledge was 'factual', rather than often a mixture of facts, values and opinions. As well as proposing other more democratic models of health education, Mayall and Foster suggest that there is now too much attention given to the surveillance of mothers and under fives, but too few child care resources which enable women to get health advice on their own terms, or which make it possible for women to work outside the home. In other words they suggest a move to new kinds of collective provision, and a move away from individualistic, 'policing' modes of intervention.

As suggested earlier in this chapter, there is also beginning to be some attention to the particular role of women professionals within health and welfare. Lorentzon suggests that nursing and social work were originally, as occupations, built on traditional notions of femininity and 'altruistic service' (1990: 53), an image represented by motherhood. She describes the way in which, in their search for professional status, these occupational groups have vigorously rejected this, and allowed it to be replaced by 'masculine rationality within bureaucratic health and welfare institutions' (ibid: 53). This suggests that professionalism rests on a fundamental dichotomy between masculine and feminine. Shaping professionalism into a 'democratic, rather than inevitably a bureaucratic, relationship', as Weeks (1989b: 132) has suggested requires a re-examination of the discourses of masculinity and femininity within which professionalism is coded. This is beginning to happen in the feminist literature on professionalism to which I referred earlier. Within health visiting such views have been around for some time, although there is little evidence that they have so far had any major impact: 'Perhaps it is time that health visitors abandoned what is essentially a masculine concern with status, and concentrated more on solidarity with their sisters' (Meerabau, 1982: 298)

The recognition in my study, and others to which I have referred, that women do not want to be 'told' how to feed their children, valuing instead the ordinariness of the views of other women, suggests that, without wanting to ditch professionalism wholesale, there is a real opportunity for change, as well as possible new directions in this literature.

There is also a danger, however, of reinforcing the essentialism implicit in most discourses of motherhood. In something of a contrast to the arguments I am presenting here Everingham (1994) suggests that professional discourse and knowledge has contradictory implications. Sometimes it can be used to undermine the idea of all women as natural mothers. This could be an important dimension of new thinking about professionalism.

This thinking will be pursued in the final chapter, following, in the next chapter, an examination of how the women in this study found ways to manage, and resist, the often contradictory expectations and discourses which shaped their infant feeding experiences.

7 Control and Resistance in Infant Feeding Regimes

> ... breastfeeding is a feminist issue because it encourages women's self reliance, confirms a woman's power to control her own body, challenges models of women as consumers and sex objects, requires a new interpretation of women's work and encourages solidarity among women. (Van Esterik, 1989: 69)

The findings of my study and the arguments I have presented here suggest that breast-feeding does not always represent these advantages to women in Western cultures. It is the intention of this chapter to review the complex discourses of power and control, discussed in earlier chapters, within which infant feeding practices have developed, and to explore the ways in which women are able to resist these. I argue here that it is important to recognize the complexity of women's situations with regard to infant feeding and to avoid the essentialism implicit in even feminist accounts such as that of Van Esterik. At the heart of her argument is a deeper foundation: 'The capacity to nurture infants and others, and to make things grow, is the basis of women's social production; it is basic to women's physiological and psychological well-being, self esteem and economic self reliance' (ibid: 68–9).

Here what women frequently do, 'nurture others' is merged with what they 'are', their being. The essence of 'woman' here is nurturing and what is fought for are the conditions in which this can be valued. As I observed in chapter one, most feminist comment on infant feeding appears to approximate to this way of thinking. I set out in my study to examine this more closely particularly from the point of view of the kinds of women who have long been seen as a problem

189

with regard to low rates of breast-feeding. This chapter and the next will examine the meaning and implications of breast and bottle feeding for the women who adopt them. For example, it is important to address the question of whether breast-feeding is an important part of women's real self, 'the very core of our identity' (Palmer, 1988: 13).

DISCOURSES OF INFANT FEEDING

I drew attention, in chapter one, to Foucault's questions concerning the links between discourses and power relations: 'What were the most immediate, the most local power relations at work? How did they make possible these kind of discourses and conversely how were these discourses used to support power relations?' (Foucault, 1981: 97). It was proposed in that chapter to examine the discursive field concerning infant feeding as one which is also a conversation about femininity. In each of the chapters that followed I have suggested aspects of this 'conversation' in the form of texts, practices, and beliefs which shape the meaning of women's experience. These have provided a highly complex and sometimes contradictory web of expectations. One important dimension of these is the idea of femininity as a 'natural' entity, but one which must be worked at by women themselves and by others such as health professionals and by those who offer health advice. Women are deemed, in some of these texts and practices, to be linked to nature, and therefore outside culture and the public sphere, although they are allowed to enter these on a conditional, controlled basis. Paradoxically even their place in the private sphere is problematic in that they have to negotiate with others what they do there: men in relation to where breast-feeding can 'safely' be undertaken; health professionals with regard to whether they are behaving as proper mothers. In this way I have suggested that although infant feeding is deemed as 'private' in the sense of an unpaid domestic responsibility, it nevertheless remains a public issue. Infant feeding practices disrupt the whole notion of separate public and private domains.

In relation to breast-feeding, there has for a long time in

the West been a contradiction for women in the way that they live their lives between the belief that good mothers should breast-feed and the fact that they need to do this in private. However greater complexity appears to have opened up with regard to the (hetero)sexualization of breasts, even though this cannot be seen as one single process or as having arisen at a specific, once and for all, historical moment. It has accompanied a changing discourse with regard to sexuality, so that from the early part of this century there was an increasing expectation that even respectable women were expected to be actively sexual within marriage (Mort, 1987; Weeks, 1989a; Clark, 1993). From the late 1960s this expectation of women's sexuality has broadened, so that taboos on pre-marital and extra-marital sex have been reduced, bringing less restrictions on women's sexuality but at the same time increased demands on them to participate in a broad range of (hetero)sexual behaviour. This discursive adaptation has also occurred as a result of what Walby (1990) has described as the shift from private to public forms of patriarchy. Within this breast-feeding itself has become a (hetero)sexualized activity.

In relation to mothering, expectations have also been contradictory. Breast-feeding has remained a symbolic policy goal, but has clashed with regimentation and lack of support brought about by the insistence on hospital births. In chapter two and chapter six I suggested that although state concern about infant feeding has remained evident, this policy has for the most part been individualistic rather than collective. Paradoxically, in Britain the provision of cheap baby milk for a long time formed the only real resource for infant feeding, tending to undermine, rather than support breast-feeding. Another main plank of policy has been through 'advice' from various health professionals which was often not appreciated by the women in my study. Popular health advice literature has simultaneously and continuously defined and redefined breast-feeding in relation to both sexuality and mothering. It is possible to see infant feeding experiences as having been shaped by two major sets of discourses, one relating to mothering; and one to (hetero)sexuality. Although these are sometimes contradictory, they are both manifestations of a deeper pre-occupation with controlling women through the construction, and maintenance, of particular forms of femininity.

Whilst all this produces a very demanding set of expectations for women, its sheer complexity also provides space and possibility for resistance. Weedon (1987) suggests that poststructuralist methods of analyzing power, those of Foucault for example, can be used by feminists to recognize the possibility of multiple forms of resistance. This approach enables feminism to continually question the taken-for-granted of femininity, rather than attempt to construct an alternative meta-narrative of women. This is achieved through understanding how femininity has been, and is continually, constructed and reconstructed; and through pushing beyond its boundaries. In this sense both breast and bottle feeding might be connected with oppressive practices, but both might also be seen as linked to forms of resistance. Although Weedon identifies the discourses of femininity as being extremely powerful in constructing meaning in relation to women's bodies in ways which have resulted in their exclusion from many aspects of public life, she nevertheless recognizes the contradictions, and possible forms of challenge within dominant discursive fields. Particular discourses offer more than one subject position, even while rewarding one form of subjectivity over others. This is evident in relation to infant feeding where good mothers can avoid breast-feeding through appropriate negotiation. Resistance can also be produced when there is a space or contradiction between the subject position offered by the discourse and the experience or interests of a particular individual. Again this is important with regard to infant feeding where babies' needs, and demands for modesty and/or sexual presentation, frequently conflict. Or when a woman experiences breast-feeding as a pleasurable, even sexual, activity in the absence of a male sexual partner. In these ways multiple forms of resistance can be produced.

There are also possibilities of resistance through reverse discourses (Weedon, 1987). Foucault (1981) identified homosexuality as having formed such a reverse discourse in the nineteenth century, at the same time, and often in the same terms, as were being used to produce and control it. This reverse discourse argued for the legitimacy and 'naturalness' of homosexuality. Weedon sees some aspects of feminism as a similar reverse discourse. Hence cultural, or gynocentric, feminists have challenged the devaluing of female subject positions by redefining them, and contesting the linguistic, legal, political, and cultural systems which denigrate the female (see Daly, 1979; Rich, 1979; Griffin, 1984; Young, 1990b). However in reversing dominant values such approaches draw on the same assumptions and categories. This is particularly important in dominant discourses concerning biological sex differences, since these are extremely significant in constituting subjectivity, and in the construction and maintenance of patriarchal social relations. For this reason feminist discourses about the body are potentially powerful in challenging domination, but have major difficulties in freeing themselves from patriarchal thinking.

In chapter five I suggested that Rich's work could be seen as working within, and for, a reverse discourse with regard to experiences of motherhood, including breast-feeding. She directs our attention to re-evaluating those parts of our experience which have tended to be ignored, manipulated and even destroyed. This is important in reminding us of the ways in which the breast-feeding powers of women have been denigrated. But it slides easily into a system of control which accompanies the notion of women as closer to nature.

As I noted at the beginning of this book there have been few attempts to relate feminist theory and practice to infant feeding. I have suggested that those few that do exist are limited by their assumptions of the 'truth' of breast-feeding as part of women's real selves. I argue below that the experience of working class women and others regarded as inadequate with regards to their breast-feeding rates can be better understood through the idea of multiple forms of resistance, rather than the idea of breast-feeding as part of the universal truth of womanhood.

Van Esterik (1989: 69–77) suggests six reasons why breast-feeding is potentially empowering for women. I will comment on each of her points in turn, drawing on arguments which have been made in earlier chapters.

Van Esterik's first argument is that breast-feeding requires changes which will mean improved conditions for women. She includes: rest after childbirth; assistance with the newborn and priority for women in the distribution of food. Breast-feeding, she argues, encourages women's self reliance and confidence in their ability to meet the needs of infants.

Experiences reported in my study show that the expectation that women breast-feed is often not accompanied by these conditions. The cross cultural work of Raphael (1985), which I explored particularly in chapter three suggests that these resources have tended to be offered to women only when breast-feeding is necessary for survival *and* when such support is actually available. My study suggests that women use whatever resources they can to preserve their own and their babies health; this may or may not involve breast-feeding. Nevertheless one can readily agree that these conditions are desirable both for breast-feeding and for mothering generally.

Second, she suggests that breast-feeding challenges medical hegemony and confirms women's power to control their own bodies through reducing further medicalization. As women gain control of their bodies they are in a better position to care for their children. The material reported in chapter six suggests that breast-feeding is as susceptible to medicalization as bottle feeding. Indeed for some women bottle feeding, when accompanied by 'acceptable' reasons for not breast-feeding, released them from what they saw as medical intrusions.

Her third point is that breast-feeding challenges the predominant view of women as consumer. She indentifies the whole process of modernization as involving women in achieving status through acquiring goods. Deciding not to spend money on bottle feeding rejects this. I would argue however that women's construction as consumers is much more deeply rooted than could be challenged simply by not bottle feeding, although this might of course play a small part in a rejection of consumerism. There was no suggestion in my study that women acquired status through bottle feeding; the opposite in fact appears to be the case, such is the symbolic link between breast-feeding and good mothering.

The fourth argument she makes is that breast-feeding challenges the view of breasts as sexual objects. As we have seen westernization and modernization have led to these changing attitudes to women's bodies, where breast-feeding in public is seen as akin to excretion. I would agree that there are examples of breast-feeding desexualizing the breasts. However for the most part women are left to cope with the complex effects of sexualization individually, so breast-feeding in itself does not automatically challenge this. Bottle feeding enables some women to avoid this complexity. It may however be that some women miss important aspects of female sexuality through not breast-feeding, which in itself reinforces male oriented domination of sexuality. However such positive experiences are likely to result from the context and meaning ascribed to breast-feeding rather than simply from breast-feeding in itself.

Fifth, she suggests that breast-feeding requires a redefinition of women's work to better integrate women's productive and reproductive activities. She notes the importance of recognizing that women do have the capacity to provide food for infants and this should be valued as work. I have argued in chapter four that the relationship between public and private spheres, between what is seen as work and what is not, is important in understanding infant feeding. The lack of resources for breast-feeding is part of a more fundamental absence of resources for caring work generally. Addressing breast-feeding within the broader context of public/private divisions avoids the functionalism and essentialism of focusing exclusively on women's biology. In many situations, breast-feeding does not bring this re-evaluation of women's work.

Finally, Van Esterik argues that breast-feeding encourages solidarity and co-operation between women, and may provide an opportunity for women to meet on their own terms. The evidence from my study is that although women may well sometimes share breast-feeding experiences as part of particular household and neighbourhood arrangements, this is not linked to breast-feeding in itself. In lots of situations women do not gather together in order to breast-feed but for many other reasons. Although there are current examples of organizations in the West which provide this sort of support for breast-feeding (NCT and La Leche League which have been discussed in earlier chapters) these have tended to be linked to a particular model of mothering and therefore have limited appeal for women who do not identify with this model. Attaching the goal of women's co-operation purely to breast-feeding seems to overlook more fundamental

purposes and meanings of women's co-operation, which
concern their broader needs.

Although Van Esterik claims her arguments are based on
a socialist feminist perspective and what she describes as a
social constructionist understanding of femininity, she has
some difficulty in resolving the contradiction between her
pro breast-feeding position and the dangerous ground of
biological determinism. She speaks of the need for women
to tune into 'vague murmurings – the submerged discourse
about their power to nurture' (1989: 107). Although she
warns of the dangers of over romanticizing breast-feeding it
seems to me that this is precisely the trap into which she
falls through her use of this language. The difficulty is that
she attributes to breast-feeding a 'truth' of the self which
she argues is in itself empowering to women. Hence she
suggests that women breast-feeding in public in North America
is a political act since it counteracts dominant norms. What
Van Esterik fails to address here is that the political nature
of this act results not simply from women reclaiming breast-
feeding, but from resisting dominant norms of femininity,
one of which is that public breasts should be sexual and
not reproductive. It is important to recognize that breast-
feeding is not of itself a form of resistance. One has only to
reflect on the fact that breast-feeding was obligatory under
the Nazis to recognize that the activity in itself can be far
from liberating for women; it can be achieved through extremely coercive social relations (Sichtermann, 1983: 61).
Pressure to breast-feed can be overt or covert and can be
exerted for a whole variety of reasons, not all of them to do
with women's interests as we have seen at various points in
this book.

Rather than seeing breast-feeding as in itself a form of
resistance to patriarchy, a more useful approach is to look
at the forms of social control which are expressed through
infant feeding regimes at any particular period and at the
multiple forms of resistance to these mechanisms of control. This study suggests that a major dimension of the local discursive power relations is the surveillance of women's
sexuality by men, and their mothering by health professionals
and by policy makers. Although these are in some ways in
contradiction with each other, both involve women check-

ing on each other, particularly working class, black and young women by white, middle class, educated women. Surveillance of mothering is not only conducted by female health professionals but by researchers and activists in relation to infant feeding. Deviant bottle feeders are asked to explain their 'irrationality'. Their lives are scrutinized in order that we can find ways to persuade them, like middle class mothers, to achieve the 'truth' of breast-feeding and themselves. Feminism, when it is pro breast-feeding, can perhaps unwittingly be linked to mechanisms for the control of women, through the denial of difference. I will argue in the next chapter that although this means that choice about feeding method is important, it is not in itself enough. Through recognizing and resisting the links between current feeding practices and various forms of social control, we can identify broader agendas about women's health and well being, identifying the ways in which breast-feeding fits with these.

FORMS OF RESISTANCE

Martin suggests from her research, which relates to women's experiences of the ways in which their bodies are managed within medical systems, that there are many different ways in which women 'express consciousness of their position and opposition to oppression' (1989: 183). She suggests six forms of consciousness and resistance (ibid: 184–8) which I have summarized below:

1. Acceptance. Things are as they are and do not need to be changed, nor can they be changed, 'that's life, that's what every woman has to go through'.

2. Lament. Expressing grief and pain, maybe with consciousness that things need not have been as they were.

3. Non-action. Not participating in or attending an organization if it is perceived to be against one's interests.

4. Sabotage. Actions or words intended to go undetected which are aimed at foiling some process.

5. Resistance. Refusing to accept a label or to co-operate in an act and saying so. Might be done individually or as part of a group.

6. Rebellion. Forcing or persuading people or organizations to change.

Although Martin reserves the term resistance for those acts which express more open opposition and overt expression of anger, she recognizes varied ways in which women manage oppressive and controlling practices. A major question for her was the relationship between opposition and social class. She concludes, albeit tentatively, that, 'working class women are at least as likely to express opposition as are middle class women' (ibid: 191).

There are interesting parallels between the concerns about working class women and their apparent irrationality in not breast-feeding and the commonly expressed frustration about their low attendance at ante-natal clinics. Oakley (1984) has suggested that it might be more useful to ask why women do attend clinics rather than why they do not. Similarly it might be illuminating to find out why middle class women do breast-feed, rather than asking working class women why they are more likely to bottle feed. From Oakley's perspective non attendance can be seen as a form of resistance, albeit a somewhat reactive one, to the social control function of ante-natal care: 'This "voting with one's feet" may be viewed as passive rather than active resistance. Women's behaviour tends to be socially interpreted in terms of passivity, although women themselves may see it differently as active manipulation of the system' (Oakley, 1984: 271). Oakley identifies the very many reasons why women might make a rational decision not to attend clinics based on their experience of them: over-crowded waiting areas, poor appointment systems, little continuity, no provision for other children. She therefore suggests that, rather than seeing the problem of non-attendance as located within women themselves, it might be better to identify deficiencies in the services. In similar vein, Macintyre (1982) has pointed out that pro breast-feeding efforts could be re-directed towards changing the many external barriers to breast-feeding, rather than continuing to focus on women's attitudes.

Since women have to find a subject position within complex and changing discourses linked to both mothering and heterosexuality, simply adopting breast-feeding or bottle feeding may prove unsatisfactory. Bottle feeding enables some women to find an acceptable subject position within the discourses of modesty and heterosexuality, but is more complex with regard to the discourse of mothering; good mothers are supposed to breast-feed. Breast-feeding will enable a woman to adopt the position of good and natural mother but may well produce complexity with regard to the discourse of heterosexuality. This complexity makes it less likely that women will express open resistance or rebellion in relation to all of the discourses. Some women in my study resisted the surveillance of health professionals very assertively, as indicated in chapter six. Resistance to heterosexual discourses of the body on the other hand was not expressed in terms of rebellion or conscious rejection, although many women expressed uneasiness at some of its practices, for example in their unhappiness with representations of women's bodies, which some saw as akin to pornography, and of course in the sheer discomfort of some women with the whole idea of breast-feeding. Perhaps the most common way of handling this complexity was through non-action, simply opting out of breast-feeding altogether. The difficulty then was to do this whilst retaining a subject position as good mother. The process of achieving this is explored in the next section.

WOMEN'S STORIES

Most mothers have a feeding story, just as they have a child-birth story. I discussed in earlier chapters my view that, rather than simply treat these stories as true in some objective sense, we recognize that they are accounts of experience constructed within, and sometimes in spite of, the scripts concerning femininity which shape women's lives. Feminist researchers have drawn on women's story telling abilities with regard to their childbirth experience (Oakley, 1980). Such stories appear to have a compulsive quality for many women and a particular genre of literature on women's health, particularly childbirth, has used women's apparent wish to talk about and to hear such accounts (Oakley, 1981a; Beels, 1980; Kenner, 1985; Cosslett, 1994).

Feeding stories exist not only because women can readily recall events which are important to them, but because they appear to need a feeding story to tell, polish up and tell again. Why? Where can this need for such a story come from? Oakley suggests that women's need to talk about childbirth after the event is a need for a kind of therapy, because of the traumatic nature of the events, particularly when heavily medicalized (1980: 297). Feeding stories are not usually quite so filled with trauma as childbirth stories. Instead they appear to reflect a wish to defend and explain. Women need to have a story at the ready to defend themselves against possible criticism, to explain themselves as a mother and a woman. For many women defending yourself against possible criticism is part of life. The criticisms may come from many different quarters and, as in the case of infant feeding, may contradict with each other. It is assumed that there are right answers about how babies are to be fed. The 'wrong' answer must be accompanied by a suitable explanation. Women also have to devise stories to tell themselves. Perhaps their experience does not fit with their own views about what good mothers do. So I am one of a number of people who has already asked for, and heard, this story.

I was particularly struck by the fact that women frequently used language which suggested that they themselves played only a small part in decision making about their own infant feeding experience. Things happened to them rather than being initiated, controlled and managed by them. For example:

I just got on with it. *The baby finds* its own way. (Bertha Combe, 1922)

I *hadn't made my mind up, hadn't thought. You didn't in them days.* I fed her for six weeks, and then *the milk left us.* (Lucy Cooper, 1930)

Yes I had made my mind up. It was *the done thing in my family.* (Mary Moreland, 1936)

When I saw Dr Tiplady the second time *he said, 'don't be*

surprised if you can't feed her on account of your age. Therefore I don't want you to eat any more. Just try. When you think she's not getting enough put her on artificial feeds'. (Jane Harrison, 1936)

I can't feed – none of my children's been fed 'cos when I'm pregnant my nipples go in and *the hospital put them straight on the bottle.* (Florence Hope, 1943)

For two weeks when I was in bed I fed the baby. When I got on my feet *the milk left us. It just left us.* (Tessa Rowe, 1944)

I picked him up that much, I got sore and *they had to take the milk away* and give him the bottle. (Annie Sinclair, 1947)

I breast-fed because that was the thing. (Jean Richards, 1949)

I fed him when I first came home but he was a very hungry baby, took a lot of filling and *they told me he wasn't getting enough.* It was very weak. It wasn't much good so I put him on the bottle. (Monica Andrews, 1951)

In those days *there was only breast-feeding.* Only the idle rich bottle fed. *I didn't make a decision.* (Audrey Soulsby, 1951)

I decided to breast-feed. *It just seemed the right thing to do.* (Gina Godfrey, 1969)

I never thought about it. When the baby was born *hospital usually say breast-feed.* I breast-fed for three to four months. (Naheed Akhtar, 1970)

Doctor says vitamins and things and *mother in law says* it's healthy. (Rukhsana Rehman, 1980)

Here there are clearly perceived to be a variety of agents other than the woman herself. Such agents include: the baby; the general culture and expectations of the time; family tradition; doctors; nipples; quality and quantity of milk; and of course 'them'. The meaning of the use of these 'agents' is not necessarily the same for each woman. Sometimes the agent is used to justify some action taken by the woman which she perceives may be unacceptable in some way. At other times the agent is clearly somewhat more coercive. One set of agents may be used against another; there is an implicit hierarchy. So the baby as agent might be used to defeat family tradition or 'them'. Perhaps the most important agent of all is biology. Cosslett writes of labour itself being talked of as a major actor in women's stories of childbirth (Cosslett, 1994; 159).

It is not surprising that women are ambivalent about expressing themselves as positive decision makers given that there are sometimes contradictions between their actions and the dominant discourse of natural mothering. Discourses of femininity are also complex with regard to autonomy and decision making. Women are expected to be responsible for themselves as well as for others but, paradoxically, to be dependent on others particularly for approval. Good girls have to simultaneously act responsibly in their own right but also to do as they are told. Carlen and Worrall describe the way that women are on the one hand expected to be 'more than men' in being independent, coping and caring. On the other hand they are expected to be 'less than a man' in being dependent 'childlike, incapable, fragile and capricious' (1987: 3). Calling on biology to explain their actions is therefore a way of managing these contradictions since this provides a discourse with which they are very familiar, and which is highly acceptable in relation to gendered experience. In other words to resist control mechanisms women may sometimes have to make use of the same language as that which is used to control. In addition they can even use discourses of femininity against other women, for example in their relations with women health professionals, which I explored in chapter six. So avoiding breast-feeding whilst having someone or something else take responsibility for this decision is rather more than non-action in Martin's terms (Martin, 1989). It successfully manages the contradictory discourses and simultaneously reduces the intrusiveness of health professionals. This should not be seen simply as a process of finding an excuse. Whilst some women did not want to breast-feed, others did. The fact that they felt they could not do so was the result of many factors: the interpretation by themselves and others of particular aspects of the process – a lack of milk; a crying baby; sore nipples; little confidence on their own part; a general lack of faith in mothers; insufficient skill on behalf of relevant professionals; too little support and privacy. The process was one of finding the right terms for negotiation between mothers and the relevant health professionals. These terms were frequently biological and involved reinforcing particular aspects of femininity.

I indicated in chapter six that some women made use of the doctor's authority to defeat potential criticism. There were some particularly striking examples of this with regard to babies' illnesses. Almost all the women told me that their babies were healthy in infancy whatever their feeding method. Two women however had babies, both bottle fed, who had gastro-enteritis which is believed to be associated with bottle feeding (Palmer, 1988; McConville, 1994). Both were reassured by their doctors that their mothering habits could not have caused this. This was very important to them in dealing with these events. Both concluded, on the basis of the doctors' reassurance, that they were being 'too careful' as mothers. Their self image as good mothers therefore remained intact:

> The doctor says sometimes babies are kept too clean. We used to keep everything so clean with gauze over everything. (Monica Andrews, 1951).

> I was so shocked 'cos there was no-one more particular. The doctor told me that he must have caught the germ from someone else. I was over-careful, stupid now when I look back. I think I tried to be a perfect mother. I just wanted everything to be right for her. (Margaret Pearson, 1975).

There were four women who expressed greater decisiveness in their own right. Three of them exercised this against the whole idea of breast-feeding. In answer to my question about whether she had made up her mind about feeding the baby before the birth Patricia Poole answered most decisively:

Yes, I had. I wanted to bottle feed. I didn't want to have anything to do with breast-feeding at all. I just made up my own mind. It just didn't appeal to me. It revolted me, the thought of doing it myself. I was very clear. (1965).

However her clarity at this stage still gave way to a softening of her decision making by reference to biology: 'As it worked out I couldn't have breast-fed anyway so the choice was taken away.' It appears as though, reflecting on these events now, she is reluctant to stick with her own decisiveness and is ambivalent about choice, not the actual choice she made but the fact of having made it. Her concept of choice is interesting in another way. When I asked whether all of this had been discussed with her by health professionals, she said: 'I can't remember being *given any choice.* They just told me to bottle feed and gave me tablets.' Again this is an indication that choice is believed to be owned by others, even in the face of strong feelings and plans of your own. But rather than seeing this as a lack of autonomy on behalf of this woman we might see it as a way of managing a complex discursive field, by warding off potential criticism and intervention.

Also in 1965, Evelyn Moore was clear about not wanting to breast-feed. Again biology played a part in her story in two ways. First, she had an abscess on her breast in her teens, and 'I had a scar in the nipple area'. She was still able to describe very vividly the pain of having it 'lanced and packed'. The language of biology also played another part; 'I just didn't have that instinct'. However she clearly continued to gather evidence about the negative impact of breast-feeding:

Most of my friends bottle fed. I can't remember anyone breast-feeding . . . I can – there was a girl I was friendly with who had a baby round about the time that David was born. She breast-fed and she had the most whining brat I've ever heard – he used to scream.

PC. *Did you think this was to do with breast-feeding?*

It was. She was told eventually she hadn't enough to give him.

One of the ironic things here is that later in the interview, when I asked about her baby's health, she told me he had terrible colic and used to scream at night. She did not apparently attribute this to bottle feeding; her son was not a 'whining brat'. So biology, this time in the form of colic, again had useful explanatory powers; his screaming was not blamed on her feeding habits.

Shirley Hill (in 1973) was obviously comfortable from the beginning with her bottle feeding decision: 'I wasn't going to breast-feed, oh no. My friends had a lot of trouble, one in particular, they had to draw the milk off.' Going out was an activity which Shirley valued and breast-feeding would interfere with this, since she was not happy feeding in front of people. Her experience of bottle feeding in this context was rated positively, 'I put him on Cow and Gate Premium and then on SMA and he was smashing.'

Only one woman, Ada Brown (1959), appeared to exercise great decisiveness in favour of breast-feeding and to stick to her plans when difficulties arose. I have discussed her experience in earlier chapters. What is important here is that she wanted to 'own' her decision: 'I wanted to breast-feed her not because it was the done thing. I'd seen mam breast-feed all of us, and I'd seen other people who for other reasons had to bottle feed, and I thought I'm just going to breast-feed.' It is worth noting that Ada Brown is a community activist who has a clear idea that an oppositional stance is sometimes appropriate. She also managed the demands of heterosexuality; she was able to joke about her leaking breasts during sex with her husband. Her discussions about bodies generally were positive. For example, she described her experience of caring for her mother who had recently been quite seriously ill, 'the sight of my mother's naked body wouldn't shock us or bother us'.

What is most important to note about this discussion is that the language which women use in relation to their experiences rarely depicts them as owning their own decisions. Ambivalence and anxiety is often revealed even after they have initially stated their intentions positively. Weedon (1987) points out that the expectation in Western liberal discourse is that one's subject position is coherent and whole. Working class women who do not breast-feed are assumed to be irrational. Breast-feeding is so obviously a good thing that their failure to do it, to take notice of good health advice, must be explained. An inadequate explanation might be a sign of irrationality. But the explanation cannot fully expose the contradictions of the discourse nor, because of other expectations regarding femininity, must women be seen to be doing something for themselves. Hence a woman must be the unitary decision-making subject of western liberalism but must 'naturally' put others, that is her baby, first. A number of women simultaneously acquiesced in relation to the professional discourse of health, but at the same time resisted its most intrusive aspects by not breast-feeding and expressing their reluctance to do so in its own, that is medical and biological, terms. Women might therefore be seen not as acquiescing to medical power and definitions but as making use of them for their own ends at least in relation to infant feeding.

The usual assumption is that middle class women who breast-feed are behaving rationally in acting on health information. But their behaviour could be interpreted differently. It may be, as I have suggested in chapter three, that there is a greater fit between the material conditions of their lives and the subject position of good mother in that they may have more control over space, time and resources. The discourse of heterosexuality may also have less pitfalls for them. Their respectability is woven into their class position whereas working class, black and young women have to continually renegotiate their respectability. It is important to raise questions about the implicit assumptions of working class irrationality and middle class rationality in relation to breast-feeding as Oakley (1984) has done in relation to antenatal clinics. In any case, as we have seen, the patterns are complex, some working class women do want to breast-feed and some achieve this.

These stories can therefore be seen as an attempt by women to find their way through the myriad potential criticisms of their mothering and femininity. This is not always achieved comfortably however and over time new demands emerge. Having managed the potential criticisms of one's own generation, women find themselves with an often different set of expectations by a new generation of health advice and behavioural expectations. I asked whether women would do the same if they 'had their time over again'. Most women felt that they would. This applied whether or not they breast-fed:

I would have breast-fed, it's best. I know some [younger women] that had them on bottles. They should have fed the children, it would have been better for them. (Bertha Combe, 1922).

Yes, I still think breast-feeding's best. (Eleanor Kershaw, 1940)

No regrets. (Maureen Watson, 1941)

Oh yes, I'd take no notice of them now [about the hospital staff with whom she had a struggle]. (Ada Brown, 1959)

Yes I think so. I had no problems. At least you know how much they're getting. (Evelyn Moore, 1965)

Yes, I'd do the same. With breast-feeding you've got to want to do it. It just doesn't appeal to me. (Patricia Poole, 1965)

It worked for me. (Carol Cook, 1973)

Yes. There was just something there. I just didn't want to breast-feed. (Margaret Pearson, 1975)

It is perhaps not surprising, and again part of a process of resistance, that women wish to believe that they have done their best for their children. Part of their construction of a story is to achieve this. One woman expressed this view strongly, 'I don't think anyone has got any right to make any mother feel that she's giving her baby any less than the best' (Ada Brown, 1959). These views might be seen as acceptance (of the terms of the discourse of natural mothering) but are also an expression of resistance to the idea that one's mothering might be questioned by others.

Despite this apparent need for a tidy story some women expressed a wish that they had done things differently. Polly

Williams (1932) who had stopped breast-feeding because of a septic breast said, 'I was disappointed at the time. Yes I would. I think breast-feeding is a good start in life. Worth all the tea in China. Can't beat a mother's milk'. Annie Sinclair (1947) also had a 'bad breast' and was disappointed, 'I would try breast-feeding. It sickened me when I had that bad breast. I was frightened. They wouldn't let us feed. They could have said, your breasts will get better, but they didn't and I never thought to ask. Breast-feeding is best'. Some women had been left with uncomfortable feelings and were now using the opportunity of the interview not only to express these feelings, but to think about how things might have been different and why they ought to have been. Rajina Mondal (1977), described in chapter three, was particularly regretful about what had happened, 'I'm sorry fail [sic]. My daughter still says, Mum you gave me your milk. So I'm sorry fail'. She was very emotional as she told me that she could not bring herself to tell her daughter (then aged ten) that she had not been breast-fed. These statements might be seen as similar to Martin's category of lament (1989), in the sense of sadness that lack of support and other negative conditions did not permit them to do what they perceived as best for their babies.

Beatrice Callender (1968) would also have wanted a different experience. She attributed the difficulties the first time around to her age, 'I'd have breast-fed if I was older. I was much more sure of myself then'. Beatrice certainly took a reflective approach to her experience and raised at least tentative questions about the terms of the health discourse in relation to breast-feeding, even though she was at a bit of a loss as to know how to challenge it: 'I don't know whether breast-feeding's better. I don't think it's necessarily better. It's got more immunities and that . . . but that's just what I've read' (1968). It is interesting to note that Beatrice Callender, like Ada Brown, who I identified earlier as a community activist, also has experience of raising questions about dominant discourses and practices. She now works as clerical worker in a small community development project where critical discussions about the work in the context of challenging inequality are frequent. Similarly Gina Godfrey (1969) regretted that she had not breast-fed any of her three children and, like Beatrice, she attributed this to her youth and lack of confidence when she gave birth. She told me that she later became pregnant for a fourth time, and was determined to do it 'all her own way', including breast-feeding. Unfortunately she miscarried and therefore did not have the opportunity to try this out. It is worth noting that Gina Godfrey has taken part in local women's health groups, part of community development work in the area in which she lives.

Those particularly likely to adopt a very assertive line about their own practice were women who had bottle fed from the start.

> Bottle feeding is better. You know what they're getting. With the other they're just sucking and not getting fed. (Elizabeth White, 1939)

> There are no disadvantages with bottle feeding. Breast-feeding's inconvenient, if you're going out anyway. They don't cater for it. My friend once was asked to leave a cafe or go and sit in a toilet. You can't do that. (Shirley Hill, 1973)

> There's nothing bad about bottle feeding. Breast-feeding is disgusting. If there are facilities to do it in private, then good luck to them. It's not very pleasant if you're on a bus and someone's feeding a baby. (Carol Cook, 1973)

> I suppose it (breast-feeding) would be better in the long run. But I never really went into that. There was something there. I didn't want to do it. And she was very contented on the bottle. (Margaret Pearson, 1975)

Although these comments might be seen as defensiveness they can also be understood as resistance to the terms of the dominant discourses of health and mothering. Some of their attitudes were also shaped by the more submerged discourses of heterosexuality which made breast-feeding embarrassing. Their assertiveness about bottle feeding can therefore be seen as a way of managing the complexities of both discourses. It may be that this extra assertiveness resulted from the more obvious contradiction from the 1960s onwards between the need for breasts to be overtly and actively sexual and the demands of breast-feeding. Although this sexualization of breasts might be seen as negative it might also be seen as an opportunity for women to assert that their breasts are neither simply 'for' breast-feeding, nor on the other hand simply there 'for' sex.

Some of those who had tried and 'failed' to breast-feed (see chapter three for discussion of those who breast-fed for less than four months) defended their own experience and still supported breast-feeding, again often using the terms of the medical discourse, and the language of natural mothering.

Anyone who can should feed them. I don't know why they don't try. Milk from a mother's breast is life to a baby.' (Tessa Rowe, 1944, breast-fed for two weeks)

Mine used to be sick [on the bottle]. I was glad when she was off the bottle. (Annie Sinclair, 1947, breast-fed for two days)

It's natural. You don't have to get up in the middle of the night and make bottles. (Jean Richards, 1949, breast-fed for two weeks)

Most women who expressed pro breast-feeding views did so in 'health education' language, or their own version of it. For example, Gina Godfrey had almost a textbook knowledge:

Obviously better for the baby. As my Dad says that's nature's way, that's the way it's supposed to be done. It brings you and the baby closer together. It's better for your own body because you've got to eat properly. Better for your own body physically. I remember reading somewhere that the baby sucking at your breast helps your stomach muscles contract. It's better all round. (1969)

If the mother's healthy, the milk must be healthy. (Bertha Combe, 1922)

Breast-feeding is a good start and it's far more convenient.

Children or animals, can't beat mother's milk. (Polly Williams, 1932)

They're getting everything you're eating. I don't think it's the same with a bottle. (Eleanor Kershaw, 1940)

You've got all the properties in the breast milk that you don't get in the bottles. Psychologists say the baby needs the comfort of the mother and you don't get that with the bottle. It's more comforting than a bottle stuck in its mouth. (Monica Andrews, 1951)

Overall some of these modes of resistance may appear rather weak in Martin's terms (Martin, 1989). Perhaps this is unsurprising given the importance of women defending their own mothering practices. Indeed my research, in asking women to explain 'themselves', could be seen as part of the whole set of practices which checks on mothers. But even though most of the women can be seen as expressing 'acceptance' or 'lament' perhaps there are signs of greater resistance than Martin's hierarchical model suggests. Some women openly and honestly recognized that things had not gone well. Many women wanted to learn and felt that they had learned more since the events described. Some women challenged or disputed received wisdoms of various kinds. Many women joked about their experiences, or expressed anger about what had happened to them. Some women avoided the intrusiveness of health professionals, and those who might want to 'look' at, and judge, their habits in public places by bottle feeding.

FEMINISM, BREAST-FEEDING AND RESISTANCE

The pro breast-feeding lobby, even when, as in the case of Van Esterik it has been influenced by feminism, tends to see women only as victims in the sense of being deprived of their breast-feeding rights by baby milk manufacturers and doctors. I have tried to recognize that, in the face of this complexity, women have pursued 'concrete freedoms' (Rajchman, 1985): assertive bottle feeding; rejecting health advice; defending their right to do what they like; avoiding the complex body management which breast-feeding demands by not doing it; using one medical reason to defeat another; sometimes having the confidence to breast-feed even when medical and other systems militate against it. On the other hand, the women in this study do not have a language out-side of these discourses with which they might challenge some of their underpinning assumptions. What is more, their resistances are for the most part individual and reactive rather than conscious, collective and political.

In this study, as I described in earlier chapters, I have emphasized the necessity of working with differences amongst women. However it appears that feminist approaches to breast-feeding exemplify the fact that, despite the attention to differ-ences amongst women within feminist theory and practice during the last decade, there remains an 'essential unitary woman' at its heart. Differences addressed are of class, race and sexual orientation but feminists are only beginning to address more complex differences, including examining the implications of the unifying category of 'woman' itself. Although femininity and masculinity have been theorized as socially constructed, the social construction of femininity has been difficult for feminists to handle politically. As Riley has noted: 'Below the newly pluralised surfaces, the old pro-blems linger' (1988: 99). For Riley, the concept of 'women's experience' and, as she sees it, the insistence on the import-ance of the distinctiveness of women's bodies by some fem-inists, for example the work of Iragary (1985), represents the tenacious hold of essentialism even while recognizing difference. Despite increasing recognition among feminists of the dangers of generalizing from the experience of (usually) white middle class women there remains a 'con-viction that there is a real or potential common essence to being a woman, which must not suffer eclipse' (ibid: 99).

There are perhaps three main reasons for this reluctance within feminism to abandon at least some aspects of essen-tialism. The first has been highlighted earlier in this chap-ter; it relates to the position of some dimensions of feminism as a reverse discourse in relation to femininity. Some fem-inist thinking turns the values attached to the female on their head, although in so doing accepts the categories of the dominant discourse, in an endorsement of some true underlying femininity. The second reason is the very real political danger of abandoning the category 'woman'. What is feminism is about if it's not about 'woman'? This danger is real, even if we substitute 'women' for 'woman' because of the dominant discourse of western liberalism within which the unified subject is male. To abandon ourselves as women is to disappear into the male subject, possibly denying the significance of reproduction and female sexuality. In undermining the importance of uniquely female activities like breastfeeding we may overlook the human needs and possibilities which arise from these, and further perpetuate the importance of production over and above reproduction. The third reason is that the category 'woman', even if not 'real', is pragmatic and strategic. Since this is how we are designated this is a position from which we can fight our oppression, strategic essentialism as suggested by Fuss (1990), and described in chapter five. Nevertheless, the unchallenged category of 'essential woman' in even feminist writing about infant feeding, has led to a collusive relationship between feminism and dominant discourses.

In relation to infant feeding key questions are whether all women could, and/or would want to, breast-feed were the conditions surrounding it improved. Is breast-feeding in women's interests? These questions will be pursued in the final chapter.

8 Feminism and Infant Feeding: Theory and Policy

In this final chapter I summarize and conclude the arguments presented so far. One important aspect of this study is that we have been able to see the behaviour of those women who fail to conform to normative expectations regarding infant feeding not as irrational and in need of change, but as expressing various forms of resistance to the dominant discourses of femininity within which infant feeding practices are framed. This way of seeing infant feeding leaves us with the major question of whether this is simply an argument in support of women being able to choose between breast-feeding and bottle feeding. This is addressed later in this chapter.

I also return, in this chapter, to the question which has formed a central strand throughout this book: whether women's interests are best served through embracing and valuing sexual difference; or whether gender equality is more effectively sought through playing down the significance of sexual difference. In the opening chapter it was suggested that the breast/bottle controversy symbolized this important and longstanding debate within feminism. On the one hand, bottle feeding might appear to potentially free women from the constraints of reproduction, thus minimizing sexual difference. On the other hand, bottle feeding might deny an important part of womanliness, exposing mothers to exploitation by baby milk manufacturers and to male definitions of sexuality.

SUMMARY OF MAIN ARGUMENTS

In chapter one I contrasted the considerable attention to infant feeding by policy makers and health professionals with the dearth of material concerning women's own experience of infant feeding. The lack of feminist attention to infant feeding was particularly noted. The failure of working class women, young women, and in some cases black and other ethnic minority women, to breast-feed, the focus of much contemporary concern, has in fact been a 'problem' since at least the beginning of the century. We have also seen that in earlier periods unmarried mothers and working mothers were also the focus of attention. Moreover evidence noted in chapter one suggests that disquiet about women's reluctance to do their motherly duty in this respect has been expressed over and over again since at least the eighteenth century.

Whilst not rejecting the importance of the rise of baby milk manufacture, which has been identified as a major element in the decline of breast-feeding, it appeared that other ways of understanding the breast/bottle controversy had been overlooked. An important dimension of infant feeding debates is that they are also debates about women, a 'conversation about femininity' as I described it in earlier chapters. I therefore set out to scrutinize infant feeding texts with this in mind, and to explore women's experiences within the context of practices concerned with femininity. Where feminist comment about infant feeding does exist, it appears to share an essentialist paradigm with much of the mainstream literature. This links breast-feeding with good 'ideal' mothering and sees women's natural capacities as having been oppressed, undermined and exploited by baby milk manufacturers.

There appeared to be a number of immediate problems with this. First, efforts to make women breast-feed and other ways of controlling their feeding habits appear to have existed well before the rise of large scale milk manufacture. Second, the women who are subject to this research and policy attention are often working class, are black, or are younger and less educated; in other words women whose mothering is generally seen as more inherently problematic. Pro breast-feeding policies are therefore pursued through practices geared to checking on mothers, particularly 'deviant', often working class, mothers. Feminists have paid little attention to this. They have seen bottle feeders largely as victims of capitalism and have not been explicitly concerned with the impact of patriarchal relations on infant feeding. Nor have they addressed the importance of differences between women.

Having identified the lack of attention to women's own perspectives on infant feeding, I set out to see their experiences in the contexts of their own lives. This required a theoretical approach which would allow the dominant discourses concerned with breasts and breast-feeding to be deconstructed. Poststructuralist feminist thinking was identified as providing the potential for a fruitful examination of: bodily practices in the context of power relations; the construction of femininity; and indeed with the category of 'women' itself (de Beauvoir, 1953; Brownmiller, 1984; Weedon, 1987; Bartky, 1988; Diamond and Quinby, 1988; Gatens, 1988; Riley, 1988; Smith, 1988; Walkerdine and Lucey, 1989; Butler, 1990b; Flax, 1990; Hekman, 1990; Nicholson, 1990; Threadgold and Cranny-Francis, 1990; Gatens, 1991).

In chapter two I explored the complex discourses about women in terms of motherhood, class and race which are written into the infant feeding literature. This chapter also provided a historical account of infant feeding policies and literature. Although there have been changes in the actual feeding method advocated at particular periods there was some consistency in portraying breast-feeding and women as part of nature, but as needing the assistance of science and professionals to carry out this natural function effectively and appropriately. This has resulted in constant scrutiny of mothers, but few resources provided for infant care. A changing discourse with regard to women's bodies was also identified as being important in shaping infant feeding experiences. Although modesty was a prominent requirement earlier this century, breasts have increasingly been given meaning within a discourse which defines women's bodies in general, and their breasts in particular, as part of active (hetero)sexuality.

The infant feeding experiences of women in a particular locality were explored in several ways. In chapter three their accounts were examined particularly with regard to the 'working conditions' in which infant feeding took place. For the most part these women did not appear to make 'decisions' about infant feeding, which they then pursued in an autonomous fashion. Rather they appeared to have balanced one set of demands against another and adopted practices which best met their own efforts to keep some control over their situation in the face of often competing expectations. Major contradictions existed between the need to maintain respectability in the way their bodies were 'viewed', and on the other hand to offer their babies the 'best' – mother's milk. Lack of control over physical space combined with little support geared specifically to breast-feeding were particularly important in this respect.

As well as similarities within the group, there were also differences. For example, generational differences were most noticeable in that women whose babies were born in the later part of the study period (post 1960s) were more assertive about using bottle feeding as a way of improving their social life; breast-feeding was seen as very restrictive. Within this group there were also women who were conscious of their lack of a language to talk about sexuality and reproduction.

Asian women had very similar experiences of the process of making decisions about infant feeding and, like white women, had a similar lack of control over physical space. For some of the Asian women there were differences from white women in that they had much stronger 'cultural' beliefs about the significance of breast-feeding in mother/child relationships and memories of a country where women had more collective control over private space in which breast-feeding could take place. Despite this, their practices, and reasons for them, were very similar to those of white women, although some of them were left with considerable sadness about the loss they felt that they, and their babies, had suffered in not breast-feeding. It is interesting that their memories are mainly of Pakistan, a Muslim country with considerable restrictions on the ways in which women can present their bodies in 'public'. Breast-feeding in this context therefore does not express freedom and control over one's body, rather a different arrangement of public and private space. Some white women who had babies in the early part of the period covered by the study had similar memories of household space where women breast-fed together, again a different arrangement of public and private.

As well as these variations, there were also many individual differences. What was common was that all the women had to negotiate their way through similar expectations regarding good mothering, modesty and sexual display. But some were able to do this more easily than others because they had greater control over household space and more sympathetic relatives. In addition it was noted that some of those women who successfully breast-fed for longer periods had better resources in terms of material conditions, more support, and fewer health problems.

Through examining the construction of public and private spheres, chapter four took forward the question of how the working conditions of infant feeding have been shaped. This process has rested to a considerable extent on the connection of embodied women with private space, and their exclusion from the public world. How women manage their bodies in public and private space was explored in this chapter and the possibilities of women making use of the 'need' for privacy for their own interests, for example to get time out from work, was considered. It was suggested that the women in this study were so much a part of the private sphere with responsibilities for unpaid domestic work that breast-feeding did not offer 'time out'. It was for many women seen as an extra and very time consuming chore. What is more, it is clear that private worlds are not places where women have control over the space. The complexity of body management was as much an issue in many households as it was in more recognizably public space. It appears that women's space has reduced during the period covered by the study with more merging of men's and women's space even in private households. Moreover, movement of women into the public world, for example into the labour market, has resulted in more apparent merging of the two spheres, but in ways which continue to treat women as inherently embodied and problematic. This chapter concluded by looking at the discursive production of femininity, which has allowed for changes in public and private boundaries whilst women remain defined and controlled as feminine beings. The question of whether femininity is entirely negative for women, in the way, for example, it appears in the work of de Beauvoir (1953), and as it looked for the most part in this chapter, was raised. This issue was pursued in relation to feeding experiences in chapter five.

In chapter five, women's experiences of infant feeding were explored for the ways in which they are, or have become, sexualized. A major dimension of the sexualization of breast-feeding concerned the expectation that women manage their bodies in ways which mean they are 'looked at' at the right time and by the 'right people'. For women who had babies in the earlier period of the study this expectation particularly concerned modesty, the need to be discreet and private. Whilst there was no sharp break, for women who had babies in the later part of the period it was suggested that a shift had occurred which in some respects produced greater complexity. This concerned the more evident demands for attractiveness within a discourse of active heterosexuality. Hence expectations of femininity have changed to incorporate specific forms of overt female sexuality. Being 'looked at' for these women involved slightly different demands, not just for modesty, but also to be both a good mother and a sexy looking woman.

This chapter concluded by re-examining one aspect of the debate about femininity which was introduced in the previous chapter, and which is important in the gender neutrality versus sexual difference debate. This is the question of whether breast-feeding is a 'lost' aspect of female sensuality/sexuality, and whether feminists should therefore fight for conditions under which women can breast-feed, as an assertion of female, rather than male, defined sexuality. It was suggested that it might be possible, through this argument, to deploy a form of strategic essentialism for feminist purposes. It was concluded that, although some forms and uses of essentialist language about female sexuality and mothering might help disrupt current dominant discourses of breasts as heterosexual equipment, recognition of the differences among women suggest that totally basing theory and strategy on this approach could readily become an arm of social control of women. Although we do not know what women's sexuality/sensuality might 'become', what its potential and possibility is, it seems important to avoid basing strategies for resistance on the body as a biological entity, if this is framed within the discourse of nature which has been dominant for several centuries (Keller, 1992). It was suggested that resistance to the discourses of femininity cannot be based on demanding the freedom to be 'natural' since this is to accept the very dichotomies public/private, culture/nature, rational/irrational, mind/body, which are fundamental to the structuring of gender inequality. Rather, it was argued that there are many ways in which women seek control of their lives and, in any case, women live in a range of material and discursive situations. It is difficult to visualize that one goal could be appropriate for all with regard to infant feeding. I address this debate later in this chapter.

In chapter six another aspect of the control of femininity, mothering, was examined. Surveillance of infant feeding as part of a more general pre-occupation with motherhood was identified in chapter two. This can be seen as part of a complex process of medicalization. During this century childbirth has become highly medicalized and, since early feeding experiences have increasingly taken place in hospital settings, the social relations and contexts of infant feeding are medical ones. Infant feeding has thus been drawn into medical arenas. However, somewhat paradoxically, women in this study appeared sometimes to retain more control through bottle feeding. Bottle feeding freed them from what they perceived as the intrusiveness of health professionals, since breast-feeding is deemed by almost everyone as complex and as needing greater levels of professional support/ supervision than bottle feeding. In this way, women appeared to find ways of 'managing' the controls of health professionals providing they were able to resolve the expectation that good mothers ought to breast-feed. They were also able to use the discourses of femininity to fend off and diminish the impact of women health professionals, by dismissing their advice if they were not seen as proper women themselves.

In the final section of this chapter I examined current professional thinking with regard to infant feeding. A particular question concerned why health professionals have not themselves always 'pushed' breast-feeding, despite pro breast-feeding policies. It was suggested that this is partially explained by the fact that there is, for some professionals, evidence of unease about their place within the surveillance of motherhood. This discussion also returned us to consideration of the discourses of femininity. I had noted in this chapter that women as clients use the discourses of femininity to judge women as professionals. The gender neutrality versus sexual difference debate is activated again here. The question of whether it is possible for female dominated professions to become like male professions was raised. I tentatively suggested that women as professionals may be in a position to build different relationships with women as patients or clients, through distancing themselves from the apparently gender neutral, but frequently patriarchal, practices associated with professionalism. Some suggestions for professional practice arising from this study are discussed below.

Chapter seven pursued the debate about the multiple types of resistance to the often contradictory forms of control which operate through infant feeding and (hetero)sexual regimes identified in chapters five and six. Through identifying the complex and often conflicting discourses of breasts and breast-feeding, I suggested that bottle feeders can be seen not as victims, but as women resisting oppression through managing the varied demands of femininity which seek to prescribe their behaviour and shape their subjectivity. It was suggested that the increasing contradiction between breasts as (hetero)sexual objects and breasts for feeding babies produces more complexity, but may also produce greater resistance. There was certainly evidence that women have become increasingly more capable of asserting their own needs. They had no way of fundamentally challenging these discourses however, and for the most part their resistances were individual and reactive. The lack of feminist informed discourse regarding infant feeding is an issue here. Even feminist influenced pro-breast-feeding discourses contain within them a view of breast-feeding as part of the truth of 'woman', an essentialism which then easily becomes bound up with control: the idea that all mothers *can* breast-feed, breast-feeding is good for mothers and babies, and therefore all women *should* breast-feed.

IS CHOICE BETWEEN BREAST-FEEDING AND BOTTLE FEEDING ENOUGH?

When a mother uses a breast milk substitute, money goes from a mother's pocket into that of a manufacturer. (Palmer, 1993: 288)

While this is not strictly true, since in the UK the subsidizing of infant foods has meant that money has often shifted from government to farmers and manufacturers, the broad point remains important however. The manufacture of infant formula is a very profitable business and attempts by organizations like WHO to undermine these profits through control of advertizing and distribution have been vigorously resisted by baby milk manufacturers. What is more, as markets are restricted in the West, those in developing countries are increasingly targeted. Other strategies such as diversification from breast milk substitutes to 'follow on' milk for older children also enables manufacturers to keep a tight hold on the market (*Guardian*, 1985; Community Outlook, 1990). Although there have been very considerable efforts by activists and health organizations to find mechanisms to control the activities of baby milk manufacturers in promoting their products, the effects have remained patchy and progress is continually under threat.

The joint UNICEF/WHO code, adopted in 1981, aimed at restricting the marketing of breast milk substitutes (WHO, 1981a). It called for a ban on general advertizing and on free samples of baby milk in hospitals. It was opposed only by the United States. In 1986 the WHO strengthened this code somewhat but it nevertheless continues to be abused, albeit in a less overt form. In some countries, including the UK, baby milk manufacturers helped government to draft their codes in this way adopting an image of responsibility.

Infant feeding practices are thus shaped to a very large extent by the economic relations of capitalist profit seeking. Whether this economic relationship has totally determined infant feeding patterns is another question. I have quoted a number of pieces of evidence which suggest that this would be too simplistic. The Durham MoH talking in 1907, and quoted at the beginning of chapter two, suggests that women were looking for other ways to feed their babies well before large scale baby milk manufacture. Cadogan's essay in 1749, from which I quoted in chapter one, suggests that frustration with women's failures to breast-feed has a long history. The extensive wet nursing industry in France during the nineteenth and early twentieth centuries similarly indicates that the failure of women to breast-feed their children is not simply a Nestle's product. What is evident in these examples, and is also indicated in this study, is the extent to which persuasion to breast-feed is woven into mechanisms concerned with the control of mothering. Sexual control of women's bodies often conflicts with this, but nevertheless still defines women in terms of their bodies, and of nature.

The social relations of pro-breast-feeding policies involve the attempted control of women by medical and health professionals and by policy makers; control which women sometimes seek to avoid. These mechanisms are part of a range of attentions to mothering, which frequently focus particularly on working class women or others who are identified as deviant. Where breast-feeding is popularly defended and promoted by women it is frequently middle class women who are at the forefront; the evidence of the largely middle class membership of the La Leche League and the National Childbirth Trust discussed in earlier chapters provides strong evidence of this (Gorham and Kellner Andrews, 1990; Kitzinger, 1990). These divisions between women constitute a major problem in addressing this controversy. It is important to recognize that it is the broader social relations surrounding infant feeding which have themselves allowed the development of this profitable industry. Rather than see manufacturers as having created the problem it is more useful to understand that the social relations involving the control of women have allowed the development of the market. In chapter one I referred to Foucault's method of analyzing power which requires an exploration of the webs of power at both micro and macro levels, linked together through complex discourses. In relation to economic systems, Foucault makes an 'ascending analysis of power': 'power relations do indeed 'serve', but not at all because they are 'in the service of' an economic interest taken as primary, rather because they are capable of being utilized in strategies' (Foucault in Gordon, 1980: 142).

Hence, merely to address the economic interests of baby milk manufacture without identifying the power relations which make it possible that this economic interest is profitable is to overlook the larger picture. This larger picture involves many aspects of gender relations as these are experienced within the lives of women. The work of Raphael (1985), based on a cross cultural anthropological study and referred to in earlier chapters, points to the need to understand breast and bottle feeding practices as resulting from very complex social and economic situations. She argues that we should trust mothers to make the best decisions in their own circumstances: 'we must also become more situational in our outlook about feeding behavior, paying attention to such important variables as a mother's lifestyle, her partner's economic status, her network of support, and the amount, availability and accessibility of foods for her and her infant, (Raphael, 1985: 147).

I have suggested, particularly in chapter two, that one facet of most thinking about infant feeding is that it invokes a particular discourse of the natural with regard to women and breast-feeding, and that this is specifically linked to race and class dimensions. Central to the view of breast-feeding as simply 'natural' for women, requiring little in the way of resources and support, is the idea that all women 'in their natural state' can successfully breast-feed. This perception of the naturalness of women gathers further impetus for black women and working class women from the wide-spread and deeply rooted idea that they are closer to nature than their more cultured sisters. Just as in de Beauvoir's terms women are the 'other', the second sex in relation to men, in much of the infant feeding literature, even that influenced by feminism, there is a tendency for black women in particular to become the 'other' in relation to breast-feeding. The breast-feeding habits of third world women are depicted as at times uncontaminated by distorted Western values. Where they are seen as moving away from breast-feeding, lured by baby milk manufacturers, they have become the object of efforts to save them from the effects of western capitalism; western pro-breast-feeding activists and feminists help them to continue to perform their natural functions. In this way they have come to represent the category of natural woman who can be saved for the sake of her children, and to preserve the world's resources. There is a similar tendency for middle class feminists to see poorer women in the West as victims of both baby milk manufacturers and of distorted views about sexuality; again they are 'the other' – women who have not caught on to the possibility of liberation through rediscovering nature. Two further points can be made about this situation.

The first is that the attraction for middle class Western women, particularly socialist feminists, of the natural has come to seem rather suspect, particularly in the wake of the collapse of communist regimes in Eastern Europe (Campbell, 1991; Cockburn, 1991). In the same way that eyebrows are raised in horror at the prospect of poor women in third world cities bottle feeding their babies, Campbell talks of Western socialists 'scolding the people of Eastern Europe for succumbing to the plastic bag and the lure of filthy lucre' (Campbell, 1991: 120). She continues: 'All those people scurrying to the West just to get their hands on things!' (ibid: 120), but reminds us that it was the absence of 'things' which was part of the crisis. In other words, from our relatively luxurious material conditions, and from a fairly privileged position in relation to the discourses of femininity, Western middle class feminists suggest that poorer women do not 'need' baby milk because they have the natural means to feed their babies.

The second point draws on Raphael's findings. She and her colleagues found that in all cultures there were some women who were more successful at breast-feeding than others, and that some babies were more easily breast-fed than others, even by the same mother (Raphael, 1985). In other words, it is not the case that breast-feeding is so natural that all women can do it with the same level of ease and success. Nor, on the other hand, are women's bodies like machines which in the correct conditions will always perform to the same level. Whilst undoubtedly more women could breast-feed than do so, especially given the poor levels of support and advice which have often been offered, this is not the same as saying that there is simply an essential, real, breast-feeding woman inside each of the varied individuals which women are.

We need to ask however whether simply being satisfied that women in our society have a choice about feeding method is enough, given that a major element shaping this choice is a well defended profit motive on a very large scale. Choosing to buy is in fact a very limited choice for women. Walkerdine

and Lucey (1989), in their examination of the influence of
developmental psychology on professional understandings
of child rearing, argue a similar case to the one I have made
about the gendered social class relations of infant feeding.
They show the ways in which working class mothers are
pathologized through practices which demand 'sensitivity'
on the part of mothers. Working class mothers are deemed
insensitive on the basis of middle class norms of mother/
daughter interaction. This results in working class mothers
being regulated by middle class female professionals through
a set of beliefs about mothering 'which set woman against
woman, rendering one normal and the other pathological,
making one responsible for the regulation and the oppression
of the other' (Walkerdine and Lucey, 1989: 5). However
Walkerdine and Lucey are also resistant to what might seem
the logical conclusion to recognizing this, which is to see
working class women as 'equal but different'. They suggest
that this 'denies oppression in a liberal endeavour to produce equality out of a misplaced pluralism' (ibid: 7).

In other words, many working class practices arise out of
restriction and a lack of resources. This does not necessarily imply that it would be better if they could become like
middle class women. Rather, it suggests that feminists cannot simply celebrate bottle feeding amongst working class
women. Although bottle feeding can be used as a part of
resistance to complex demands regarding mothering, it is
important to recognize that it is a form of resistance which
often emerges from relatively little control over resources
and sometimes from poorer health. Some of the conditions
which shape infant feeding practices and experiences are
clearly undesirable. For example, the varied discourses of
femininity which allow women little control over space are
not ones which we can simply ignore on the grounds that
at least women have the choice to bottle feed. Material conditions, including demands on time and resources which
make breast-feeding exhausting and difficult, are only very
minimally addressed through having a choice. The sometimes unhelpful practices of health professionals in relation
to infant feeding are not the best use of the few collective
resources and policies for mothers and children. In other
words we need to expand women's choices and opportunities,

and enhance their confidence in making them, not simply restrict them to the very limited ones available to the women in this study. Whether a pro breast-feeding policy can address these issues without resorting to essentialism and control of difference will be addressed in the following section which looks at current developments in feminist theory.

THEORETICAL CONCLUSIONS: THE SEXUAL DIFFERENCE VERSUS GENDER NEUTRALITY DEBATE

In the final section of the preceding chapter I looked at the implications for feminist theory and practice of attempts to challenge essentialism through radical deconstruction of the category of 'woman'. This is currently a very live and central debate within feminism (Pateman, 1988; Riley, 1988; Scott, 1988; Evans, 1990; Flax, 1990; Lewis and Davies, 1991; Soper, 1991; Bock and James, 1992; Butler, 1993). Feminist theory which argues from a poststructuralist perspective has highlighted the necessity of looking beyond the simple dichotomies of man and woman to recognize the possibility of a vast array of sexual differences and experiences even, perhaps, a proliferation of genders. There is a recognition that the particular feminized category of woman which now dominates gender relations is a product of thinking which took shape in the enlightenment, and which has been reworked, but not fundamentally challenged, since then.

Feminist struggles, for at least the last hundred years, have been dominated by the idea that we should either deny sexual difference and enter the public world as far as possible on the same terms as men, or we should recognize that there are real and important sexual differences associated particularly with the needs arising from reproduction, which should be valued and allowed to flourish. There are now attempts to suggest alternative ways of thinking our way through these apparently opposed strategies. These have partly been encouraged by the rapidly changing nature of our political world, the changes in Eastern Europe for example, and the lessons which can be learned from these developments. What has become clear is that we can neither simply ignore sexual difference, nor build a whole world upon it. It is beginning to be more forcefully argued that what must be addressed are those other categories within which gender relations are wrapped: the relationship between public and private; culture and nature; and mind and body. The meta-narratives of both communism and capitalism have been built on the basis of these dichotomies, with the maintenance of more or less sharp divisions between them. Both of these economic and social systems have been involved in the domination of what is identified as nature, ignoring and exploiting reproduction, in its broadest sense. Whilst in both systems women are no longer trapped entirely within the private world, they nevertheless remain responsible for it and have few resources to go with these responsibilities. They are also continually monitored within the private world, and enter the public world on an entirely unequal basis: 'The form of patriarchy in contemporary Britain is public rather than private. Women are no longer restricted to the domestic hearth, but have the whole society in which to roam and be exploited' (Walby, 1990: 201).

A number of feminist writers now argue that we must change the terms of the debate. Pateman suggests that the question of whether to choose between 'femininity as sub-ordination and the sex-neuter individual' (1988: 226) is the wrong question. As she describes it, in modern patriarchal societies to choose one is *also* to choose the other, since the 'individual' in civil society is male. To ignore sexual difference is to leave it intact. Lewis and Davies (1990) argue that the terms of the equality versus difference debate should be transcended. They argue for a third model, that of 'diversity' in which the range of obligations and activities over an adult's lifetime are recognized and pre-existing inequalities are compensated for. In other words the needs of reproduction and care should be addressed, but should be detached from biological definitions; biology should be seen as cultural rather than only as natural.

Scott (1988) also argues that, since it does not make sense for feminists to give up either equality or difference, it is important to refuse this oppositional dichotomy. She suggests that feminists should not 'buy into the political argument that sameness is a requirement for equality' (Scott, 1988: 48). Gatens (1991) also argues for a conceptualization of the political world which is based on diversity, rather than a narrow, and basically male, idea of the citizen in liberal discourse. She expresses her idea of difference in this way: 'If there is to be a genuinely polymorphous socio-political body, it is clear that it will need to be capable of discriminating and respecting differences amongst its members' (Gatens, 1991: 139).

Other feminists have expressed these notions differently. Kahn (1989) talks of the need for mixed zoning of both public and private time and space, allowing time and resources for activities like breast-feeding, but ensuring that women can also live in what she calls 'linear time', that which dominates the industrial world. In a much earlier examination of the public and the private, Rosaldo argued that for gender equality to be sought, 'the nature of work itself will have to be altered and the asymmetry between work and home reduced' (1974: 42).

The key strands in these arguments appear to be for the need to disrupt the fixity of gender relations, whilst at the same time boosting the importance of reproduction. This also implies that we should not see reproduction as rooted in women's biological capacities, but can accept the importance of these where appropriate. This is best achieved, it is argued, through a merging of the public and private spheres, resulting in new forms of shared, collective responsibilities for caring work.

One important aspect of thinking about these issues in relation to infant feeding is to recognize the extent to which the private and public spheres are already merged and the way in which gendered power relations, particularly in relation to women's bodies, are currently enacted. In this developing language of 'diversity' and 'mixed zoning' there is a danger of building a new kind of 'meta-narrative' in the sense of a new grand Utopian plan, rather than analyzing and building on the forms of resistance which currently arise in the reality of these already merged spheres. Whilst the discourses of femininity are controlling of women, current changes in the social world also allow for forms of resistance to them. In chapter four I suggested that we recognize the increased merging of public and private worlds in ways which depict women's bodies as always problematic and always sexualized. As the private and public worlds have become more integrated and inseparable, discourses of gender and sexuality have not weakened; they may even have intensified. Pateman argues that we have to recognize that at the heart of the 'social contract' the 'story' which has been used to account for the structuring of modern civil society, is a sexual contract, where: 'Civil freedom includes right of sexual access to women and, more broadly, the enjoyment of mastery as a sex' (Pateman, 1988: 225). Because of this, womanhood – female sexuality – is inevitably politically significant. This cannot be changed through grand revolution but through building on individual and collective resistances which challenge the terms on which womanhood is based, without pretending that we are just like men.

I have suggested that in the changing public/private divisions women's bodies have been increasingly shaped by a discourse of active heterosexuality. This changing discourse has played a part in infant feeding practices and experiences through sexualizing breasts. Two points need to be made here. First although I have suggested that this process of sexualization has been oppressive in some respects it is not all embracing. It is both coercive and liberating. Even within the data presented here we can see that for some women these changes have presented the possibility of being more comfortable with one's body and of enabling questions to be asked, even though many women do not have a language which enables them to escape totally from the restrictions of the discourses of heterosexuality. Some women at least have a greater desire to be a subject rather than an object as a body. Flax describes the problem with seeing sexual relations as totally exploitative and controlling. Such a restricted view, she says: 'leaves unexplained how women could ever feel lust for other women and the wide variety of other sensual experiences women claim to have – for example, in masturbation, breast feeding, or playing with children' (Flax, 1990: 53). Hence, although discourses of heterosexuality may complicate breast-feeding, the reverse is also true. Breast-feeding may, at times, offer women a different relationship to their bodies than that defined through the (hetero)sexualization of breasts.

The second point to be made is that these discourses of

heterosexuality are on the move in the context of the changing boundaries of public and private worlds. Whilst patriarchal social relations are able to adapt to the changing position of women they do not go unchallenged. There are a number of examples of fairly fundamental challenges to dominant discourses regarding sexuality. For example, sexual harassment, which has been recognized as a social issue in the workplace for about the last ten years, is currently the subject of considerable attention. More workplaces are adopting policies and devising training programmes which at the very least allow current gender relations to be scrutinized and shifted from the taken-for-granted (Sedley and Benn, 1982; Wise and Stanley, 1987; Stanko, 1988; Rutter, 1989; Curtis, 1993). Related concepts such as 'date (or acquaintance) rape' a term used to describe coercive sex when women have not given consent even when they have chosen to spend time with the man in question are now being aired (Warshaw, 1988; *Guardian*, 14.5.91; *Guardian* 13.10.91). Rape within marriage is now considered to be a criminal offence in this country (House of Lords, 1991).

Although these are similar to other feminist campaigns in relation to rape and child sexual abuse, what is distinctive about these issues is that they all address the 'ordinary' in terms of sex, although of course there is always pressure to push them back into the 'monster' pathological category (Wise and Stanley, 1987). I am not of course suggesting that this is the onward march towards a sexual Utopia. Rather, it is a changing discursive field which gives room for new forms of resistance as well as changing forms of power. With regard to infant feeding this new field offers more possible ways of women thinking about their bodies, which might for some women challenge dominant views. At least the idea that women's bodies are not simply there to be used by others is more frequently articulated. In this study women who said 'I wanted to be out' and 'you can't feed in the toilet' were expressing this.

One major difficulty in collectively challenging discourses relating to the body and sexuality is that feminists have become extraordinarily entangled in the politics of pornography and censorship, as I noted in chapter five. Given the wide range of firmly held beliefs within this and other debates about the body, it is not surprising that the women in this study found it difficult to talk confidently about their bodies when, for example, they were confronted with pictures of women in childbirth. Feminism, as a discursive field in relation to representations of the body, is still caught up with fairly essentialist views about sexuality. This tendency to see pornography on the one hand as an expression of totally exploitative sexual relations, or on the other hand as of little significance, are both based on a view of sexuality as existing in its own right either separate from, or totally dominating, all other relations. Working class women in my study appear to want to talk about bodies, and about sexuality, although they were also afraid of doing so, of being thought a prude, or of not wanting, like Beatrice Callender, to be thought a 'pervert' for having good feelings about breasts. They were cautious about a world and language already heavily sexualized and therefore full of dangers. Ways of talking about sexuality need to understand the connectedness of bodies and sexuality to other areas of women's lives. In relation to breasts and breast-feeding we need a language which helps to take sensuality and pleasure out of a completely (hetero)sexualized arena.

I would add two points to this which relate specifically to breast-feeding. First, it is important to discuss breasts, breast-feeding and sexuality without pressing for an understanding of the 'real' feelings of breast-feeding. We should not try to pin down the truth of breast-feeding. Instead feminists can be open to possibility and difference. The second point follows from this. It is not enough on the other hand to adopt a relativist view. Women's experiences of breasts and breast-feeding have been controlled, shaped, given meaning and contained, to a very considerable extent, through these discourses of femininity, modesty, and (hetero)sexuality. Hence disrupting these discourses through identifying the sensuality of breast-feeding can have an effect on women and lead perhaps to changed practices and experiences of infant feeding. In arguing *against* the mechanisms of control which often arise from active pro-breast-feeding policies, I am not arguing *for* the status quo as far as breasts, bodies and infant feeding are concerned. I am proposing the sort of endless questioning suggested in the last chapter as a strategy for change. This endless questioning is already beginning to happen as part of the changes in private and public boundaries, where new meanings about bodies and sexuality, and about men and women, can be constructed. This endless questioning about breast-feeding should also involve a broader range of women than health professionals and/or middle class breast-feeders.

Three main themes emerge from this discussion of feminist theory which will be used to inform the next section. The first theme is that of disrupting our current gendered categories, particularly of resisting the negative and controlling effects of discourses of femininity. We need to think in terms of expanding difference and possibility with regard to sexuality and gendered subject positions. The second point is that the context for this is a changing relationship between public and private spheres and between culture and nature. What is important here is that, as Pateman (1988) has argued, we cannot simply deny womanhood as a social and political category within these debates. To do so is to almost inevitably deny the significance of reproduction and the real needs and possibilities, both individual and collective, which these involve. Women do not disappear through this process, 'the category of woman does not become useless through deconstruction, but becomes one whose uses are no longer reified' (Butler, 1993: 29). Disrupting the fixity of gendered categories also demands that we question other political categories of which they are a part; the separation of reproduction from public responsibilities, for example. The third point is that it is useful to build on those forms of resistance which already exist, expanding these, and recognizing their local and strategic significance. Hence bottle feeding was used by some women in this study to gain more control and to resist oppressive social relations. It does not therefore follow that bottle feeding is in itself an answer to the many forms of social control which women in this study experienced in their particular position as women with babies, as I have argued above. It did not liberate them to become like men; bottle feeding is not a route to gender neutrality. Rather, it is useful to analyze the complexity of power relations both at micro and macro levels at the same time as identifying resistances.

POLICY AND PRACTICE CONCLUSIONS: STRATEGIES FOR CHANGE

I have argued here that to a considerable extent pro breast-feeding policies have been caught up in mechanisms of control based on essentialist notions of the 'real' and 'natural' woman and that this has tended to be reinforced, rather than challenged, by most feminist discourse. I have also, however, argued that, although 'choice' of breast or bottle offers women a way of managing their lives, it does not tackle the mechanisms of control and the lack of resources which limit, rather than expand, women's choices in relation to how they care for their children, and how they use their bodies. The strategies suggested below are not another over optimistic remedy for poor breast-feeding rates. Aiming to increase breast-feeding is simultaneously far too narrow a goal but also too grand a plan. The aim of these strategies is to enhance the possibility of women, both individually and collectively, defining their own needs and having them met. My suggestions attempt to link individual resistances with collective ones and to work in small ways towards new public/private relations, challenging the controlling aspects of the discourses of femininity.

Questions about the effectiveness of breast-feeding policies can in part be examined in relation to other health education and promotion strategies; indeed breast-feeding can be seen as one of the most long standing health education issues. Critiques of health education have suggested that it is frequently too individualistic and potentially victim blaming in stressing those aspects of people's lives which they choose, or apparently choose, ignoring the more fundamental ways in which health is affected by factors completely beyond the control of individuals (Crawford, 1977; Rodmell and Watt, 1986; Townsend *et al.*, 1988; Blaxter, 1990; Blackburn, 1991). Instead, it is suggested that health education should be conducted in ways which acknowledge that achieving good health is frequently beyond the control of individuals. A better strategy is seen as using and developing methods which specifically address health inequality. One strand in this is the use of community development approaches to health issues (Watt, 1986; Community Health

Action, 1990; Beattie, 1991; Open University Health Education Unit, 1991). Such methods draw on broader community development strategies and on the women's health movement, building on collective action around women's health issues. There are a range of usually small scale projects, often working in the voluntary sector, which adopt this approach to health issues.

The key features of this work are working *with* people on issues identified *by* them, and on working towards change in ways which enhance the control which relatively powerless groups of people have over their own lives. If breastfeeding were to feature in this kind of work, it would be understood as affected by the underpinning issues identified here: lack of space and other resources for mothers and children; the effects of poverty and deprivation; lack of leisure facilities and educational opportunities for women; problematic relations with health and social service professionals: as well as many issues concerning power and sexuality. Working with women on these issues seems more relevant to their needs than just advising them to breast-feed. Within my study clinics as places where women could share space and use professional resources without the same level of intrusiveness as home visits carried positive memories. This indicates that new types of collective resource might be welcomed.

Community development and health strategies can also draw on informal and community education approaches (Freire, 1972; Freire, 1974; Mackie, 1980; Thompson, 1983; Jarvis, 1987). Within these approaches links are made between health issues and literacy campaigns as well as broader political and community education. Although these principles have had their greatest influence in third world countries they have had some impact on educational practice at community levels in the West. The fundamental principles of such strategies are concerned with involving communities in political change in relation to those aspects of social and economic organisation which produce bad health.

There are attempts to identify those aspects of the work of welfare professionals which might be seen as informal education. For example, Jeffs and Smith (1990) argue that informal education can be, and sometimes already is, part of the practice of social workers, youth workers, residential care workers and probation officers. They identify a number of characteristics of informal education which could be made relevant to the work of health professionals, particularly those, like health visitors, whose work is concerned with health education and promotion. In relation to infant feeding this would mean that the health education task would go beyond the technical one of passing on certain pieces of information or advice. As we have seen, simply conveying 'facts' about the goodness of breast-feeding does not take into account the woman's own knowledge and situation, and fails to engage with her broader needs. The task of the informal educator is to promote learning and understanding, rather than simply to convey information. This is based on the idea of education as dialogue. Foster and Mayall (1990) have recently explored the possibilities of using such an approach in health work and make the following statement about the health visitor: 'Through dialogue with people, particularly in groups, she may be able to devise with them means of tackling both structural and individual problems' (Foster and Mayall, 1990: 291). If a health professional adopted this approach to infant feeding discussions she might see the opportunity as one in which a woman's understanding of her body and sexuality could be enhanced, as could her knowledge of why her choices were constrained in a variety of ways. It would of course be an exaggeration to imagine that every encounter between women and health professionals regarding infant feeding might be as momentous as this. But using opportunities to enhance understanding might be a better goal than checking on mothering practices or giving advice in a technical way.

From the interviews conducted for this study, it is possible to see that a process of discussion and reflection produces material which an informal educator could use to deepen women's understanding and enhance their control through greater autonomy. The use of the childbirth pictures described in chapter five is a specific example of the potential for this approach. It might be argued from this that we need to try to produce more relevant pictures. However it is clear that it is not possible to produce neutral images. A more useful strategy might be to find ways to use such material as part of dialogue. From the reactions of the women here one can envisage that greater understanding of why women become the object of the male gaze, of how this affects them, and of fears of exposure and vulnerability, might have developed from a discussion of these pictures in an appropriate setting. Grundy (1987) describes a particular use of photographs of a drunken person by a health educator concerned with alcoholism. The responses of the group were to do with the connections between drunkenness, poverty and powerlessness (ibid: 105). In this situation the educator did not impose meaning; rather the multiple meanings of the photograph were explored and negotiated. Pregnancy, childbirth and infant feeding are opportunities for a more dialogical approach to sex education than women are usually offered. However before one could make a firm suggestion that health professionals view their work in this way, it would be important to ensure that they had opportunity, during their professional training for example, to explore the social construction of sexuality in the context of class, gender, race, (dis)ability and heterosexuality. Reflecting on the way in which all forms of sex education have been policitised in recent years should help us to recognize its potential for challenging and resisting power (Weeks, 1993).

In order for health professionals to work in this way it is important for them to recognize their own place within the normative discourse of health, as some of them are clearly beginning to do. They can attempt to develop complex understandings of health in order to work with a broad range of women. In conveying bodies of health knowledge to others they can find ways to explore its meaning, taking into account the relationship between physical, social and emotional well being. For example, it is not simply a 'fact' that breast-feeding is better for babies. Rather, this needs to be explored, evaluated and its meaning deconstructed in relation to particular contexts. Again race, class and ethnicity are highly significant in doing this. Health professionals need also to be equipped with skills in enabling women to breast-feed. It is not a natural accomplishment. But they need to be able to use these skills in ways which enhance women's confidence and control. It is also important to expand discussions about whether and how women professionals can usefully build on commonality with women as clients and patients. Part of this process must include consideration of racism. The Asian women in this study encountered only white professionals; this clearly offers an even narrower base for common concerns and experiences than work between white professionals and their clients.

There has been significant development in the importance of seeing health education as best pursued as a dialogical process, conducted on a community development basis in relation to AIDS and HIV (Watney, 1987; Aggleton and Homans, 1988; Carter and Watney, 1989; Blaxter, 1991). For example, Watney talks of the need to shift from disciplinary to community based HIV/AIDS education (1989). Although developments which attempt to do this are currently piecemeal and frequently unco-ordinated, their example, and the learning which is arising from them, are important in developing other health and health education strategies.

What is needed, in relation to infant feeding practices, is more imaginative thinking. Women's infant feeding experiences, as reported in this study, reflect the narrowly based and somewhat authoritarian forms of service characteristic of earlier periods of social welfare. Both material and ideological aspects of breast-feeding need to be addressed in the context of mothering more generally. For example, Doyal, drawing on research carried out by the Maternity Alliance (Durward, 1988), noted that 'despite the existence of the British welfare state some women were still not able to feed themselves adequately during pregnancy' (Doyal, 1990: 511). This clearly does not provide an adequate base for breast-feeding. Raphael (1985) points out that breast-feeding requires extra nutrition for mothers which they frequently do not have. A midwife wrote of the hidden costs of breast-feeding which she discovered from her own experience (Scott, 1989). She suggests that women ideally need three nursing bras and money for breast pads and shells. She also found that she needed a larger wardrobe of clothes, such as loose tops, suitable for breast-feeding and that these needed extra washing because of milk leaking from her breasts. It is perhaps unsurprising that breast-feeding rates in America and in Britain have fallen or failed to rise during the latter 1980s given the welfare policies of Regan and Thatcher and consequent

poverty among women and children. Women's needs in relation to the costs of infant care have barely been addressed.
Nor have their needs for various kinds of domestic assistance, as well as company, and opportunities for rest and
leisure. All of these can be pursued with women, not simply
in order that they breast-feed, although one would antici-
pate that more breast-feeding would follow from a situation
where these real needs were negotiated and taken seriously.

Professional strategies and the construction of infant feeding
policies could be conducted on a 'dialogical' basis, in the
sense that knowledge, experience and needs are, where
possible, explored collectively. In this way pro breast-feeding arguments can be subjected to shared scrutiny and judgement rather than being viewed as a set of facts conveyed by
one group of women, health professionals, to another, often
working class women. These strategies can only be slow and
piecemeal however in the context of current government
policy where targeting, performance indicators and objective setting constrain such approaches (Cole-Hamilton, 1991).
They also carry with them the danger of becoming another
arm of normative surveillance, producing new ways in which
women are forced to control their own bodies, in the interests
of others. For this reason it is important that this is not
restricted to health issues but relates to other ways in which
femininity can be deconstructed and challenged. Opportunities for women to experience their bodies outside of discourses of motherhood, femininity and heterosexuality can
therefore be developed. In this way women's football teams
or new forms of cultural representation are just as important as health related efforts.

CONCLUDING COMMENTS

I set out in this book to explore infant feeding from the
perspective of those women who have long been seen as a
problem in relation to their low rates of breast-feeding. I
suggested, in chapter one, that a useful analysis would be
achieved through drawing on feminist perspectives which
have made use of poststructuralist thinking. I have argued
that this approach was necessary to dislodge the tenacity of

the notion of natural woman which is at the heart of infant feeding debates, including the few feminist contributions to these. As well as using this theoretical approach I also argued that we needed to maintain some distance from the dominant pro breast-feeding stance in order to examine the terms within which this position has been constructed.

This perspective has allowed us to question the way in which the category of woman has been devised in relation to infant feeding and to draw attention to differences between women. This has been important in developing a critical analysis of the conditions in which infant feeding takes place. This analysis has not however rested on the notion that all women would breast-feed if these conditions were changed. Instead, attention to differences between women and to women's wish to have control over their bodies and their lives, has alerted us to the need to expand women's choices about how they engage with reproduction and sexuality, rather than limit them to what appears as natural womanly behaviour. Recognizing the inter-connectedness of femininity with the construction of public/private and nature/culture dichotomies indicates that the social and political changes necessary for this expansion of choices are multi-faceted. I set out not only to look at what makes women breast or bottle feed but at how they experienced these. This has revealed great complexity in women's experiences which suggests that neither form of feeding can in itself represent a goal for feminism.

Infant feeding, whilst in some ways a very small part of women's lives, symbolizes many of the central concerns of feminist theory and practice. It also provides the opportunity for more creative thinking about the work of professionals within health and welfare policy. I have shown in this chapter, and in the study as a whole, that, by using theoretical developments which attempt to overcome the limitations of the 'difference versus equality' discourse, it is possible to root feminist strategy in women's own experiences, needs, and practices. Enhancing women's autonomy and control over their own lives presents a more appropriate feminist goal than does more, and longer, breast-feeding. We may however find that these are not always in contradiction with one another.

Bibliography

ABBOTT, P. and R. Sapsford, (1990) 'Health Visiting; Policing the Family?', in P. Abbott and C. Wallace (eds) *The Sociology of the Caring Professions* (Basingstoke: Falmer Press)

ABBOTT, P. and C. WALLACE, (eds) (1990) *The Sociology of the Caring Professions* (Basingstoke: Falmer Press)

AGGLETON, P. and H. HOMANS, (eds) (1988) *Social Aspects of AIDS* (Lewes: Falmer Press)

AHMAD, W.I.U. (1993) (ed) *'Race' and Health in Contemporary Britain* (Buckingham: Open University press)

ALCOCK, P. (1993) *Understanding Poverty* (Basingstoke: Macmillan)

ALDER, E. and J. BANCROFT, (1988) 'The relationship between breast feeding persistence, sexuality and mood in postpartum women', *Psychological Medicine* 18, 2: 389–96

APPLE, R.D. (1987) *Mothers and Medicine: A Social History of Infant Feeding. 1890–1950* (Wisconsin: The University of Wisconsin Press)

ARDITTI, R., R. DUELLI KLEIN, and S. MINDEN, (eds) (1984) *Test Tube Women* (London: Pandora Press)

ASHTON, J. and H. SEYMOUR, (1988) *The New Public Health* (Milton Keynes: Open University Press)

ASSITER, A. (1989) *Pornography, Feminism and the Individual* (London: Pluto Press)

ATTAR, D. (1988) 'Who's Holding the Bottle?', *Trouble and Strife* 13, Spring: 33–46

BACON, C.J. and J.M. WYLIE, (1976) 'Mothers' attitudes to infant feeding at Newcastle General Hospital in summer 1975', *British Medical Journal* 7, February: 308–309

BARRETT, M. and M. MCINTOSH, (1982) *The Anti-Social Family* (London: Verso)

BARTKY, S.L. (1988) 'Foucault, Femininity and the Modernization of Patriarchal Power' in I. Diamond and L. Quinby (eds) *Feminism and Foucault, Reflections on Resistance* (Boston: Northeastern University Press)

BEATTIE, A. (1991) 'Knowledge and control in health promotion: a test case for social policy and social theory' in J. Gape, M. Calnan and M. Bury (eds) *The Sociology of the Health Service* (London: Routledge)

BEDDOE, D. (1989) *Back to Home and Duty – Women Between the Wars 1918–1939* (London: Pandora)

BEELS, C. (1980) *The Childbirth Book* (St Albans, Herts: Granada Publishing)

BENWELL COMMUNITY PROJECT (1978a) *Private Housing and the Working Class* Newcastle on Tyne: Benwell Community Project.

BENWELL COMMUNITY PROJECT (1978b) *Slums on the Drawing Board* Newcastle in Tyne: Benwell Community Projects.

BENWELL COMMUNITY PROJECT (1981) *West Newcastle in Growth and Decline,* Benwell Newcastle on Tyne: Benwell Community Project)

BERGER, J. (1972) *Ways of Seeing* (Harmondsworth: Penguin)
BETTERTON, R. (Ed) (1987) *Looking On: Images of Femininity in the Visual Arts and Media* (London: Pandora)
BILLINGHAM, K. (1986) 'The Politics of Breast Feeding', *Health Visitor* 59, June: 184–186
BISSETT, L. (1986) 'Public Virtue, Private Vice', *New Socialist* June: 28–30
BLACKBURN, C. (1991) *Poverty and Health, Working with Families* (Buckingham: Open University Press)
BLAXTER, M. (1990) *Health and Lifestyles* (London: Routledge)
BLAXTER, M. (1991) *AIDS: Worldwide Policies and Problems* (London: Office of Health Economics)
BLAXTER, M. and E. PATERSON, (1982) *Mothers and Daughters: A Three-Generational Study of Health Attitudes and Behaviour* (London: Heinemann)
BOCK, G. and S. JAMES, (1992) (eds) *Beyond Equality and Difference* (London: Routledge)
BORCHORST, A. and B. Siime, (1987) 'Women and the advanced welfare state – a new kind of patriarchal power?' in A. Showstack Sassoon (ed) *Women and the State* (London: Hutchinson)
BROCKWAY, L. (1986) 'Hair colour and problems in breast feeding', *Midwives Chronicle* March, 99 (1178): 66–7
BROWN, R.E. (1988) 'Breastfeeding in the United States' in D.B. Jelliffe and E.F.P. Jelliffe (eds) *Programmes to Promote Breastfeeding* (Oxford: Oxford University Press)
BROWN, G. and T. HARRIS, (1978) *The Social Origins of Depression* (London: Tavistock)
BROWNMILLER, S. (1984) *Femininity* (London: Paladin Grafton Books)
BRYAN, B., S. DADZIE, and S. SCAFE (1985) *The Heart of the Race: Black Women's Lives in Britain* (London: Virago)
BRUCE, M. (1968) *The Coming of the Welfare State* (London: Batsford)
BUREAU OF SOCIAL RESEARCH FOR TYNESIDE (1927) *Infant Welfare on Tyneside*, Tyneside Papers, 8 (Newcastle on Tyne: Bureau of Social Research for Tyneside)
BUTLER, J. (1990a) 'Gender Trouble, Feminist Theory, and Psychoanalytic Discourse' in L. Nicholson (ed) *Feminism/ Postmodernism* (London: Routledge)
BUTLER, J. (1990b) *Gender Trouble, Feminism and the Subversion of Identity* (London: Routledge)
BUTLER, J. (1993) *Bodies That Matter* (London: Routledge)
CADOGAN, W. (1749) 'An Essay upon Nursing' in W. Kessen (ed) (1965) *The Child* (New York: Wiley and Sons)
CAIN, M. (ed) (1989) *Growing Up Good. Policing the Behaviour of Girls in Europe* (London: Sage)
CAMPBELL, B. (1987) 'A Feminist Sexual Politics: Now You See It, Now You Don't' in Feminist Review (ed) *Sexuality, A Reader* (London: Virago)
CAMPBELL, B. (1988) *Unofficial Secrets* (London: Virago)
CAMPBELL, B. (1991) '1989 and All That', Feminist Review Special Issue 39, Winter: 119–123

CAMPBELL, C.E. (1984) 'Nestle and Breast vs Bottle Feeding: Mainstream and Marxist Perspectives' *International Journal of Health Services* 14, 4: 547–567

CARLEN, P. and A. WORRALL, (eds) (1987) *Gender, Crime and Justice* (Milton Keynes: Open University Press)

CARTER, P. (1992) *Breast and Bottle Feeding in West Newcastle 1920–1980: A Study of Women's Experiences* (unpublished PhD thesis, Newcastle Polytechnic)

CARTER, E. and S. WATNEY, (eds) (1989) *Taking Liberties: Aids and Cultural Politics* (London: Serpent's Tail)

CHAMBERLAIN, M. (1981) *Old Wives Tales. Their History, Remedies and Spells* (London: Virago)

CHESTER, G. and J. DICKEY, (eds) (1988) *Feminism and Censorship. The Current Debate* (Bridport: Prism Press)

CHETLEY, A. (1986) *The Politics of Baby Foods: Successful challenges to Marketing Strategies* (London: Frances Pinter)

CHILD POVERTY ACTION GROUP (1985) *Poverty and Food* (London: CPAG)

CITY OF NEWCASTLE ON TYNE (1988) *Newcastle upon Tyne 'City Profiles', Results from the 1986 Household Survey*, Policy Services Department

CLARK, D. (1993) '"With My Body I Thee Worship": The Social Construction of Marital Sex Problems' in D. Morgan and S. Scott (eds) *Body Matters: Essays on the Sociology of the Body* (Buningstone: Falmer)

COCKBURN, C. (1991) 'In Listening Mode' in *Feminist Review* Special 39, Winter: 124–126

COLE-HAMILTON, I. and T. LANG, (1986) *Tightening Belts – a Report on the Impact of Poverty on Food* (London: London Food Commission)

COLE-HAMILTON, I. (1991) *Poverty can Seriously Damage Your Health* (London: Child Poverty Action Group)

COMMUNITY HEALTH ACTION (1990) *Community Participation in Health for All by the Year 2000* 15, Spring (London: National Community Health Resource)

COMMUNITY OUTLOOK (1990) *Follow on milk* January 16:8

COREA, G., R., DUELLI KLEIN, J., HANMER, H.B., HOLMES, B., HOSKINS, M., KISHWAR, J., RAYMOND, R. ROWLAND, and R. STEINBACHER, (1985) *Man-Made Women: how new reproductive technologies affect women* (London: Hutchinson)

COREIL, J. and J.E. MURPHY, (1988) 'Maternal commitment, lactation practices and breastfeeding duration' *Journal of Obstetric, Gynecologic and Neonatal Nursing (JOGNN)* July–August, 17,4: 273–8

COSSLETT, T. (1994) *Women Writing Childbirth*, (Manchester: Manchester University Press)

COSTELLO, A., M. SHAHJAHAN, and B. WALLACE (1992) 'Nutrition for Bandladeshi Babies', *Community Outlook*, April, 21–23

COUNTY COUNCIL OF DURHAM (1907) *Report of the County Medical Officer on the High Infant Mortality in the Administrative County of Durham*

COVENEY, L., M., JACKSON, S., JEFFREYS, L. KAYE, L. and P.

MAHONEY, (1984) *The Sexuality Papers. Male Sexuality and the Social Control of Women* (London: Hutchinson)

COWARD, R. (1984) *Female Desire* (London: Granada)

COWARD, R. (1987) 'What is pornography?' in R. Betterton, (ed) *Looking On: Images of Femininity in the Visual Arts and Media* (London: Pandora)

COWARD, R. (1989) *The Whole Truth* (London: Faber and Faber)

COWARD, R. and J. SPENCE, (1987) 'Body Talk' in J. Spence, P. Holland and S. Watney (eds) *Photography/ Politics two* (London: Comedia)

CRAWFORD, R. (1977) 'You are dangerous to your health: the ideology and politics of victim blaming', *International Journal of Health Service* 7, 4: 663–680

CROW, G. (1989) 'The Post-War Development of the Modern Domestic Ideal' in G. Allan and G. Crow (eds) *Home and Family: Creating the Domestic Sphere* (Basingstoke: Macmillan)

CUNNINGHAM, A.S. (1988) 'An historical overview of breastfeeding promotion in Western Europe and North America' in D.B. Jelliffe and E.F.P. Jelliffe (eds) *Programmes to Promote Breastfeeding* (Oxford: Oxford University Press)

CURTIS, L.A. (1993) *Making Advances* (London: BBC Books)

DALE, J. and P. FOSTER, (1986) *Feminists and State Welfare* (London: Routledge and Kegan Paul)

DALY, M. (1979) *Gyn/Ecology: The Meraetics of Radical Feminism* (London: The Women's Press)

DARKE, S. (1988) 'Return to breast feeding in the United Kingdom: reasons, implementation, and prospects' in D.B. Jelliffe and E.F.P. Jelliffe (eds) *Programmes to Promote Breastfeeding* (Oxford: Oxford University Press)

DAVIDOFF, L. (1983) 'Class and Gender in Victorian England', in J. L. Newton, M.P. Ryan and J.R. Walkowitz (eds) *Sex and Class in Women's History* (London: Routledge and Kegan Paul)

DAVIES, K. (1990) *Women, Time and the Weaving of the Strands of Everyday Life* (Aldershot: Gower)

DE BEAUVOIR, S. (1953) *The Second Sex* (London: Jonathan Cape)

DENNIS, N. F., HENRIQUES, and C. SLAUGHTER, (1956) *Coal is our Life* (London: Eyre and Spottiswoode)

DHSS (1974) *Present Day Practice in Infant Feeding* (London: HMSO [Reports on Health and Social Subjects: No 9])

DHSS (1976) *Prevention and Health: Everybody's Business* (London: HMSO)

DHSS (1980) *Present Day Practice in Infant Feeding: 1980* (London: HMSO [Reports on Health and Social Subjects: No 20])

DHSS (1988) *Present Day Practice in Infant Feeding: Third Report* (London: HMSO [Reports on Health and Social Subjects: No 32])

DoH (1988) *Caring for the Breastfeeding Mother: 'The Lost 25 per cent,'* Report of a conference on 18th October 1988 to launch a Joint Breastfeeding Initiative

DoH (1993) *Changing Childbirth: Report of the Expert Maternity Group*, (HMSO)

DIAMOND, I. and L. QUINBY, (eds) (1988) *Feminism and Foucault, Re-*

flections on Resistance (Boston: Northeastern University Press)

DINGWALL, R.W.J. (1977) 'Collectivism, Regionalism and Feminism: Health Visiting and British Social Policy 1850–1975', *Journal of Social Policy* 6, 3: 291–315

DOMINELLI, L. (1991) *Women Across the Continents. Feminist Comparative Social Policy* (Hemel Hempstead: Wheatsheaf)

DOMINELLI, L. and E. MCLEOD, (1989) *Feminist Social Work* (Basingstoke: Macmillan)

DONNISON, J. (1977) *Midwives and Medical Men – A History of Inter-Professional Rivalries and Women's Rights* (London: Heinemann Educational Books)

DONZELOT, J. (1980) *The Policing of Families* (London: Hutchinson)

DOUGLAS, M. (1975) *Implicit Meanings* (London: Routledge and Kegan Paul)

DOYAL, L. (1983) 'Women, health and the sexual division of labour: a case study of the women's health movement in Britain', *Critical Social Policy* 7, Summer: 21–23

DOYAL, L. (1985) 'Women and the National Health Service: The Carers and the Careless' in E. Lewin and V. Oleson (eds) *Women, Health and Healing* (London: Tavistock)

DOYAL, L. (1987) 'Infertility – a Life Sentence? Women and the National Health Service' in Stanworth, M. (ed) *Reproductive Technologies, Gender, Motherhood and Medicine* (Cambridge: Polity/Oxford: Blackwell)

DOYAL, L. (1990) 'Hazards of Hearth and Home (Health at Home and in Waged Work Part One)', *Women's Studies International Forum* 13,5: 501– 517

DURWARD, L. (1988) *Poverty in Pregnancy* (London: Maternity Alliance)

DYBALL, C. (1992) *Breastfeeding and the Social Control of Women* (Unpublished PhD thesis, Open University)

DYHOUSE, C. (1981) *Girls Growing up in Late Victoria and Edwardian England* (London: Routledge & Kegan Paul)

EHRENREICH, B. and D. ENGLISH (1979) *For Her Own Good 150 Years of Experts' Advice to Women* (London: Pluto)

EIGER, M.S. and S.W. OLDS (1972) *The Complete Book of Breastfeeding* (New York: Workman)

ELLIS, H. (1903) *Studies in the Psychology of Sex, vol 111, Analysis of the Sexual Impulse in Women* (Philadelphia: F.A. Davies)

EVANS, M. (1985) *Simone de Beauvoir: A Feminist Mandarin* (Tavistock: London)

EVANS, M. (1990) 'The Problem of Gender for Women's Studies', *Women's Studies International Forum* 13,5: 457–462

EVANS, N., I.R. WALPOLE, M.O. QUERESH, H.M. MORON and H. W. EVELY JONES (1976) 'Lack of breast feeding and early weaning of Infants of Asian immigrants to Wolverhampton', *Archives of Disease in Childhood* 51: 608–612

EVANS, S. (1980) 'Breastfeeding', *Spare Rib* 101, Dec: 49–52

EVERINGHAM, C. (1994) *Motherhood and Modernity* (Buckingham: Open University Press)

FAIRWEATHER, E., R. McDONOUGH and M. McFADYEAN (1984) *Only the Rivers Run Free. Northern Ireland: The Women's War* (London: Pluto)

FIELD, S., J. DRAPER, M. KERR and M.J. HARE (1982) 'A Consumer View of the Health Visiting Service', *Health Visitor* 55: 299–301

FILDES, V. (1986) *Breasts, Bottles and Babies. A History of Infant Feeding* (Edinburgh: Edinburgh University Press)

FILDES, V. (1987) 'Infant Feeding in the Bible', *Midwife, Health Visitor and Community Nurse* July, 23: 7

FILDES, V. (1988) *Wet Nursing – A History from Antiquity to the Present* (Oxford: Basil Blackwell)

FINCH, J. (1989) *Family Obligations and Social Change* (Cambridge: Polity Press)

FINCH, J. and D. GROVES (eds) (1983) *A Labour of Love: Women, Work and Caring* (London: Routledge and Kegan Paul)

FISHER, C. (1985) 'How did we go wrong with breast feeding?', *Midwifery* 1: 48–51

FISHER, C. (1986) 'On demand breastfeeding' *Midwife Health Visitor and Community Nurse* 22, June: 194–198

FLAX, J. (1990) 'Postmodernism and Gender Relations in Feminist Theory' in L. Nicholson (ed) *Feminism/Postmodernism* (London: Routledge)

FOOD AND AGRICULTURE ORGANIZATION OF THE UNITED NATIONS (FAO) (1979) *Women in Food Production, Food Handling and Nutrition* (Rome: FAO)

FORMAN, F.J. and C. SOWTON (eds) (1989) *Taking our Time: Feminist Perspectives on Temporality* (Oxford: Pergamon)

FOSTER, M.-C. and B. MAYALL (1990) 'Health visitors as educators', *Journal of Advanced Nursing* 15: 286–292

FOUCAULT, M. (1977) *The Archaeology of Knowledge* (London: Tavistock)

FOUCAULT, M. (1979) *Discipline and Punish* (Harmondsworth: Penguin)

FOUCAULT, M. (1981) *The History of Sexuality Volume 1, An Introduction* (Harmondsworth: Penguin)

FRANKENBERG, R. (1993) 'Growing up White! Feminism, Racism and the Social Geography of Childhood', *Feminine Review*, 45: 51–84

FREEMAN, C.K. and N.K. LOWE (1993) Breastfeeding Care in Ohio Hospitals: A Gap Between Research and Practice', *JOGNN*; September/October, 22: 5, 447–455

FREIRE, P. (1972) *Pedagogy of the Oppressed* (Harmondsworth: Penguin)

FREIRE, P. (1974) *Education: The Practice of Freedom* (London: Writers and Readers Publishing Cooperative)

FUSS, D. (1989) *Essentially Speaking. Feminism, Nature and Difference* (London: Routledge)

GAMARNIKOW, E., D. MORGAN, J. PURVIS and D. TAYLORSON (eds) (1983) *The Public and the Private* (London: Heinemann)

GARFORTH, S. and J. GARCIA (1989) 'Breastfeeding policies in practice – "No wonder they get confused"', *Midwifery* 5: 75–83

GASKIN, I.M. (1988) 'Midwifery Reinvented' in S. Kitzinger (ed) *The Midwife Challenge* (London: Pandora)

GATENS, M. (1988) 'Towards a feminist philosophy of the body' in B. Caine, E. A. Grosz and M. de Lepervanche (eds) *Crossing Boundaries: Feminism and the Critiques of Knowledges* (Sydney: Allen and Unwin)

GATENS, M. (1991) *Feminism and Philosophy* (Cambridge: Polity Oxford: Basil Blackwell)

GIEVE, K. (1987) 'Rethinking Feminist Attitudes Towards Mothering', *Feminist Review*, 25: Spring, 38–45

GOEL, K.M., F. HOUSE and R.A. SHANKS (1978) 'Infant Feeding Practices among Immigrants in Glasgow', *British Medical Journal* 2: 1181–1183

GOLDFARB, J. and E. TIBBETTS (1980) *Breastfeeding Handbook. A Practical Reference Book for Physicians, Nurses and other Health Professionals* (Montagne, France: Ensloe Publishers)

GOMM, R. (1976) 'Breast – Best or Bestial?' *Midwife, Health Visitor and Community Nurse*, October, 12: 317–321

GORDON, C. (ed) (1980) *Power/Knowledge Selected Interviews and Other Writings 1972–77 Michel Foucault* (Brighton: Harvester Press)

GORDON, L. (1985) 'The Struggle for Reproductive Freedom: Three Stages of Feminism' in Z.R. Eisenstein (ed) *Capitalist Patriarchy and the Case for Socialist Feminism* (New York: New York Monthly Review Press) cited in H. Eisenstein *Contemporary Feminist Thought* (Hemel Hempstead: Unwin)

GORDON, L. (1989) *Heroes of their own Lives: the Politics and History of Family Violence* (London: Virago)

GORHAM, D. and F. KELLNER and REWS (1990) 'The La Leche League: A Feminist Perspective' in K. Arnup, A. Levesque and R. Roach Pierson (eds) *Delivering Motherhood – Maternal ideologies and Practices in the 19th and 20th Centuries* (London: Routledge)

GRAHAM, H. (1976) 'Smoking in Pregnancy: The Attitudes of Expectant Mothers', *Social Science and Medicine* 10: 399–405

GRAHAM, H. (1984) *Women, Health and the Family* (Brighton: Wheatsheaf)

GRAHAM, H. (1993) *When Life's a Drag: Women Smoking and Disadvantage* (London: DoH HMSO)

GRAHAM H. and A. OAKLEY (1981) 'Competing ideologies of reproduction: medical and maternal perspectives on pregnancy' in H. Roberts (eds) *Women Health and Reproduction* (London: Routledge and Kegan Paul)

GREER, G. (1984) *Sex and Destiny* (London: Secker and Warburg)

GREGSON, B. and S. BOND (1989) *Infant Feeding Survey: Interim Report to the North Tees Health Authority, Department of Midwifery* (Newcastle on Tyne: Centre for Health Care Research, University of Newcastle on Tyne)

GRIFFIN, S. (1984) *Woman and Nature: The Roaring Insider Her* (London: The Universities)

GRIMSLEY, M. and A. BHAT (1988) 'Health in Britain's Black Population: A New Perspective' in A. Bhat, R. Carr-Hill and S. Ohri (eds) The Radical Statistics Race Group *Britain's Black Population* (Aldershot: Gower)

GRUNDY, S. (1987) *Curriculum: Product or Praxis* (Lewes: Falmer Press)

GUARDIAN (28th Nov 1985) 'Anger as ministry backs new baby milk'

GUARDIAN (6th Feb 1990) 'Hide and seek'

HALL, R. (ed) (1981) *Dear Dr Stopes* (Harmondsworth: Penguin)

HALL, D.J. and B.A. BERRY (1985) 'Breast feeding: differences in prevalence between caucasian and negroid women in Paddington and North Kensington, London', *Journal of Advanced Nursing* 10: 173–177

HALLY, M.R., J. BOND, E. BROWN, J. CRAWLEY, B.A. GREGSON, P. PHILIPS and I. RUSSELL (1981) *A Study of Infant Feeding* (Newcastle upon Tyne: Health Care Research Unit, University of Newcastle upon Tyne)

HANMER, J. and D. STATHAM (1988) *Women and Social Work* (Basingstoke: BASW/Macmillan)

HARDYMENT, C. (1983) *Dream Babies* (Oxford: Oxford University Press)

HARTMANN, H. (1981) 'The family as the locus of gender, class and political struggle: the example of housework', *Signs* 6,3: 366–91

HAWKINS, L.M., F.H. NICHOLS and J.L. TANNER (1987) 'Predictors of the Duration of Breastfeeding in Low-income Women', *Birth* 14,4, December: 204–9

HEALTH EDUCATION COUNCIL (HEC) (1984) *Pregnancy Book* (London: Health Education Council)

HEALTH VISITOR (1991) *EC draft threatens breastfeeding*, 64,3 March: 64

HEARN, J. (1985) 'Patriarchy, Professionalisation and the Semi-Professions' in C. Ungerson (ed) *Women and Social Policy* (London: Macmillan)

HEARN, J. (1987) *The Gender of Oppression* (Brighton: Wheatsheaf)

HEARN, J. and W. PARKIN (1987) *'Sex' at 'Work'. The Power and Paradox of Organisation Sexuality* (Brighton: Wheatsheaf)

HEARN, J., D.L. SHEPPARD, TANCRED-SHERIFF P. and BURRELL, G. (eds) (1989) *The Sexuality of Organisation* (London: Sage)

HEITLINGER, A. (1987) *Reproduction, Medicine and the Socialist State* (Basingstoke: Macmillan)

HEKMAN, S.J. (1990) *Gender and Knowledge: Elements of a Postmodern Feminism* (Cambridge: Polity Press)

HELLINGS, P. (1985) 'A discriminant model to predict breast feeding success', *Community Nurse Research* Fall, 18: 15–24

HELSING, E. and F. SAVAGE KING (1982) *Breast-Feeding in Practice* (Oxford: Oxford University Press)

HENRIQUES, F. (1959) *The Sociology of Sex* (London: MacGibbon and Kee)

HENSCHEL, D. (1989) 'Breast Feeding in Adversity – Out of the Doldrums?' *Midwives Chronicle and Nursing Notes* December: 402–407

HEWAT, R.J., and D.J. ELLIS (1986) 'Similarities and differences between women who breastfeed for short and long duration', *Midwifery*, 2: 37–43

HEWITT, M. (1958) *Wives and Mothers in Victorian Industry* (Letchworth: Loxley Bros)

HICKSON, W. (1840) *Handloom Weavers Report* (London: Report from the Commissioners on the State of Handloom Weavers)

HILLMAN, J. (1989) 'Family Life' in A. While (ed) *Health in the Inner City* (Oxford: Heinemann)

HOMANS, H. (ed) (1985) *The Sexual Politics of Reproduction* (Aldershot: Gower)

HOOKS, B. (1982) *Ain't I a Woman. Black Women and Feminism* (London: Pluto)

HOUSE OF LORDS (1991) *R v. R* (rape: marital exemption)

HUNT, M. (1990) 'The De-eroticisation of Womens Liberation: Social

Purity Movements and the Revolutionary Feminism of Sheila Jeffreys', *Feminist Review* 34: 23–46

HUTTER, B and G. WILLIAMS (eds) (1981) *Controlling Women: The Normal and the Deviant* (London: Croom Helm)

IMRAY, L. and A. MIDDLETON (1983) 'Public and Private: Marking the Boundaries' in E. Gamarnikow, D. Morgan, J. Purvis and D. Taylorson (eds) *The Public and the Private* (London: Heinemann)

IRIGARY, L. (1985) *This Sex Which Is Not One*, trans. Catherine Porter with Carolyn Burke (Ithaca: Cornell University Press)

JARVIS, P. (ed) (1987) *Twentieth Century Thinkers in Adult Education* (London: Croom Helm)

JELLIFFE, D.B. and E.F.P. JELLIFFE (1978) *Human Milk in the Modern World* (Oxford: Oxford University Press)

JELLIFFE, D.B. and E.F.P. JELLIFFE (eds) (1988) *Programmes to Promote Breastfeeding* (Oxford: Oxford University Press)

JEFFREYS, S. (1985) *The Spinster and her Enemies. Feminism and Sexuality 1880–1930* (London: Pandora)

JEFFS, T. and M. SMITH (eds) (1990) *Using Informal Education* (Buckingham: Open University Press)

JENNER, S. (1988) 'The influence of additional information, advice and support on the success of breastfeeding in working class primaparas', *Child: care, health and development* 14: 319–328

JIVANI, S.K. (1978) 'The practice of infant feeding among Asian immigrants', *Archives of Disease in Childhood* 53: 69–73

JOINT BREASTFEEDING INITIATIVE (1990) *Survey on Restaurant Facilities* (London: Joint Breastfeeding Initiative)

JOLLY, H. (1980) *Book of Child Care – the complete guide for today's parents* (London: Sphere Books)

JONES, R.A.K. and E.M. BELSEY (1977) 'Breast Feeding in an Inner London Borough – A Study of Cultural Factors' *Social Science in Medicine*, 11: 175–179

JONES, D.A., R.R. WEST and R.G. NEWCOMBE (1986) 'Maternal Characteristics associated with the duration of breast-feeding', *Midwifery* 2: 141–146

JONES, D.A. (1987) 'The choice to breast feed or bottle feed and influences on that choice: a survey of 1525 mothers', *Child: Care health and development* 13: 75–85

JORDAN, P. (1986) 'Breastfeeding as a Risk Factor for Fathers', *Journal of Obstetric, Gynecologic and Neonatal Nursing (JOGNN)* March/April: 94–96

JORDAN, J. (1974) *The White Man's Burden* (New York: Oxford University Press)

KAHN, R.P. (1989) 'Women and Time in Childbirth and During Lactation' in F.J. Forman and C. Sowton, C. (eds) *Taking our Time: Feminist Perspectives on Temporality* (Oxford: Pergamon)

KELLER, E.F. (1992) *Secrets of Life, Secrets of Death* (London: Routledge)

KENNER, C. (1985) *No Time for Women – Exploring Women's health in the 1930s and Today* (London: Pandora)

KERR, M. (1958) *The People of Ship Street* (London: Routledge and Kegan Paul)

KESSEN, W. (1965) *The Child* (New York: John Wiley and Sons)

KHATIB-CHAHIDI, J. (1992) 'Milk Kinship in Shi'ite Islamic Iran' in V. Maher (ed) *The Anthropology of Breast-Feeding* (Oxford: Berg)

KINSEY, A., W.B. POMEROY, C.E. MARTIN and P.H. GEBHARD (1953) *Sexual Behaviour in the Human Female* (Philadelphia: W.B. Saunders and Co)

KITZINGER, J. (1990) 'Strategies of the Early Childbirth Movement: A Case-Study of the National Childbirth Trust' in J. Garcia, R. Kilpatrick and M. Richards (eds) *The Politics of Maternity Services for Childbearing Women in Twentieth Century Britain* (Oxford: Clarendon Press)

KITZINGER, S. (1979) *The Experience of Breastfeeding* (Harmondsworth: Penguin)

KLEIN, R. (1989) *The Politics of the NHS* (Harlow: Longman)

KNAUER, M. (1985) 'Breastfeeding and the Return of Menstruation in Urban Canadian Mothers practising "Natural Mothering"' in V. Hull and M. Simpson (eds) *Breastfeeding, Child Health and Spacing* (Beckenham: Croom Helm)

KURINJI, N., P.H. SHIONO and G.G. RHOADS (1988) 'Breast-feeding incidence and duration in Black and White women', *Pediatrics* March 81,3: 365–71

KWAKWA, J.F. (1984) 'Don't Push Breast Feeding!', *Midwives Chronicle and Nursing Notes* April: 126

LANG, T. (1984) *Jam Tomorrow?* (Manchester: Food Policy Unit Manchester Polytechnic)

LANG, T. (1986/7) 'The new food policies', *Critical Social Policy* Winter, 18: 32–47

LAQUEUR, T. (1986) 'Orgasm, Generation, and the Politics of Reproductive Biology', *Representations*, 14: 1–14

LAQUEUR, T. (1990) *Making Sex* (Cambridge, Massachusetts: Harvard University Press)

LASCH, C. (1977) *Haven in a Heartless World* (New York: Basic Books)

LAWRENCE, R.A. (1988) 'Influences: major difficulties in promoting breastfeeding: US perspectives' in D.B. Jelliffe and E.F.P. Jelliffe (eds) *Programmes to Promote Breastfeeding* (Oxford: Oxford University Press)

LEATHARD, A. (1990) *Health Care Provision, Past Present and Future* (London: Chapman and Hall)

LEEPER, J.D., MILO T. and COLLINS, T.R. (1983) 'Infant Feeding and Maternal Attitudes Among Mothers of Low-Income' *Psychological Reports*, 53, 259–265

LESLIE, A. (1986) 'Survey on Infant feeding', *Health Visitor*, June, 59: 173–174

LEWIS, J. (1980) *The Politics of Motherhood: Child and Maternal Welfare in England, 1900–1939* (London: Croom Helm)

LEWIS, J. (1984) *Women in England 1870–1950: Sexual Divisions and Social Change* (Brighton: Wheatsheaf)

LEWIS, J. (1990) 'Mothers and Maternity Policies in the Twentieth Century' in J. Garcia, R. Kilpatrick and M. Richards (eds) *The Politics of Maternity Services for Childbearing Women in Twentieth Century Britain* (Oxford: Clarendon Press)

Bibliography 251

LEWIS, J. and C. DAVIES (1991) 'Protective Legislation in Britain, 1870–1990: equality, difference and their implication for women', *Policy and Politics* 19,1: 13–25

LEWIS, J. and B. MEREDITH (1988) *Daughters who Care* (London: Routledge)

LEWIS, J. (1992) *Women in Britain since 1945* (Oxford: Blackwell)

LLEWELYN DAVIES, M. (ed) (1978) *Maternity – Letters from Working Women* (London: Virago)

LIN, M.M. (1991) 'Breast feeding and weaning practices among Pakistani and Chinese communities in Newcastle upon Tyne' (unpublished M.Sc. dissertation: University of London)

LITTLE, J., L. PEAKE and P. RICHARDSON (eds) (1988) *Women in Cities* (London: Macmillan)

LORDE, A. (1980) *The Cancer Journals* (Argyle, NY: Spinsters Ink)

LORENTZON, M. (1990) 'Professional Status and Managerial Tasks: Feminine Service Ideology in British Nursing and Social Work' in P. Abbott and C. Wallace (eds) *The Sociology of the Caring Professions* (Basingstoke: Falmer Press)

LUKER, K. and J. ORR (eds) (1985) *Health Visiting* (Oxford: Blackwell)

LUTHERA, M.S. (1988) 'Race, community, housing and the state – a historical overview' in A. Bhat, R. Carr-Hill and S. Ohri (eds) *Britain's Black Population* (Aldershot: Gower)

MACCANNELL, D. and J. MACCANNELL (1987) 'The Beauty System' in N. Armstrong and L. Tennenhouse (eds) *The Ideology of Conduct* (London: Methuen)

MACINTYRE, S. (1982) 'Rhetoric and Reality. Mothers' Breastfeeding Intentions and Experiences', *Research and the Midwife Conference Proceedings*: 39–62

MACKIE, R. (ed) (1980) *Literacy and Revolution. The Pedagogy of Paulo Freire* (London: Pluto Press)

MACKINNON, C. (1982) 'Feminism, Marxism, Method, and the State', *Signs*, 7, 3, Spring: 515–544

MACKINNON, C. (1994) *Only Words* (Harvard: Harvard University Press)

MACLEAN, M. and D. GROVES (1991) *Women's Issues in Social Policy* (London: Routledge)

MACLEOD, M. and E. SARAGA (1988) 'Challenging the Orthodoxy: Towards a Feminist Theory and Practice', *Feminist Review*, 28: 16–55

MACLEOD, M. and E. SARAGA (1991) 'Clearing a path through the undergrowth: a feminist reading of recent literature on child sexual abuse' in P. Carter, T. Jeffs and M.K. Smith (eds) *Social Work and Social Welfare Yearbook 3* (Buckingham: Open University Press)

MAHER, V. (1992) (ed) *The Anthropology of Breast-Feeding* (Oxford: Berg)

MANDERSON, L. (1985) 'To Nurse and to Nurture: Breastfeeding in Australian Society', in V. Hull and M. Simpson (eds) *Breastfeeding, Child Health and Spacing* (Beckenham: Croom Helm)

MARTIN, E. (1989) *The Woman in the Body* (Milton Keynes: Open University Press)

MARTIN, J. (1978) *Infant Feeding 1975: attitudes and practices in England and Wales* (London: OPCS)

MARTIN, J. and J. MONK (1982) *Infant Feeding 1980* (London: OPCS)

MARTIN, J., and A. WHITE (1988) *Infant Feeding 1985* (London: OPCS)

MASTERS, W.H. and V.E. JOHNSON (1966) *Human Sexual Response* (London: J.A. Churchill)

MAYALL, B. and M.-C. FOSTER (1989) *Child Health Care, Living with Children, Working for Children* (Oxford: Heinemann Nursing)

McCONVILLE, B. (1994) *Mixed Messages; Our Breasts in Our Lives* (London: Penguin)

McDOWALL, J. (1991) 'Ten Point Quality Plan for Midwives in Relation to Breast-feeding' *Midwives Chronicle and Nursing Notes*, December: 361–365

McINTOSH, J. (1985) 'Decisions on Breastfeeding in a Group of First-Time Mothers' *Research and the Midwife Conference Proceedings*: 46–63

McNAUGHT, A. (1988) *Race and Health Policy* (Beckenham: Croom Helm)

MEAD, M. (1950) *Male and Female* (Harmondsworth: Penguin)

MEERABAU, L. (1982) 'Improving the Image', *Health Visitor*, June, 55: 298

MIDWIFE HEALTH VISITOR and COMMUNITY NURSE (1976) *Editorial*, October, 12: 309

MILES, A. (1991) *Women, Health and Medicine* (Buckingham: Open University)

MILES, R. (1989) *Racism* (London: Routledge and Kegan Paul)

MILLETT, K. (1977) *Sexual Politics* (London: Virago)

MILLMAN, S. (1985) 'Breastfeeding and Infant Mortality: Untangling the Complex Web of Causality', *The Sociological Quarterly* 26, 1: 65–79

MINISTRY OF HEALTH (1920) 'Annual Report of the Maternity and Child Welfare Department' in *The State of Public Health 1919* (London: HMSO)

MINISTRY OF HEALTH (1943) 'The Breast Feeding of Infants', *Report of the Advisory Committee on Mothers and Young Children* (London: HMSO)

MORGAN, G. (1983) 'Research Strategies: Modes of Engagement' in G. Morgan (ed) *Beyond Method: Strategies for Social Research* (Newbury Park, CA: Sage)

MORRIS, J. (1991) *Pride Against Prejudice* (London: The Women's Press)

MORRIS, J. (1991/92) '"Us" and "them"? Feminist research, community care and disability', *Critical Social Policy* 33, Winter: 22–39

MORRIS, S.E. (1993) 'Dutch and UK Breast-feeding practices compared' in *Midwives and Nursing Notes, Midwives Chronicle*, August: 296–300

MORT, F. (1987) *Dangerous Sexualities Medico-Moral Politics in England since 1830* (London: Routledge and Kegan Paul)

NARAYANAN, I., K. PRAKASH, N.S. MURTHY and V.V. GUJRAL (1984) 'Randomized controlled trial of effect on raw and Holder pasteurized human milk and fromula supplements on incidnece of neonatal infection', *Lancet* ii: 1111–3

NEWALL, F. (1990) 'Wet nursing and child care in Aldenham, Hertfordshire', 1595–1726: some evidence on the circumstances and effects of seventeenth-century child rearing practices' in V. Fildes (ed) *Women as Mothers in Pre-Industrial England* (London: Routledge)

NEWMAN, G. (1906) *Infant Mortality – a Social Problem* (London: Methuen)

NEWSON, J. and E. NEWSON (1963) *Patterns of Infant Care in an Urban Community* (Harmondsworth: Penguin)

NICHOLSON, L.J. (1990) *Feminism/Postmodernism* (London: Routledge)

OAKLEY, A. (1974) *The Sociology of Housework* (Oxford: Martin Robertson)

OAKLEY, A. (1976a) *Housewife* (Harmondsworth: Penguin)

OAKLEY, A. (1976b) 'Wisewoman and Medicine Man' in J. Mitchell and A. Oakley (eds) *The Rights and Wrongs of Women* (Harmondsworth: Penguin)

OAKLEY, A. (1980) *Women Confined: Towards a Sociology of Childbirth* (Oxford: Martin Robertson)

OAKLEY, A. (1981a) *From Here to Maternity: Becoming a Mother* (Harmondsworth: Penguin)

OAKLEY, A. (1981b) 'Normal Motherhood: an exercise in self-control' in Hutter, B. and Williams, G. (eds) *Controlling Women: the Normal and the Deviant* (London: Croom Helm)

OAKLEY, A. (1984) *The Captured Womb* (Oxford: Basil Blackwell)

OAKLEY, A. (1987) 'From Walking Wombs to Test Tube Babies' in M. Stanworth (ed) *Reproductive Technologies* (Cambridge: Polity, Oxford: Basil Blackwell)

OAKLEY, A. (1993) 'Birth as a normal process' in *Essays on Women, Health and Medicine* (Edinburgh: Edinburgh University Press)

OLESON, E. and V. LEWIN (eds) (1985) *Women, Health and Healing* (London: Tavistock)

OPCS (1971) *Census Small Area Statistics* (Ward Library)

OPCS Monitor DH3 84/85 (1984), *Birthweight Statistics 1983* (London: HMSO)

OPCS Monitor, DH3 85/6 (1985) *Birthweight Statistics 1984* (London: HMSO)

OPCS (1986) *Birth Statisitics 1986* (London: HMSO)

OPEN UNIVERSITY HEALTH EDUCATION UNIT (1991) *Roots and Branches: Community Development and Health – The Winter School Papers* (Milton Keynes: Open University Health Education Unit)

OPPENHEIM, C. (1990a) *Poverty: The Facts* (London: Child Poverty Action Group)

OPPENHEIM, C. (1990b) *The Cost of a Child* (London: Child Poverty Action Group)

ORR, J. (1980a) *Health Visiting in Focus* (London: Royal College of Nursing)

ORR, J. (1980b) 'Feminism and Health Visiting', *Health Visitor*, April, 54: 156–157

ORR, J. (1986) 'Feminism and Health Visiting' in C. Webb (ed) *Feminist Practice in Women's Health Care* (Chichester: Wiley)

PALMER, G. (1988) *The Politics of Breastfeeding*, new edn 1993 (London: Pandora)

PARSONS, T. and R.F. BALES (1956) *Family Socialization and Interaction Process* (London: Routledge and Kegan Paul)

PASCALL, G. (1986) *Social Policy A Feminist Analysis* (London: Tavistock)

PAYNE, S. (1991) *Women, Health and Poverty* (Hemel Hempstead: Harvester Wheatsheaf)

PATEMAN, C. (1988) *The Sexual Contract* (Cambridge: Polity Press)

PETCHESKY, R.P. (1980) 'Reproductive Freedom: Beyond "A Woman's Right to Choose"', *Signs: Journal of Women in Culture and Society* 5,4: 661– 685

PETCHESKY, R.P. (1986) *Abortion and Women's Choice: The State, Sexuality and Reproductive Freedom* (London: Verso)

PETCHESKY, R.P. (1987) 'Foetal Images: the Power of Visual Culture in the Politics of Reproduction' in M. Stanworth (ed) *Reproductive Technologies* (Cambridge: Polity/Oxford: Basil Blackwell)

PHILLIMORE, P., A. BEATTIE and P. TOWNSEND (1994) 'Widening inequality of health in northern England' in *British Medical Journal*, 30 April

PHILLIPS, A. and J. RAKUSEN Boston Women's Health Collective (1978) *Our Bodies Ourselves* (Harmondsworth: Penguin)

PHILLIPS, A. and J. RAKUSEN (1989) Boston Women's Health Collective (1989) *The New Our Bodies Ourselves* (London: Penguin)

PHOENIX, A. (1990) 'Black Women and the Maternity Services' in J. Garcia, R. Kilpatrick, M. Richards (eds) *The Politics of Maternity Care* (Oxford: Clarendon Press)

POOR LAW COMMISION (1912) *Minority Report 1909* (London: Fabian Society)

POOVEY, M. (1984) *The Proper Lady and the Woman Writer* (Chicago: University of Chicago Press)

PRENDERGAST, S. and A. PROUT (1990) 'Learning about Birth: Parenthood and Sex Education in English Secondary Schools' in J. Garcia, R. Kilpatrick and M. Richards (eds) *The Poltics of Maternity Care* (Oxford: Clarendon Press)

PRINCE, J. (1976) 'Infant Feeding through the Ages', *Midwives Chronicle and Nursing Notes*, December: 283–285

RAJAN, L. and A. OAKLEY (1990) 'Infant feeding practices in mothers at risk of low birth weight delivery', *Midwifery* 6: 18–27

RAJCHMAN, J. (1985) *Michel Foucault: the freedom of philosophy* (New York: Columbia University Press)

RAKUSEN, J. (1981) 'Depo-Provera: The Extent of the Problem. A Casestudy in the Politics of Birth Control' in H. Roberts (ed) *Women, Health and Reproduction* (London: Routledge and Kegan Paul)

RAPHAEL, D. (ed) (1973) *The Tender Gift – Breast feeding* (Englewood Cliffs N.J.: Prentice Hall)

RAPHAEL, D. (1978) *The Lactation Review*, 111,1: 1

RAPHAEL, D. (1985) *Only Mothers Know* (Westwood, Conneticut: The Human Lactation Centre, Greenwood Press)

REES, A.D. (1950) *A Life in the Welsh Countryside* (Cardiff: University of Wales Press)

REISSMAN, C.K. (1983) 'Women and Medicalisation: A New perspective', *Social Policy*, Summer: 3–18

RHODES, C. (1982) 'The Benefits of Breast-Feeding', *Journal of Practical Nursing* July–August: 19–55

RICH, A. (1979) *Of Woman Born: Motherhood as Experience and Institution* (London: Virago)

RICH, A. (1980) 'Compulsory Heterosexuality and Lesbian Existence',

Signs: A Journal of Women in Culture and Society, Summer: 631–57

RICH, A. (1984) *On Lies, Secrets and Silences* (London: Virago)

RILEY, D. (1983) *War in the Nursery* (London: Virago)

RILEY, D. (1988) *Am I that Name? Feminism and the Category of Women in History* (Basingstoke: Macmillan)

RIORDAN, J. (1983) (ed) *A Practical Guide to Breastfeeding* (St Louis Missouri: C.V. Mosby Company)

RIORDAN, J. and B. COUNTRYMAN (1983) 'Infant feeding patterns: past and present' in J. Riordan (ed) *A Practical Guide to Breastfeeding* (St Louis Missouri: C.V. Mosby Company)

ROBERTSON, C. (1988) *Health Visiting in Practice* (Edinburgh: Churchill Livingstone)

ROBINSON, S. (1990) 'Maintaining the Independence of the Midwifery Profession: A Continuing Struggle' in J. Garcia, R. Kilpatrick and M. Richards (eds) *The Politics of Maternity Services for Childbearing Women in Twentieth Century Britain* (Oxford: Clarendon Press)

ROCHERON, Y. (1988) 'The Asian Mother and Baby Campaign: the construction of ethnic minorities' health needs' *Critical Social Policy* 22, Summer; 4–23

RODMELL, S. and A. WATT (1986) 'Conventional Health Education: Problems and Possibilties' in S. Rodmell and A. Watt (eds) *The politics of health education; raising the issues* (London: Routledge and Kegan Paul)

ROIPHE, K. (1994) *The Morning After: Sex, Fear and Feminism* (London: Hamish Hamilton)

ROSALDO, M.Z. (1974) 'Women, Culture and Society: a theoretical overview' in M.Z. Rosaldo and L. Lamphere (eds) *Women, Culture and Society* (Stanford: Stanford University Press)

ROSSITER, J.C. (1993) 'Breast-feeding, the better option: getting the message across', *World Health Forum* 14: 316–318

ROUSSEAU, J.-J. (1762) *Emile ou l'education* (translated into English, London: T. Bechet)

RUTTER, M. and N. MADGE (1977) *Cycles of Disadvantage* (London: Heinemann)

RUTTER, P. (1989) *Sex in the Forbidden Zone* (London: Unwin)

RYAN, A.S., D. RUSH, M.S. KRIEGER and G.E. LEWANDOWSKI (1991) 'Recent Declines in Breast-Feeding in the United States, 1984 Through 1989 in Pediatrics 88: 4 October: 719–727

SAYERS, J. (1982) *Biological Politics: Feminist and Anti-Feminist Perspectives* (London: Tavistock)

SCHIEBINGER, L. (1989) *The Mind Has No Sex* (Harvard: Harvard University Press)

SCOTT, H.R. (1989) 'Breast-Feeding: Not all Romance', *Midwives Chronicle and Nursing Notes* December: 413–414

SCOTT, J.W. (1988) 'Deconstructing Equality-versus-Difference: Or, The Uses of Poststructuralist Theory for Feminism', *Feminist Studies*, 14, 1, Spring: 33–50

SCOTT, J.W. (1989) 'Gender: A Useful Category of Historical Analysis' in E. Weed (ed) *Coming to Terms: Feminism, Theory and Politics* (London: Routledge)

SCOWEN, P. (1989) 'Twenty five years of infant feeding 1964–1989', *Midwife, Health Visitor and Community Nurse* 25, 7: 293–302

SECRETARY OF STATE FOR HEALTH (1991) *The Health of the Nation; A consultative document for health in England* (HMSO)

SECRETARY OF STATE FOR HEALTH (1992) *The Health of the Nation: A strategy for health in England* (HMSO)

SEDLEY, A. and M. BENN (1982) *Sexual Harassment at Work* (London: National Council for Civil Liberties)

SEGAL, L. (1987) *Is the Future Female? Troubled Thoughts on Contemporary Feminism* (London: Virago)

SEGAL, L. and MCINTOSH, M. (1992) (eds) *Sex Exposed: Sexuality and the Pornography Debate* (London: Virago)

SHAHJAHAN, M. (1991) 'Infant and Toddler Feeding Patterns and Related Issues in the Bangladeshi Community in Newcastle' (Unpublished MSc dissertation: University of Newcastle upon Tyne)

SHORT, C., K. TUNKS and D. HUTCHINSON (eds) (1991) *Dear Clare . . . this is what women feel about Page 3* (London: Radius)

SICHTERMANN, B. (1983) *Femininity: The Politics of the Personal* (Cambridge: Polity Press)

SILVERTON, L. (1985) 'Breast feeding yesterday and today', *Midwifery* 1: 162–166

SMITH, D.E. (1988) 'Femininity as Discourse' in L.G. Roman, L.K. Christian Smith, and E. Ellsworth (eds) *Becoming Feminine – The Politics of Popular Culture* (Lewes, Sussex: Falmer Press)

SONTAG, S. (1979) *On Photography* (Harmondsworth: Penguin)

SOPER, K. (1991) 'Postmodernism and its Discontents', *Feminist Review*, 39: 97–108

SPENCE, J. (1986) *Putting Myself in the Picture. A Political Personal and Photographic Autobiography* (London: Camden Press)

SPIRO, A. (1987) 'Playing the same tune . . . consistent advice and support from health visitors and community midwives', *Community Outlook* March: 18–19

SPRING RICE, M. (1981) *Working Class Wives* (London: Virago)

STANKO, E. (1988) 'Keeping women in and out of line: sexual harassment and occupational segregation' in S. Walby (ed) *Gender Segregation at Work* (Milton Keynes: Open University Press)

STANWAY, P. and A. STANWAY (1978) *Breast is Best* (London: Pan)

STANWORTH, M. (ed) (1987) *Reproductive Technologies: Gender, Motherhood and Medicine* (Cambridge: Polity/Oxford: Basil Blackwell)

STOPES, M. (1939) *Your baby's first year* (Putnam; London)

SUSSMAN, G.D. (1982) *Selling Mothers' Milk: The Wet Nurse Business in France 1715–1914* (Chicago: University of Illinois Press)

SWEENEY, M.A. and C. GULINO (1987) 'The health belief model as an explanation for breast-feeding practices in a Hispanic population', *Advances In Nursing Science* 9,4: 35–50

THOMPSON, J. (1983) *Learning Liberation: Women's Responses to Men's Education* (Beckenham: Croom Helm)

THORNTON, L. (1987) 'Breast Feeding in South Africa', *Midwives Chronicle and Nursing Notes*: April, 88–92

THREADGOLD, T. and A. CRANNY-FRANCIS (eds) (1990) *Feminine, Masculine and Representation* (Sydney: Allen and Unwin)

TOWNSEND, P. and N. DAVIDSON (1982) *Inequalities in Health: The Black Report* (Harmondsworth: Penguin)

TOWNSEND, P., D. SIMPSON and N. TIBBS (1984) *Inequalities in Health in the City of Bristol* (Bristol: Department of Social Administration, Univeristy of Bristol)

TOWNSEND, P., P. PHILLIMORE and A. BEATTIE (1988) *Health and Deprivation: Inequality in the North* (Beckenham: Croom Helm)

TREUHERZ, J., T.R. CULLINAN and D.I. SAUNDERS (1982) 'Determininants of Infant-Feeding Practice in East London', *Human Nutrition: Applied Nutrition*, 36,A: 281–286

TURNER, B.S. (1984) *The Body in Society* (Oxford: Basil Blackwell)

TURNER, B. (1987) *Medical Power and Social Knowledge* (London: Sage)

TURNATURI, G. (1987) 'Between public and private: the birth of the professional housewife and the female consumer' in A. Showstack Sassoon (ed) *Women and the State* (London: Hutchinson)

UNITED NATIONS CHILDREN'S FUND (UNICEF) (1990) *The State of the World's Children* (Oxford: Oxford University Press)

URWIN, C. (1985) 'Constructing motherhood: the persuasion of normal development' in C. Steedman, C. Urwin and V. Walkerdine (eds) *Language, Gender and Childhood* (London: Routledge and Kegan Paul)

UNITED STATES DEPARTMENT OF HEALTH AND HUMAN SERVICES (1990) *Healthy People 2000: National Health Promotion and Disease Prevention Objectives*

VAN ESTERIK, P. (1989) *Motherpower and Infant Feeding* (London: Zed Books)

WALBY, S. (1986) *Patriarchy at Work* (Cambridge: Polity Press)

WALBY, S. (1990) *Theorising Patriarchy* (Oxford: Basil Blackwell)

WALKER, C. and G. CANNON (1986) *The Food Scandal* (London: Century Arrow)

WALKERDINE, V. and H. LUCEY (1989) *Democracy in the Kitchen: Regulating Mothers and Socialising Daughters* (London: Virago)

WALTERS, M. (1976) 'The Rights and Wrongs of Women: Mary Wollstancroft, Harriet Martineau, Simone de Beauvior' in J. Mitchell and A. Oakley (eds) *The Rights and Wrongs of Women* (Harmondsworth: Penguin)

WARING, M. (1988) *If Women Counted: A New Feminist Economics* (London: Macmillan)

WARSHAW, R. (1988) *I Never Called it Rape* (New York: Harper Row)

WATNEY, S. (1987) *Policing Desire: Pornography, AIDS and the Media* (London: Methuen)

WATNEY, S. (1989) 'Taking Liberties: An Introduction' in E. Carter and S. Watney (eds) *Taking Liberties: AIDS and Cultural Politics* (London: Serpent's Tail)

WATT, A. (1986) 'Community health education: a time for caution' in S. Rodmell and A. Watt (eds) *The Politics of Health Education: raising the issues* (London: Routledge and Kegan Paul)

WEBB, C. (ed) (1986) *Feminist Practice in Health Care* (Chichester: John Wiley and Sons)

WEBER, M. (1968) *Religious Ethics and the World: Sexuality and Art in Economy and Society* (Glencoe, Illinois: Free Press)

WEEDON, C. (1987) *Feminist Practice and Poststructuralist Theory* (Oxford: Basil Blackwell)

WEEKS, J. (1989a) *Sex, Politics and Society: The regulation of sexuality since 1800* second edition (Harlow: Longman)

WEEKS, J. (1989b) 'AIDS, Altruism and the New Right' in E. Carter and S. Watney (eds) *Taking Liberties* (London: Serpents Tail)

WEEKS, J. (1993) 'AIDS and the regulation of sexuality' in Berridge V. and Strong, P. (eds) *AIDS and contemporary History* (Cambridge: Cambridge University Press).

WHITE, A., S. FREETH and M. O'BRIEN (1992) *Infant Feeding 1990* (OPCS: HMSO)

WHITEHEAD, M. (1988) *The Health Divide* (Harmondsworth: Penguin)

WICKES, I.G. (1953) 'A History of Infant Feeding', *Archives of Disease in Childhood*: 151–158; 232–240; 332–340; 416–422; 495–501

WILKINSON, R.G. (1989) 'Class Mortality Differentials, Income Distribution and Trends in Poverty 1921–81', *Journal of Social Policy*, July, 18, 3: 307–335

WILLIAMS, F. (1989) *Social Policy: A Critical Introduction* (Cambridge: Polity Press)

WILLIAMS, F. (1992) 'Women with Learning Difficulties are Women too' in M. Langar and L. Day (eds) *Women, Oppression and Social Work* (London: Routledge).

WILSON, E. (1977) *Women and the Welfare State* (London: Tavistock)

WISE, S. and L. STANLEY (1987) *Georgie Porgie Sexual Harassment in Everyday Life* (London: Pandora)

WISE, S. and L. STANLEY (1990) 'Sexual Harassment, sexual conduct and gender in social work settings' in P. Carter, T. Jeffs and M. Smith (eds) *Social Work and Social Welfare Yearbook 2* (Milton Keynes: Open University Press)

WORLD HEALTH ORGANIZATION (1974) *Resolution on Infant Feeding* (Geneva: WHO)

WORLD HEALTH ORGANIZATION/UNITED NATIONS CHILDREN'S FUND (1979) *Meeting on Infant and Young Child Feeding Background Paper* (Geneva: WHO)

WORLD HEALTH ORGANIZATION (1981a) *Resolution on Infant Feeding: Handbook of Resolutions and Decisions of the WHO, 1978* (Geneva: WHO)

WORLD HEALTH ORGANIZATION/UNITED NATIONS CHILDREN'S FUND (1981b) *International Code of Breast-Milk Substitutes* (Geneva: WHO)

WORLD HEALTH ORGANIZATION (1981c) *Contemporary Patterns of Breast-Feeding. Report on the WHO Collaborative Study on Breast-feeding* (Geneva: WHO)

WORLD HEALTH ORGANIZATION/UNITED NATIONS CHILDREN'S FUND (1989) 'Ten Steps to Successful Breast Feeding', reported in

UNICEF (1990) *The State of the World's Children* (Oxford: Oxford University Press)

WORLD HEALTH ORGANIZATION (1988) *From Almatra to the Year 2000* (Geneva: WHO)

WORRALL, A. (1987) 'Sisters in Law? Women Defendants and Women Magistrates' in P. Carlen and A. Worrall (eds) *Gender, Crime and Justice* (Milton Keynes: Open University Press)

WRIGHT, A.L., C. HOLBERG and TAUSSIG (1988) 'Infant-feeding practices amongst middle-class Anglos and Hispanics', *Pediatrics*, Sept, 82, 3, 2: 496–503

YOUNG, I.M. (1990a) *Throwing Like a Girl and Other Essays in Feminist Philosophy and Social Theory* (Bloomington, Indiana: Indiana Press)

YOUNG, I.M. (1990b) 'Humanism, Gynocentrism, and Feminist Politics' in *Throwing Like a Girl and Other Essays in Feminist Philosophy and Social Theory* (Bloomington, Indiana: Indiana Press)

YOUNG, I. M. (1990c) 'The Breasted Experience' in *Throwing Like a Girl and Other Essays in Feminist Philosophy and Social Theory* (Bloomington, Indiana: Indiana Press)

YOUNG, M. and P. WILLMOTT (1957) *Family and Kinship in East London* (London: Routledge and Kegan Paul)

Name Index

Subject Index

generation and social class 92–3
grandmothers 92–5

health promotion/education 61,
103, 142–3, 186–7, 234, 238
heterosexuality 53, 56, 59, 108, 119,
128, 130, 137–9, 149, 152, 153,
154, 158, 191, 199, 205, 216, 219,
221, 230, 231, 232, 237, 293
hospital practices 9, 55, 59, 88, 90,
93, 161, 162–5, 172
household/home 107, 108, 109,
110, 112

ignorance, maternal 41, 45–6, 49,
51
incest taboos 103, 114
inequalities in health 61, 93, 234
infant feeding policies 2, 3, 12–13,
34, 41, 50, 60, 70, 183–188, 234
infant formula *see* baby milk
manufacture
infant mortality 60–1, 65, 96, 131
informal/community
education 235–6, 238

La Leche League 17, 58, 195, 223
labour market changes 108, 119

material circumstances/resources for
infant feeding 45, 48, 50, 54,
76, 78, 85–7, 88, 93, 126–7,
193–4, 218, 225, 226, 238–9
medicalisation 21, 40, 48–9, 58, 61,
100, 162, 179–83, 194, 220
milk dispensaries/milk depots/guotte
de lait 44, 45, 47
modesty 97, 106, 109, 110, 112, 130,
131, 139, 151, 192, 216, 218
mothering 34, 42, 46, 56, 57, 60,
71, 125, 155, 160, 161, 175–6,
177, 191, 195, 197, 215, 218,
220, 236

National Childbirth Trust
(NCT) 24, 58, 195, 223
nature/natural 1, 2, 16–17, 19, 21,
23, 26, 29, 35, 36, 38, 39, 42, 51,
56, 57, 60, 66, 67, 68, 70, 74,
116, 126, 143, 158, 180–1, 193,
199, 220, 224, 225, 227, 233,
234, 140

patriarchy 26, 106, 114, 129, 133,
193, 228

photography, representation and
bodies 142–8, 159, 199, 231,
232, 236–7, 239
pornography 150, 199, 231
poverty and breast-feeding 45, 47–8,
52, 62, 65, 80, 82, 90, 92, 101–2,
182, 234, 237, 239
power and infant feeding 29, 161,
223, 233
pre-industrial societies 37
professionalism 186–8, 238
professionals, health 4, 49, 104,
152, 161, 220, 236, 237, 239, 240
professionals and gender 172–9,
187, 191, 196–7, 203, 230, 226,
233, 238
pro-natalism 44, 46, 57

qualitative research 12, 104

race, racism 20, 46, 96–7, 224, 237
race/nation/eugenicism 46–7, 55, 56
rape 231
reproduction 1, 17, 21, 69–70, 91–2,
123, 148, 162, 214, 227, 229,
233, 240
resistance 28–9, 148, 160, 192, 193,
197–8, 219, 221, 226, 233, 234
reverse discourses 192–3

science/nature debates 35, 36, 66,
69, 216
sensuality, 141, 142, 219, 232
sex education 231
sexology 52, 136
sexual abuse 114, 231
sexual difference versus gender
neutrality 27, 214, 219, 227–34,
240
sexual harassment 231
sexual hygiene 52, 54
sexualisation of breasts 26, 52, 53,
100, 120, 128, 134–40, 148, 149,
157, 194–5, 230
sexuality of breast-feeding 51, 59,
104, 115, 117, 120, 134, 192,
219, 224
sexuality and discourse 30, 59, 115,
117, 118, 119–20, 129
space/women's space 104, 107, 108,
109, 110, 114, 121, 128, 217,
218, 229, 235
stories, infant feeding 71, 73, 74,
199–201

third world/developing
    countries 20, 49–50, 65, 67, 224
time 106, 121, 122, 123–4, 125, 218,
    226, 229

underclass *see* culture of poverty

weaning 167–8, 172
wet nursing 37–9, 117–18
whiteness 99
women, breast-feeding and meanings

about 1, 33, 7–8, 52–5, 192
women, category of 32, 212–13, 227,
    233, 240
women, differences between 20, 22,
    23, 39, 48, 60, 212, 216, 227, 240
Women's Co-operative Guild 46, 48
women's experiences 11–12, 32, 71,
    72, 148, 159–60, 21, 215, 238,
    240
women's health 1, 19, 47, 49–50,
    62, 76, 80, 88–9, 199, 218, 226